ACCOUNTING
A SYSTEMS
APPROACH

ACCOUNTING
A SYSTEMS
APPROACH

ALISON WARMAN AND JEFF DAVIES

INTERNATIONAL THOMSON BUSINESS PRESS
I(T)P® An International Thomson Publishing Company

London • Bonn • Johannesburg • Madrid • Melbourne • Mexico City • New York • Paris
Singapore • Tokyo • Toronto • Albany, NY • Belmont, CA • Cincinnati, OH • Detroit, MI

Accounting: A Systems Approach

Copyright © 1999 Alison Warman and J R Davies

I(T)P® A division of International Thomson Publishing Inc.
The ITP logo is a trademark under licence

British Library Cataloguing-in-Publication Data
A catalogue record for this book is available from the British Library

First edition published 1999

Typeset by J&L Composition Ltd, Filey, North Yorkshire
Printed in the UK by Antony Rowe Ltd, Chippenham, Wiltshire

ISBN 1–86152–037–9

International Thomson Business Press
Berkshire House
168–173 High Holborn
London WC1V 7AA
UK

http://www.itbp.com

Contents

Preface

This book has been designed as an introductory accounting text book but with a very different approach to that adopted by traditional texts. The accountant is seen in the role of information manager and the book introduces basic accounting concepts and procedures in their context as part of the information system within an organisation rather than as isolated ideas. Internal control and audit needs are integrated with the accounting material as a natural part of the day-to-day operating procedures. In addition, the book recognizes that the recording and processing functions are no longer manual exercises. It concentrates on the way in which computer based software is used to record and process information together with the additional control procedures needed to provide assurance of the integrity of the system and the information it produces. Accounting concepts are introduced and illustrated using the computer based system as an integral part of the explanation.

These differences mean that the book offers a good overview of the accounting disciplines and the way that they interrelate. Starting with the information system, the book explores the need for information for internal management use and for reporting to outside users, for internal control procedures and audit as well as introducing the need for credit control and financial management. This can form the basis for further study of these disciplines in more advanced programmes or the book can stand alone as an illustration of the accountant's role for non specialists. We have found this initial overview a useful aid in breaking down the barriers between the accounting core subject areas which otherwise students can have a tendency to compartmentalize as separate disciplines.

The first chapter introduces the approach in detail.

We are grateful to SAGE plc for permission to use one of their products as an illustration of the way in which accounting packages are used. We have chosen to use the DOS based product SAGE Line 50 previously known as SAGE Sterling, but the ideas and procedures should be transferable to other products.

The book is aimed at anyone needing a basic introduction to accounting and does not require any previous knowledge. It adopts a practical case study based approach to introducing new ideas but with further examples available for practice purposes. The case study runs throughout the text and is intended to build up to a more sophisticated situation as the student's level of knowledge and skill increases. However, it is possible to join the case study in later chapters having ignored the introductory levels if required.

The book is suitable for any first level specialist accounting or non specialist degrees, HND/HNC programmes or any professional programme requiring a working knowledge of the accounting function. Although written as a course book, it could be of use to anyone wishing to study independently and requiring help in a work based context.

The final chapter in the book relating to internal controls has been contributed by Ms Marlene Davies of the University of Glamorgan. We would like to express our thanks for the chapter and also for her useful comments on the rest of the text.

We are grateful for the continued support and advice which we received from the staff of International Thomson Publishing and their patience without which this book would not have been completed.

Finally we want to thank our long suffering families and friends for their unfailing support and forbearance while this book was planned and written.

1 Introduction to the systems approach

Learning objectives

After reading this chapter you should be able to:

1. ■ appreciate the role of the accountant in modern business
2. ■ understand what is meant by a 'system' and why the accountant can be called an information manager
3. ■ see where the Accounting Information System (AIS) and its subsystems relate to the Management Information System (MIS)
4. ■ be able to identify and list the qualities necessary for information to be effective and valuable to the user.

Introduction

This book has been written as a first year text for accounting and business studies students at degree and HND level. Its approach recognizes the rapidly changing role of the accountant and the text can be divided into two distinct parts, each part covering a semester.

You will be expected to follow the course using integrated accounting software and throughout the text we follow the fortunes of John and Azina Bale from the time they set up in business for the first time through to their change in status to a limited company and onwards.

Most students using this textbook will be studying accounting for the first time and that is our basic assumption. Those who have studied accounting previously will find this approach unique and complementary to their previous studies.

Most people's perception of an accountant is someone who has an office in the local high street, advises people about taxation and audits other people's accounts. This perception is only true for a minority of accountants. The majority of accountants work in industry or commerce as part of a management team, playing a key co-ordinating role in providing information to other managers to help them make the correct decisions. They are heavily involved with computer systems and consequently in the design and maintenance of such systems. It is an extremely challenging and exciting job.

It is important at this early stage that you have a clear picture of what modern accountancy is and the role of the accountant within it. It will place the other subjects you study in the correct perspective and hopefully demonstrate to you that the modern accountant requires many skills in addition to technical accounting knowledge. They must be able to manage, co-ordinate, communicate (both verbally and in writing) persuade, interpret and analyse. All these skills are necessary; the accountant is no longer the 'bean counter'. These skills are valuable and in great demand and a person who has acquired such skills and completed the relevant training will have many career opportunities to choose from within and outside accountancy.

It is also important that you understand why a systems approach is being taken and is essential for the modern accountant.

Accountancy and the accountant

Over the years various definitions have been made to provide an answer to the question 'what is accounting?' Each succeeding definition has been broader than the previous definition reflecting the increasing importance of the role within organizations and the contribution it makes to effective decision making and also to public expectation and social responsibility.

The history of accountancy reflects the evolutionary pattern of social developments and in this respect, illustrates how much accountancy is a product of its environment and at the same time a force for changing it.

Above, we used the term 'bean counter', this gives a very narrow view of the role of accountancy and is now regarded as a derogatory view of the accountant. We view the accountant as being an 'information manager'. Everything that happens in an organization crosses the accountant's desk. Whether you are providing goods or providing services it will be reduced to the common denominator of money, and dealt with and processed by accounting staff. Accountants are in one sense 'two faced', they must face inwards and provide information, analysis and informed judgement to managers within the organization and also face outwards in providing information to shareholders, the Inland Revenue, Custom and Excise, banks, Registrar of Companies, etc.

Consequently we like the definition given by the American Accounting Association in 1966 which interprets accounting as 'the process of identifying, measuring and communicating economic information to permit informed judgements and decisions by the users of the information'.

We interpret this definition as meaning that the accountant will sort, select and process data to produce and communicate valuable economic information for a variety of users within and outside the organization. As the role broadens so the list of skills necessary to meet these demands also grows. In recent years the introduction of information technology has increased the importance of the role of the accountant. As information managers they have been at the heart of these developments and have had to acquire new skills to communicate effectively with technical managers like programmers, systems analysts and communications experts. We are informed that the 'computer revolution' is over and that we are now at the beginning of the 'information revolution'. No one is better placed within the organization than the accountant to play a central role in this revolution.

The accountant's job, is similar in some respects to the job of a production manager. The accountant is responsible, however, not for the production of components but for the production of information and for analysing and interpreting information for other managers. The management team must take the responsibility for decisions which affects its functional areas, but such decisions are made within a framework of information and advice given by the accountant.

There are dangers in any organization that this framework may result in a management control system that is too rigid, and this will seriously affect the vitality of the unit. The accountant must be sensitive to the fact that the role is that of co-ordinator, provider and facilitator and must not dominate the decision making process.

Without this sensitivity there is a real danger that the accountant may become a production manager with a product that cannot be sold to the customers, represented by the management team, and consequently will have little opportunity to influence and advise them.

Accounting has evolved over time in response to environmental changes from stewardship accounting, with its roots in pre-industrial society, to financial accounting, with the advent of the joint stock company, and then management accounting, which belongs to the twentieth century. The birth of modern management accounting with its emphasis on detailed information for decision making provided a tremendous impetus to the development of management accounting in the early decades of this century, and in so doing considerably extended the boundaries of accounting. Management accounting shifted the focus of accounting from recording and analysing financial transactions to using information for decisions affecting the future.

Unfortunately there has also developed a tendency to view financial accounting and management accounting as two very separate disciplines with the academic approach to management accounting consisting of a series of techniques such as job costing, process costing, break even analysis, allocation of overheads, etc. Although recognizing that they serve two distinct purposes, financial accounting and management accounting work off the same database, and the design setting up, maintenance and security of that database is a common responsibility.

Our systems approach would like to emphasize not the differences but the common aspects of financial and management accounting, namely the design of the accounting system. Figure 1.1 shows in diagrammatic form the two faces of the accountant. In the left column the management team formulate objectives and then produce a series of plans and budgets to achieve those objectives. In the second column the accountant provides information to help develop the plans and the budgets and then keeps records of activity and provides feedback on performance. Periodically, accounts and reports are produced that are of interest to those listed in the third column and objectives may change as a result of organizational performance or a changing environment.

Naturally, accountants provide accounting or economic information and this is produced from within the **Accounting Information System** (AIS) which is one of many systems that make up the **Management Information System** (MIS). The AIS (i.e. chart of accounts, input procedures, design of input documentation, data capture, data security and the use of the data processed to develop specific outputs to meet the special needs of financial or management accounting as a whole) provides all sorts of information to management – both quantitative and qualitative.

The AIS however, is the organization's 'nervous system' and most organizations would soon die if it ceased to function. Accountants are at the heart of the AIS as:

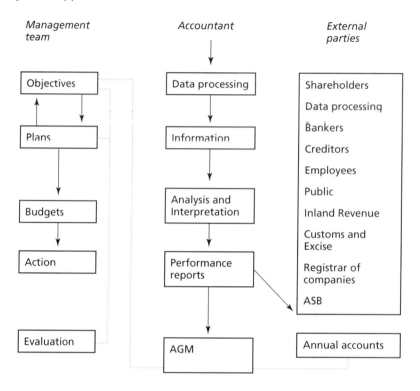

Figure 1.1
Role of the
accountant

1   users;
2   consultants;
3   designers;
4   auditors.

They cannot avoid being involved, and system considerations currently play, and will increasingly play, an even larger role in the work of accountants.

The structure and content of this textbook recognizes that:

1   Accountants are responsible for the quality of the information generated by accounting systems.
2   Accountants in industry should be, and typically are, involved in systems development to ensure that the computerized accounting system meet the needs of their organization and other users.
3   Accountants in public practice are often asked by clients for advice on acquiring computer hardware and software.
4   Accountants are expected to provide advice regarding the costs of developing, operating and enhancing accountancy information systems.
5   Professional standards require external auditors to understand the flow of transactions through accountancy systems and to evaluate the internal controls embodied in those systems before expressing an opinion on the fairness of the financial statements.
6   Accountants are expected to advise their managers on issues of control and data security.

1 Why is the term 'bean counter' no longer appropriate in describing the modern accountant?
2 Discuss the definitions of accounting given by the American Accounting Association in 1966.
3 From a systems perspective why is it wrong to view financial accounting as being one of two very distinct academic disciplines?

A systems approach

Let us now examine what we mean by a system and how this is relevant to the teaching of accountancy. We define a **system** as 'a methodically arranged set of ideas, principles methods or procedures to achieve a common goal', or in very simple terms 'a way of consistently making something which is difficult, easy'.

We have stated above that accountants produce economic information and try to effectively communicate that information to users. In other words they take **data** and following certain ideas, procedures and guidelines convert data into **information**. The system is outlined in Figure 1.2.

Although in everyday speech data and information are words that are used on an interchangeable basis it is important to distinguish clearly between the two. Data can be meaningless to a user, it is only after they have been **processed** that they become information. Data are processed by:

1 classifying;
2 sorting;
3 calculating;
4 summarising;
5 analysing.

Systems Theory is relatively new and dates back to the 1930s. It is concerned with the general properties of systems and although we are concerned with AIS and MIS the same general theory applies to other systems, e.g. biological systems, political systems and social systems.

Prior to the development of **General System Theory** (GST), people perceived systems as being mechanistic, that is, there was a clear cause and effect such that if A happened B was bound to follow. It is clear now however that systems are being developed that are dynamic, changing and interacting with each other and the environment.

GST has contributed to the principles and practice of management in several ways:

1 It drew attention to the dynamic aspects of business organization, and the factors influencing the growth and development of subsystems.
   It created an awareness of subsystems, each with potentially conflicting goals

Figure 1.2
The basic system

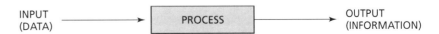
INPUT (DATA) → PROCESS → OUTPUT (INFORMATION)

which must be brought into line with each other – suboptimization remains a significant feature of much business practice today.

3   It taught managers to reject the deterministic idea that A will always cause B to happen.

4   The importance of the environment on a system was acknowledged. Before GST this self-evident truth was not properly understood.

5   GST considered the purpose or goals of systems in order to understand better how they work.

Systems are dynamic in that once a system has been introduced to meet the needs (goals) of an organization it immediately begins to become redundant as the organization changes and environmental influences affect the organization.

Companies will vary over time in size and in the product or service they supply. Changes also take place in the law and in the general public's attitude to certain issues, e.g. environmental issues, the role of women in the work place.

All these changes make the current systems less effective in meeting the organization's needs. Unless the organization recognizes this and responds by constantly reviewing and modifying its systems, it will find that its current systems will become less and less effective.

Subsystems

The AIS is a subsystem within the organization's MIS which in itself is a subsystem of the organization as a whole which is operating within an environment that is constantly changing. For example, European laws are slowly affecting our behaviour in a way that could not have been perceived ten years ago. Figure 1.3 shows the AIS as a subsystem of the MIS within an organization resident in the UK but subject to environmental influences from Europe.

This effect of other subsystems and the environment on the subsystem under observation indicates that MIS and AIS in particular are **open systems**, i.e. systems

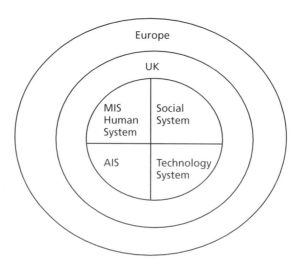

Figure 1.3
The AIS as a subsystem of the MIS resident in the UK subject to the EU environment

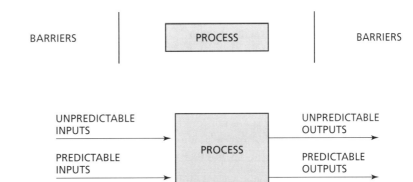

Figure 1.4
A closed system

Figure 1.5
An open system

which interact with their environment. Figure 1.4 shows a system which is not affected by its environment and which is therefore defined as a **closed system**. An example of a closed system is an economy which has surrounded itself with trade barriers and has no contact with the outside world. Closed systems rarely, if ever, exist.

Figure 1.5 shows a system that interacts with its environment and is therefore defined as being an open system. An example of an open system is found in any organization which interacts with its environment, such as a hospital, university or any business. All accounting and management information systems are open systems.

Such interaction means that boundaries must exist which enable a system to be clearly identified. Given our objective of producing and communicating economic information for decision making the boundaries of the AIS are as shown in Figure 1.6.

From unlimited data in the environment the boundary ensures that raw data become input data. Processing takes place using well-tried methods and principles and eventually the output (information) must meet the needs of the users. If it does not then feedback takes place which can affect the selection of input data for processing and perhaps the way in which data are processed.

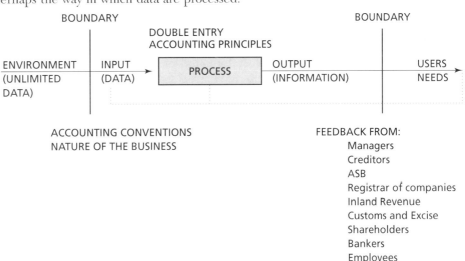

Figure 1.6
The AIS

Information is communicated so that action can be taken. An MIS should help managers do their jobs more effectively. Since managers must have information there will always be, in all organizations, an MIS.

The question, however, is 'how effective is that system'? Without thought, without formal planning:

1   some managers will prefer to keep data in their heads;
2   not all data are collected and processed;
3   information is available but not communicated;
4   information is communicated late.

Usable information is, therefore, the key. When we are planning and designing our AIS this objective must be clearly kept in mind.

Qualities of good information

Although the accountant is at the heart of the AIS, it is not his or her system; he or she must not dictate what the users need or the form in which they require it. Output can be communicated verbally, on screen, via paper, disk, microfilm, microfiche.

For information to be effective and valuable to the user it should be:

1   *Relevant for its purpose* – The information should address the relevance for the user, be in the correct format and contain sufficient detail for the purpose in hand.
2   *Complete for its purpose* – In the same way that the user does not want to access a second and third source of information because the first source is incomplete, the user also does not want excessive detail or irrelevant information which can also prove to be equally time consuming.
3   *Sufficiently accurate for its purpose* – Not every user needs the same level of accuracy because the same basic information set can be used by a number of users for completely different purposes. Someone negotiating a new contract to supply a service could require the information to be presented in a manner that showed pence, whereas the managing director may be interested in the same information, but to a level of accuracy equal to the nearest £10 000 or £1 million.
4   *The user should have confidence in it* – The method and system for generating and presenting the information has been tested so that the user will not be challenged and embarrassed by errors or inaccuracies.
5   *Communicated to a person who needs it to do their job* – Do not provide information to those who do not need it. This becomes frustrating to the recipient and devalues their perception of you as a provider of relevant information and the controller of a vital management requirement.
6   *Clear to user* – The technical terminology here is that the information should contain no 'noise'. In other words its message must be clear and unambiguous. This can be achieved by summarizing, using subtotals and graphs.
7   *Timely* – To be useful most information should be in the hands of the user by a specific agreed time and date. This gives the user an opportunity to digest the information and use it in the most effective way. In certain circumstances the user may be prepared to sacrifice a certain degree of accuracy in order to ensure that information is timely.

8 *Communicated by an appropriate channel of communication* – Many ways exist to communicate information, e.g. paper, disks, microfilm, microfiche and screen. Let the user decide what is most appropriate.

9 *Not be excessive* – In the early days of computing, users would receive huge printouts where perhaps only one or two pages were relevant to them. Alternatively it was all relevant but so badly organized and presented that it took many hours to extract what was really required. In most cases this problem was caused by a lack of communication between user and provider with the provider having only a very rough idea of what the user required.

10 *Provided at a cost which is less than the value of the benefit it provides* – In other words, do not incur costs of £100 to provide information which is going to save £20.

What should be clear from these points is that the accountant (information manager) should have a regular dialogue with the user and that it is the user who specifies what is required. This must be the case. The accountant cannot dictate to the production and marketing manager how to do their job. The information system is as much theirs as it is the accountant's and consequently they must feel ownership of the system and in control of its outputs.

This does not, of course, place the accountant in a purely subservient role. The accountant has the expertise of understanding the whole system and knowing what is and what is not possible. (The user will normally only be interested in that section of the system that directly affects their job). The accountant must consult, listen, advise and, as in the case of the last item in the above list, refuse to supply information.

Benefits of the systems approach

Our approach to teaching accounting using commercial integrated accounting software gives you the opportunity of seeing the AIS as a whole, together with its own subsystems sales ledger, purchase ledger, nominal ledger, stock control, sales order processing and purchase order processing.

Considerable time is spent on double entry bookkeeping and on you designing you own chart of accounts because this aspect is associated with the selection of your input data and how it is processed. Over the years it has become fashionable not to pay too much attention to double entry bookkeeping because it was not thought to present students with sufficient intellectual challenge. Emphasis became concentrated on the output side of Figures 1.1 and 1.4.

Accountants, however, as we have emphasized, are intimately involved with all aspects of the AIS and to achieve acceptable outputs equal attention must also be given to the input and processing stages.

Modern accounting software operates on the basis of the rules of double entry. The availability of accounting software as a teaching mechanism allows the students to appreciate the AIS as a whole, plus its subsystems, the inputs and outputs and the management of inputs and outputs. Our experience shows quite clearly that students respond to professional presentation of accounts, real time processing and using professional outputs.

Following the exercises in this book and preparing answers for the discussion sessions will ensure that this approach will give you:

1   a better understanding of the basics of accounting by using fully developed commercial software;
2   a greater appreciation of the design, control and flow of paperwork;
3   a greater appreciation of systems and the importance of controls;
4   more time for interpretation and integration of other subject areas;
5   greater reality;
6   a clearer insight into systems that are poorly designed;
7   recognition of the changing role of accountants;
8   recognition of the new demands being placed on accountants.

Activities

4   What is the process by which data is converted to information?
5   Discuss the contribution of General System Theory to the development of the principles and practices of management.
6   Explain the difference between an open system and a closed system and give examples of each.
7   You have been asked to provide a report to a member of the management team (who is not an accountant). You arrange an interview with the manager to discuss the requirement. List the main areas that you would wish to clarify to ensure that the manager receives information that is effective and valuable.

CASE STUDY

The case study involves us following the fortunes of John and Azina Bale who live in Melchester. John met Azina in his final year at University where he was studying computer science.

After leaving university, John worked for Codas Business Systems Ltd. His work involved him in system support (both hardware and software) on mainframe and minicomputer systems which at the time confined business computing to medium and larger sized companies. The introduction of the PC changed the scene completely and John was quick to spot the potential of companies of all sizes being able to afford computers and business software.

In the last few years, John has moved from technical support into sales and his technical knowledge coupled with his outgoing pleasant personality made him a very successful salesman for Codas Business Systems Ltd. He now knew he could sell. The job also exposed him to the market, the competition and potential clients and he was certain he could succeed in the growing PC business market. He was under no illusion, however, as to the level of competition but he was sure that he could provide a service that clients would be willing to pay for.

John had looked into the possibility of setting up his own business in 1987 but could not raise the finance. Although disappointed it did not dampen his enthusiasm and he continued to watch the PC market and became more sure that having his own business would be right for him.

Then, out of the blue, John heard that a relative had died leaving him a substantial sum of money. Over the following months he and Azina talked and talked about setting up in business. Azina would continue in her job in the legal department of a local authority to earn enough money to ensure that their mortgage was covered until the business was established; John would have to resign from Codas Business Systems Ltd. They both realized that there was a substantial risk. However well planned, there was no guarantee of success. They spoke to their friends about the idea, and some thought they had lost their senses, but they both knew that although they could seek other people's advice, at the end of the day they and only they would know if they were prepared to commit themselves. One thing that they both agreed on was that the new business should be set up in Melchester.

A Melchester base would improve their prospects of success. With a population of 250 000 it would have good potential in its own right, but it also had excellent motorway links with the Midlands, Bristol and the South West and Wales.

A friend of Azina's drew her attention to the Small Firm Advisory Centre in Liverpool and one lunch time Azina made an appointment and went down to speak to one of their staff. It was time well spent. The advisor was very experienced and patient and drew Azina's attention to all sorts of things that, up to now, she and John had not considered. She returned home with a load of leaflets and a list of questions to discuss with John.

The Advisory Centre had provided her with a checklist, which they discussed, and found very helpful. One of the major items on the checklist was the production of a business plan. This would certainly be required by the bank but more importantly it would tell both John and Azina if their idea was feasible. Azina was as committed to the idea of a new business as John and she realized that one of her roles was going to be keeping John's feet on the ground. He knew the market and could sell but the administration, paperwork and accounting would have to be Azina's responsibility.

The software

The software used and described throughout the text is Sage Sterling Financial Controller. Sage Sterling Accounting software is designed for the small to medium sized business and it provides a truly integrated system. All ledgers and control accounts are automatically updated with only one keyboard entry. For example, posting a sale invoice automatically:

1   updates the sales ledger;
2   posts VAT to the VAT account;
3   updates the debtor control account;
4   posts to the correct nominal account;
5   posts the transactions to the audit trail assigning a transaction number.

Sage is used as a vehicle to teach basic accounting and the use of the software and supporting materials is essential in developing a systems approach to accounting. Learning Sage is a byproduct, but an important byproduct nevertheless, because all integrated accounting software is written and operates on the same principles as double entry bookkeeping.

Important transferable skills are therefore acquired by the student relating to system design, system set up, security, management of documentation, and operational controls. Other integrated software can be used with the text but specific references relate to Sage Sterling Financial Controller. It is assumed that the software will be installed and run either on a hard disk or on a network.

This text does not pretend to be a manual for Sage. Features and functions are introduced as and when necessary and in the context of managing the flow of input data, through processing to the production of information. It is our experience that students enjoy this approach and find learning about Sage in the context of the management of the accounting function very stimulating. This is very different, there-fore, to reading a manual. You will be exposed to and will have to become involved in:

1 design of the chart of accounts;
2 design of balance sheet and profit and loss account;
3 document design and management;
4 batch control;
5 input controls;
6 security considerations i.e. fraud, theft and viruses;
7 analysis of day books and audit trails;
8 control of debtors;
9 bank reconciliation;
10 preparing returns for VAT;
11 presentation of management reports;
12 presentation of reports to comply with statutory requirements, etc.

By using commercial software, issues can be addressed and simulated in a way that would be impossible with a manual system. Students should benefit from working within a system that is as realistic as one can make it in a teaching environment.

Figure 1.7 shows the individual modules in this integrated system and how they are related. In this two semester course we shall be concentrating on what is traditionally the heart of the AIS, namely the **ledgers**: nominal ledger, sales ledger and the purchase ledger. These are subsystems of the AIS.

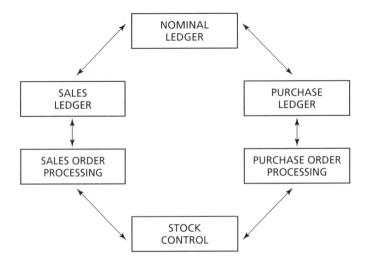

Figure 1.7
Modules in
integrated system

The parallel run

As we follow the fortunes of John and Azina Bale you will be required to computerize their manual accounts. On the introduction of a computerized system it is essential that for at least two months a **parallel run** takes place. By this is meant that the manual and computer systems are run together side by side. This can impose an enormous strain on what is probably a hard-pressed workforce but is necessary because at these early stages:

1 the hardware may cause problems;
2 the software may cause problems;
3 operator error will take place;
4 new procedures will not all be in place.

The two systems are run side by side and at the end of the month a comparison is made between the two sets of accounts. If a discrepancy exists no further processing can take place until it is detected and rectified. Reasons for the discrepancy must be established and action taken to prevent repetition. In most cases this will represent extra training for operatives and a review and revision of some of the procedures.

The parallel run continues into the second month, at the end of which another comparison is made. Hopefully at this stage very few errors exist and the management and operators will feel confident in 'cutting over' completely to the new computerized system (the maintenance of the manual system will cease).

The menu system

The final part of this section introduces you to the **menu system**. The logon procedure will vary depending on whether you are operating directly off the hard disk or on a network but once you have logged on you will be faced with the main menu. Figure 1.8 shows the Sage main menu with all the various individual components of the Accounting Information System. Use your arrow keys to move the cursor on to your selection and then press enter/carriage return. Figure 1.9 shows the menu for the

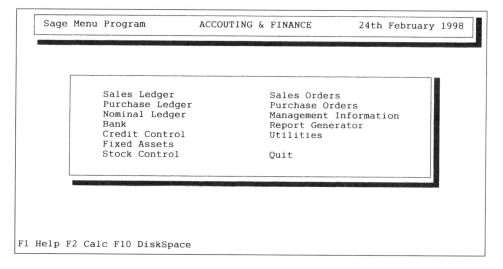

```
Sage Menu Program        ACCOUTING & FINANCE       24th February 1998


            Sales Ledger              Sales Orders
            Purchase Ledger           Purchase Orders
            Nominal Ledger            Management Information
            Bank                      Report Generator
            Credit Control            Utilities
            Fixed Assets
            Stock Control             Quit



F1 Help F2 Calc F10 DiskSpace
```

Figure 1.8
SAGE menu

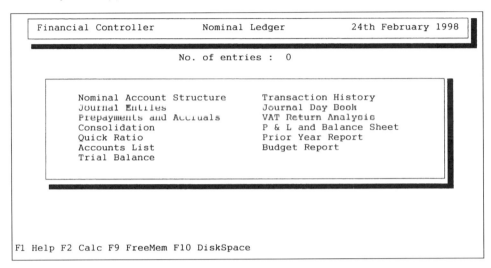

```
┌─────────────────────────────────────────────────────────────┐
│ Financial Controller      Nominal Ledger      24th February 1998 │
└─────────────────────────────────────────────────────────────┘

                      No. of entries :   0

        ┌───────────────────────────────────────────────────┐
        │   Nominal Account Structure   Transaction History   │
        │   Journal Entries             Journal Day Book       │
        │   Prepayments and Accruals    VAT Return Analysis    │
        │   Consolidation               P & L and Balance Sheet│
        │   Quick Ratio                 Prior Year Report      │
        │   Accounts List               Budget Report          │
        │   Trial Balance                                      │
        └───────────────────────────────────────────────────┘


F1 Help F2 Calc F9 FreeMem F10 DiskSpace
```

Figure 1.9
SAGE nominal ledger

nominal ledger and Figures 1.10 and 1.11 the menu for the sales ledger and purchase ledger. The sales ledger and purchase ledger are mirror images of each other, so once you have mastered one you will have mastered the other.

In newer versions of Sage the bank functions have been taken out of the individual ledgers and amalgamated in a menu of their own (Figure 1.12). Just remember that the sales receipts and purchase payments are actually part of the sales and purchase ledgers. The rest is nominal ledger.

Each option on each menu leads to further sub-menus. The software is extremely user friendly and prompts at the bottom of the screen take you through each process. Don't be worried by all the menu options you face and do not be mesmerized by the technology. This is a working AIS and the actions you will be required to perform will be dictated to you either through the documentation you receive or the requests made of you to provide information to a user. The solutions to the problems you will be faced with are accounting solutions, Sage is merely a tool to help you obtain those solutions.

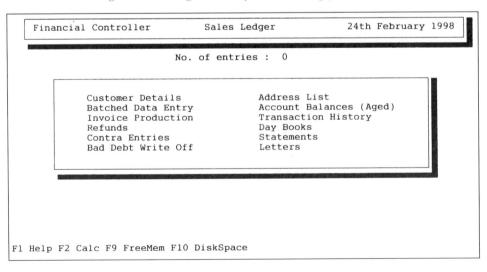

```
┌─────────────────────────────────────────────────────────────┐
│ Financial Controller       Sales Ledger       24th February 1998 │
└─────────────────────────────────────────────────────────────┘

                      No. of entries :   0

        ┌───────────────────────────────────────────────────┐
        │   Customer Details            Address List           │
        │   Batched Data Entry          Account Balances (Aged) │
        │   Invoice Production          Transaction History     │
        │   Refunds                     Day Books               │
        │   Contra Entries              Statements              │
        │   Bad Debt Write Off          Letters                 │
        └───────────────────────────────────────────────────┘



F1 Help F2 Calc F9 FreeMem F10 DiskSpace
```

Figure 1.10
SAGE sales ledger

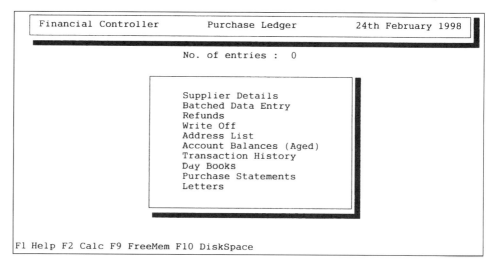

Figure 1.11
SAGE purchase
ledger

You will be amazed at how quickly you become familiar with the ledgers. As with all well designed software there is a consistency of commands and key strokes that speeds the learning process and quickly gives a reassuring familiarity which creates confidence.

Finally, do not be afraid to experiment. You will need to spend a number of weeks familiarizing yourself with the menu layouts, content, posting routines and reports. Prior to commencing the case study you should use the restore function to restore a set of empty files to the programme.

Summary

This chapter has explained how the role of the accountant has changed and what an important role the accountant plays in the whole process of producing management information.

To meet this new challenge we are adopting a systems approach to teaching

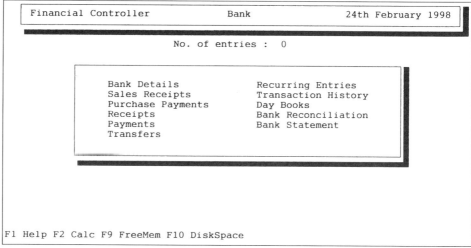

Figure 1.12
SAGE bank menu

accounting that will involve you using an integrated computerized accounting system. This method will provide you with a greater understanding of the role of information in the management decision process and consequently the importance of planning and designing systems that can meet the needs of management.

There is a clear distinction between data and information, and for information to be effective it must display certain characteristics.

You have met John and Azina Bale and we shall follow their progress and use their experiences in each chapter to build a case study that will clearly show you the value of a well designed and managed accounting information system.

At the end of each chapter summary you will find a list of new key words introduced in the chapter. Before moving on you should be very clear as to the meaning of these words. If in doubt reread the chapter.

Key words

accounting information system p. 3 • closed system p. 7 • data p. 5 • general systems theory p. 5 • information p. 5 • ledgers p. 12 • management information system p. 3 • menu systems p. 13 • open system p. 6 • parallel run p. 13 • process p. 5 • system p. 5

2 The choice of corporate form

Learning objectives

After reading this chapter you should be able to:
- understand the different types of organizational form that one can choose from and begin to evaluate the advantages and disadvantages of each
- be able to make a decision on organizational form by considering
  - legal requirements
  - operational requirements
  - risk
  - control
  - availability of finance
  - taxation.

Introduction

The choice of organizational form that every business enterprise has to make is not merely an academic exercise as much literature would have us believe. For extremely large firms, the attractions of the public company are undoubtedly overwhelming, but for the vast majority of small business enterprises in the UK the choice is by no means clear cut.

The definition of a 'small firm' is multi-dimensional and has varied over time but there is no doubt that small firms make a significant contribution to the UK economy in terms of employment and net output. Traditionally there is a rapid turnover of small firms indicating, perhaps, the high risk involved in setting up a business in an uncertain world. John and Azina certainly recognize that risk.

It is undoubtedly true that small firms possess considerably greater latitude in their choice of organizational form than do very large firms for reasons discussed below. For a sizeable proportion of UK business, the choice of organizational form is important. It is a crucial decision which will be determined largely by the objectives of the owners of the business in the light of the advantages and disadvantages of the various types of organizational form.

John Bale checked his rear view mirror, signalled right and overtook yet another juggernaught on the M5 heading south from Leeds early that morning and was now heading home after having had a very successful day meeting a new supplier and two new clients. He reflected with some pride on the events of the last three years which had seen Bale and Co. grow substantially. He smiled to himself as he remembered his interview with the manager of the Midside Bank, Sam Farwood. Sam had listened patiently to John's proposal but even before the interview had concluded, John had felt that this manager was not the type to take any chances. Luckily his friend of many years Bill Davies – an accountant who had helped him with his business plan – introduced him to Jim Buckley a manager with Blackshire Bank. Jim Buckley was new to the job, keen to promote fresh ideas and support local business. The approach had been far more positive.

The £50 000 the Bales had inherited had made the whole concept of their own business possible and they had entered into their new commitment with confidence and determination. The backing of the Blackshire Bank had been important although the funds acquired from the Blackshire Bank had been secured by personal guarantee.

Early discussion had centred around the form of business organization which should be used. John had thought a limited company would be best because it sounded more substantial to him, but he had been unaware of the implications of that choice.

Bill had pointed out that although this would give limited liability, John and Azina had already agreed to sign a personal guarantee for the bank which would mean that they did not get the full benefit of this. On the other hand they would have to register the company and comply with company law as well as sorting out the tax consequences. Bill had advised that the important thing was to be clear on their objectives in going into business.

John and Azina had sat down to clarify their objectives. Over a number of hours of discussion the following list emerged.

- We want to be in control. We want to see the business grow and we want to be the main decision makers.
- We want to minimize the risk of a financial disaster.
- For the foreseeable future the legacy and the support of the Blackshire Bank would meet their financing needs.
- We want a comfortable living but do not necessarily want to become millionaires.
- We want to make the business grow and be successful.
- We want to develop a good customer base and provide a quality service that will lead to repeat business.

Types of organizational form

The sole proprietor

The simplest kind of business enterprise is the 'sole proprietor' or **sole trader**. These are very small business organizations and, as the name suggests, are under the ownership and control of one person. The sole proprietor may have any number of people working for the business, but the essential element of ownership is in the hands of one person. In terms of numbers, this is the most common form of business organization and is found mainly in the retail trade, service industries and the professions.

The partnership

Next in complexity is the **partnership** form of organization. This is only one step removed from the sole proprietor, and like the latter it is common in the professions, e.g. doctors and lawyers, and is of comparatively little importance in the manufacturing sector, at least insofar as contribution to net output is concerned. It is possible for a partnership to extend the size of its business by taking on 'sleeping' partners, who do not participate at all in the running of the business. Such a move has implications for limited liability which we will consider below. At this point it is sufficient to say that the limited partnership has not become a popular form of business enterprise in the UK.

The joint-stock company

The most important form of organization in the UK is that of the joint-stock company. This form of organization was a direct result of the nineteenth-century Limited Liability Acts which were designed to mobilize the savings of the community into company finance.

There are two basic kinds of joint-stock company, the private company and the public company. The legal recognition of the private company came about with the Companies Act 1907. The Companies Act 1985 S 1 (1) lays down that 'any two or more persons associated for a lawful purpose may, by subscribing their names to a memorandum of association' form an incorporated company. Such a company will be a private limited company (Ltd). If the issued share capital exceeds £50 000 and the shareholders agree through a special resolution the company may become a public limited company (plc).

Unquestionably, it is the public joint-stock company that has been mainly responsible for the growth of large-scale business organization in the UK. It has been one of the major instruments responsible for the high rate of economic growth enjoyed by most modern industrial communities in the twentieth century.

Nevertheless, despite the contribution the public joint-stock company has made to modern economic development, such success has not been achieved without reservations – monopoly, exploitation, bureaucracy, etc. Moreover, despite the advantages ascribed to public companies, great private empires have continued not only to survive but to grow successfully. The continued formation of new business enterprises every year and the environmental limitations on growth of many of the existing ones, have continued to provide an outlet for the simpler forms of business organization.

Choice of organizational form

Against this background of various organizational forms we will now consider the essential factors governing the choice of corporate structure.

Why should choice be a problem?

The problem arises because the legal, financial and economic environment affords opportunities but imposes constraints. It is important, therefore, that the enterprise analyses the implications of these opportunities and constraints so that it can choose the type of organizational form which will enable it to manipulate them in an optimum manner for its particular objectives.

Legal requirements and constraints

Legal requirements and constraints differ greatly according to the type of organizational form. The sole proprietor is subject to virtually no regulations, they do not even have to register the business name. The next least constrained is the partnership, which is also subject to few legal requirements other than the contract between the partners. Under the Limited Partnership Act 1907, a business may constitute itself a limited partnership by registering with the Registrar of Companies. This involves somewhat more detailed regulation than the unlimited partnership, particularly with regard to the sums contributed by each limited partner. Nevertheless, despite these extra commitments, the legal constraint is not much greater than that of the sole proprietor.

However, when we move on to consider the joint-stock company form of organization, the legal requirements become much more onerous, with those for the public company being even greater than the private company. The formation of a joint-stock company involves the production of three documents:

1 **Memorandum of Association** – This includes the name of the company, its objectives, details of the authorized share capital and an indication that the liability of the shareholders is limited (which it nearly always is in practice).
2 **Articles of Association** – Standard Articles of Association are laid out in Table A of the Companies Act 1985 and these will be adopted unless the company has articles of its own. This document contains information on the issue and transfer of shares, alteration of capital, dividend policy, borrowing powers of the company, regulations governing shareholders' meetings and the power of the directors.

    Legally, a private company is distinct from a public company in that it has certain constraints in its Articles of Association. These constraints include restrictions on the right to transfer shares, and prohibition of public subscription for the share capital of the company.
3 *Statutory Declaration* – This is a declaration by a director or the acting solicitor for the company that the conditions laid down in the Companies Act 1985 for the formation of companies have been complied with.

Besides the costs involved in the production of the above documents there is also a registration stamp and fees and a tax of 50p per £100 of authorized capital. In addition to this the public company is required to file a prospectus and list of directors with the Registrar of Companies. The directors must also indicate that the required amount of capital has been subscribed. If the public are not invited to subscribe, then the company may issue a statement in lieu of the prospectus.

Operational constraints

In addition to these legal requirements, limited companies also face various constraints upon the operation of their business.

1   The most important requirement is the obligation to file their annual accounts with the Registrar of Companies. Prior to 1967 there existed a category of private companies called exempt private companies, which were not required to file their accounts in this manner. However, since the Companies Act 1967, all limited companies are required to conform to this procedure. This legislation removed the outstanding advantage which these exempt private companies possessed – their ability to conceal their accounts from the public.
2   There are also additional requirements for the public company if it wishes to have its shares quoted on the Stock Exchange.
3   Finally, and perhaps most importantly, as far as economic analysis of business decisions is concerned, the legal framework of joint-stock companies requires that annual general meetings of shareholders be held. In certain circumstances it is possible for such meetings to impose serious constraints on company policy, although in reality the majority of these meetings usually impose a passive rather than an active constraint.

Thus, one of the great attractions of the sole trader, and indeed the partnership form of organization, lies in the fact that they are easily and inexpensively formed and are subject to few government regulations. This is in marked contrast to the company type of organization, where the legal requirements are much greater. Perhaps the one weakness of the sole trader and the partnership lies in their impermanence. The sole proprietor form of organization is bound up with the life of the owner, and the partnership may also involve re-drafting of partnership contracts on the death of one of the partners. In this sense, of course, the joint-stock company has virtual immortality, unless the company is formally wound up either voluntarily or because it is unable to meet its liabilities. In this latter case it is said to be insolvent and is put into liquidation or receivership to realize what assets are left and pay the creditors as far as possible.

Risk for the owners

The biggest single risk which faces anyone starting a business is that which arises from unlimited liability. If a business organization does not possess **limited liability** it means that the owners are jointly liable for the debts of the firm. Thus the entire private fortune of a shareholder may be put at risk merely by the purchase of one share in an unlimited company.

In practice, of course, most companies are limited. However, the status of limited liability is not available to the sole proprietor and partnership forms of organization. It is possible for a partnership to consist of some limited partners, but *at least one* of the partners must have unlimited liability. However, the limited partner is not permitted to participate in the running of the business (known as a sleeping partner).

The principle of limited liability is an extremely important one. It means that the shareholder is liable only up to the amount stated on the par value of the share. **Par**

value is the value stated on the share certificate e.g. £1. If someone pays more than £1 for a share it is said that the share is being sold at a premium (the premium being the difference between the par value and the selling price). If someone pays less than £1 for a share it is said that the share is being sold at a discount (the discount being the difference between the par value and the selling price). Once the share is fully paid up, the shareholder has no other liability to the company. In the case of the limited partnership, the amount contributed by each limited partner must be clearly designated.

Risk in the joint-stock company

It is quite clear that from the point of view of risking everything in the fortunes of the business, the sole proprietor and the partnership are at a serious disadvantage *vis-à-vis* the limited company. If the business should founder on the uncharted seas of the business environment, the sole proprietor and the unlimited partners risk losing all they possess. Many a small business has gone to the wall, its creditors hovering around like vultures hoping to cut their losses with small pickings from the debris left behind in the bankruptcy.

In contrast, shareholders in limited companies can stand aloof if similar ill-fortune were to fall on one of the companies in which they invest. With a diversified share-holding among a number of companies, the success of some is likely to cancel out the losses incurred from one company in liquidation. Yet if just a single share in any unlimited company had been purchased, virtually everything they possessed could be seized by its creditors.

It is little wonder, then, that the introduction of limited liability played such a great part in the rapid growth of the British economy in the latter part of the nineteenth and early twentieth centuries. It was the advent of the joint-stock company and the development of limited liability that led to the channelling of small savings into investment; an investment which was so necessary for the rapid rate of economic growth which Britain enjoyed during this period.

The private investor's risk

Although it is true that shareholders in limited companies do not risk the loss of everything they possess, unlike the sole proprietor or unlimited partners, the value of the shareholdings themselves are nevertheless subject to the whims of the market. Since the Stock Exchange represents the major form of investment in the UK (other than house purchase), some investors may find that a sizeable proportion of their assets is continuously at risk. Moreover, it is not merely the prospect of the liquidation of particular companies that is the risk element here, but also the fluctuating value of the shareholdings themselves. This aspect of risk is of particular significance to those investors to whom liquidity is important, since the value of their shareholdings may not be standing at a desirable level at the time they wish to realize their assets. Indeed over the three years 1973–75 the Stock Exchange Index varied from a low of under 150 to a high of over 450, so that anyone who bought their shares in a boom market was reluctant to realize them at depressed values.

Thus, while it is true to say that the sole proprietor and the partnership form of organization are exposed to a much greater risk than are the shareholders of a limited company, in that their total realizable assets are at stake, shareholders of limited companies are themselves open to considerable losses, particularly where the extent of their shareholdings is large.

Ownership and control

We will now attempt to answer the fundamental question – do the people who own the business enterprise also control its operations?

If one desires to remain in 100 per cent control of an enterprise, the only form of business organization to satisfy this is the sole proprietor. The sole trader as the name implies, means that only one person has the authority to make all the crucial decisions. In the partnership form of organization, control is shared among the partners to the extent specified in the partnership contract.

Once one moves into the company form of organization, control by the owners can be considerably diluted. Ownership of 51 per cent of the shares or more is crucial to retaining control. The real divorce of ownership from control lies in the large public company, where there may be hundreds of thousands of shareholders. However, the structure of such shareholdings is usually such that control can be maintained with considerably less than 51 per cent of the shares. The line will vary from company to company. Whatever the figure is, the fact remains that for most shareholders in the large public company the divorce of ownership from control is more or less complete in that they have no effective control over operational policy. Their influence is limited to voting at a general meeting.

Therefore, in terms of the maintenance of control by the owners, the simpler forms of industrial organization such as the sole proprietor and the partnership are far superior to the company form.

Control over the earnings stream

This concept of control over a business representing control over earnings seems very pertinent. It is true that many small businesses have been reluctant to expand because of the fear of losing control of the earnings stream. This, of course, raises the fundamental question of whether achieving the largest possible earnings stream was the objective in the first place.

Availability of finance

More than any other factor, it was the serious limitation of the ability of the simpler organizational forms to raise adequate finance that led to the development of the public limited company.

To engage in almost any kind of business activity, the owner must be prepared to provide some of the capital from private sources. The sole trader is obviously restricted in the amount of capital he or she can provide and frequently the owner has to resort to borrowing from close friends and relatives. The partnership form of organization can provide more capital than the sole proprietor, but it, too, is restricted to the private resources of the partners.

Limitations upon the amount of ownership capital are extremely important, since they severely constrain the borrowing capacity of the business. As a broad generalization, it can be said that small businesses have adequate access to short-term finance. The major source of such finance is trade credit which generates itself in the course of the business, bank loans which for small businesses are largely determined by the personal contact between the lender and the borrower, accruals in the form of tax owed to the Inland Revenue but not yet paid, and invoice discounting and factoring whereby certain specialized finance companies will convert a certain proportion of the debts of the company into cash. In terms of short-term financing for small businesses, banks are of crucial importance, for the business can use its own resources to the limit knowing that it can fall back on the bank in times of emergency.

While small businesses have not been lacking in short-term finance there have been periods when the provision of long-term finance has been a problem. This problem of financing the long run capital requirements of small companies became so acute that the Macmillan Committee (1931) was able to talk of a positive 'gap' in the financing of these companies. The subsequent criticism of the banking sector's attitude to small firms by the Radcliffe Committee (1959) led to the setting up of a number of organizations in an attempt to bridge the 'gap' (e.g. Industrial & Commerce Finance Corporation).

In the 1980s and 1990s there was a renewed interest in the fortunes of small companies leading to the establishment of the Unlisted Securities Market (USM) in 1980. The USM was intended to enable small and medium-sized firms more easily to acquire venture capital on the London Stock Exchange. Previously, smaller firms had been discouraged by the prohibitive cost of a full listing on the Stock Exchange (upwards of £200 000) and the fact that a minimum of 25 per cent of shares had to be in the hands of the public. The cost of joining the USM was considerably below that of a full listing, perhaps as little as £12 000, and there was greater flexibility since companies need only place a minimum of 10 per cent of shares in public hands. The advantages of the USM for the small or medium-sized firm included access to share capital, which is one of the cheapest forms of company funding, the opportunity to engage in rights issues and placings, and the ability to offer shares as well as cash when seeking to grow through acquisition. Although there is no rigid limit to the size of firms joining the USM, they have ranged from £1m to £5m in terms of market capitalization. This is smaller than is normal for companies which seek a full listing.

Companies such as Reliant Motors, Acorn Computers and Intersun Leisure were amongst the 283 companies which had used the USM by mid-1985. These companies had raised over £803m from their flotations. In 1988 companies raised a total of £1.02bn in that year alone on the USM, of which £308m was raised by new companies. Since then the money raised by new companies each year has fallen, perhaps reflecting the downturn in the economy. Nearly 200 USM companies have transferred to a full listing since 1980. In the year 1990–91, 49 new companies were admitted to the USM, bringing the total listing to almost 400.

Changes in the law have also made it possible for small business owners to sell shares to outside investors and make an agreement with them that the company will buy back the shares after a certain time period. This benefits small firms which wish to raise capital but which do not want to part with their equity permanently. The situation has improved but, nevertheless, they still face genuine difficulties compared to public limited companies.

Changes in the EU directives harmonizing stock exchange requirements led to a reduced role for the USM as thresholds to the main market were reduced but those to the USM increased. In 1995 the Unlisted Securities Market was replaced by the Alternative Investment Market (AIM). AIM was established to provide a market for smaller companies. It is too early as yet to judge how effective it will be.

Advantages of the public company

The advantages of the public company become overwhelming when we consider the effect which the availability of finance has on choice of organizational form. The sole proprietor and the partnership have no access at all to the facilities of the new issue market, and the activities of the private company are severely limited. The public company can raise long-term finance merely by the issue of debentures, preference shares and equities.

Figure 2.1 shows the securities that can be sold by a company to raise long-term finance. The left hand side of the figure shows shares and the right hand side debentures. Let us concentrate initially on the left hand side.

Equity or ordinary shares are the main type of shares issued. These shares represent ownership of the business and the reward for holding these shares is a share of the profit (**dividend**). There is no guarantee of any return and equity holders shoulder all of the business risk, i.e. in the event of a liquidation, equity holders are the last to be paid from the proceeds of the liquidation. In practice this often means that they receive nothing.

The preference shareholders, as the name implies, receive preferential treatment in that they will receive a dividend before the equity can receive anything but there will be a limit on the amount of dividend that they receive.

The variations of the preference share, just like the variations of the debenture, are really a marketing device to make the product more or less attractive depending upon conditions in the market. For example, if confidence is high and there is plenty of money in the economy a less attractive package will need to be offered to potential

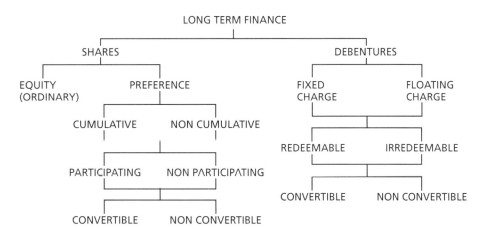

Figure 2.1
Long-term finance

investors than when confidence is low and less money is available in the economy. The following variations should be noted:

1 *Cumulative* means that if a dividend is not paid this year it will be rolled forward for payment in the following year.
2 *Participating* means that a second opportunity may exist to receive a dividend once the ordinary shares have received a stated guaranteed return. For example, a preference share may give a 5 per cent dividend but an extra share of profit will be received once the ordinary dividend reaches 12 per cent.
3 *Convertible* means that at some specific date in the future the preference share-holders will be given an opportunity to convert their preference shares to ordinary shares.

A **debenture** holder is simply a person who has made a long-term loan to the company at an agreed rate of interest. The debenture holder is a creditor of the company, not a shareholder, and is entitled to a fixed rate of interest every year. They can force the company into liquidation if they are not paid. Individuals and institutions are prepared to buy debentures from the company because they know that this is the safest form of investment; they have the first claim on the assets of the company in the event of liquidation. Note here that the debenture issues made by a public company are usually made on a floating charge (i.e. the debenture is secured against all the assets of the company whatever they happen to be), whereas the long-term debt finance available to the partnership and the sole proprietor usually take the form of a mortgage secured on a specific asset of the enterprise. Thus, the public company usually has much more flexibility and autonomy in its use of long-term debt finance. The following variations of debentures exist:

1 *Redeemable* means that the debenture when it is originally sold will have a redemption date, i.e. a date when the original loan will be repaid.
2 *Irredeemable* means that the security has an indefinite life.
3 *Convertible* and *non-convertible* have the same meaning as under preference shares.

In so far as equity financing is concerned, it is the principle of limited liability which represents the major advantage of the public company. The public limited company can issue equity shares which the public will buy because they can then participate in the profits of the company with the only risk being that of fluctuation in the value of the shares.

The preference share is a kind of hybrid security: it carries a fixed rate of dividend similar to debentures, but holders are not able to force the company into liquidation if they are not paid. The larger the ordinary shareholder investment (known as the equity base) that the firm possesses, the greater will be the amount of long-term debt it can raise, since the larger equity base will provide some security for debenture holders.

Thus if finance, or perhaps lack of finance, is the main criterion of choice of business form, the advantages of the public company are outstanding. Not only are they in a better position to attract loan finance but also the advantages of limited liability facilitate the diversification of shareholdings so necessary to the small shareholder.

Tax burden

For taxation purposes, business organizations can be divided into two categories: on the one hand sole proprietors and partnerships, on the other hand ordinary companies.

1   Sole proprietors and partnerships are taxed as individuals, and consequently are taxed according to the income of the partners involved. The amount of tax paid depends upon each partner's share of the profits and his individual tax rate. An important point to note here is that the greater the number of partners, the smaller is each individual's share of the profits and consequently the lower is his marginal tax rate. This is one of the main reason for the conversion of many sole proprietorships into partnerships and family businesses. The tax burden of these simple forms of business organization varies from the lower rate of 15 per cent income tax, through a basic rate of (in 1997/98) 23 per cent to the higher-rate tax of 40 per cent Thus, the sole proprietor and the partnership are faced with a progressive system of taxation.

2   The second taxation category is represented by ordinary companies who pay corporation tax on their trading profit at the prevailing rate. In 1997/98 this was at a standard rate of 31 per cent except for small companies (defined as companies with profits of less than £300 000 at 21 per cent. Until April 1973 the taxation system favoured profit retention, since while retained profits acquired no further tax liability once corporation tax had been paid, profits distributed as dividends were taxed at the income tax rate and possibly an investment income surcharge rate applicable to the individual shareholder. After April 1973 with the introduction of the imputation system of corporation tax, distributed and undistributed profits faced a uniform corporation tax rate.

Under the imputation system a company makes a payment to the Inland Revenue when it pays a dividend but the shareholders get an 'imputed' credit for having borne income tax at the basic rate. This tax payment on dividends is called the advance corporation tax and it can be offset against the company's eventual corporation tax liability on that year's profit, thus ensuring that there is no discrimination between distributed and undistributed profits. However there is currently a move to return to the pre-1973 model of corporation tax.

Individuals and companies are subject to various taxes and restrictions which are constantly changing and a decision on organizational form based on taxation considerations can only be made with the information available at the time. Income tax, corporation tax, national insurance, capital gains tax, inheritance tax, choice of year end and treatment of losses could all be relevant to the decision but they are beyond the brief of this textbook. Let us give you two examples to illustrate the points.

1   A sole trader or partnership can withdraw funds without tax penalty, subject in a partnership to other partners and the partnership agreement. A dividend from a company has tax consequences.

2   For a sole trader and partnership, losses accrued in the first four years of assessment may be set back against statutory total income of the previous three years.

In most cases, the choice of corporate structure is determined by factors other than tax. However, circumstances may exist in which a change of corporate structure may reduce the tax burden. In this respect, it is worth noting the recommendations of the Bolton Committee, which suggested that 'what is required above all for the health of the small firm sector is an economic and taxation system which will enable individuals to acquire or establish new businesses out of personal resources, and to develop these on the base of retained profits'.

Summary

There is no one single criterion business people can use to select the correct form of organization for their enterprise. The whole question of choice is closely related to the objectives of the owners. Generally, most businesses start up with the simpler forms of organization such as sole proprietor and partnership, where ease of formation and maintenance of control are important. They work their way to the private company and eventually the public company, as the expansion drive of the enterprise becomes stifled by lack of capital and exorbitant taxation. However, there is no clearly defined point at which one moves from one organizational form to another.

There are many sole proprietors who are content to be their own boss and do their own thing rather than expand the enterprise with the inevitable dilution of control that this entails. Similarly, there are many extremely large private companies that are struggling against lack of capital to maintain their own private empires. One of the classic examples of a large private company being forced to go public by lack of capital was Lord Cowdray's company, Pearson.

The company had been private for over 130 years, but the need to guard against the inevitability of death duties forced the company to go public. When the company offered ten million of its ordinary shares to the public in August 1969 it was one of the biggest issues the stock market had ever seen, and put a price tag of £71.6m on Cowdray's business interests. If a wealth tax is introduced, it will make it even more difficult for the large private empires to avoid going public. Nevertheless, the example of Pearson provides evidence of the ability of business to survive in the organizational form of their choice, even when the sheer size of operations suggests that a more appropriate organizational form is required. Other large private empires which have turned public include Pilkington Brothers and J Sainsbury.

Thus, in the final analysis, choice of organizational form is very much a personal issue, although the time must come when every family business will begin to feel the pressure of the factors outlined above. John and Azina, after much discussion, finally classified their own objectives and chose to set up initially as a sole trader. We say 'initially' because this question relating to organizational form is dynamic and must be reviewed as the business develops and circumstances change. A partnership would have been an obvious choice, however, Azina is hoping to continue to work until the business can produce a reliable cash flow but her employer is not keen for employees to have second jobs. Azina does not want to jeopardize her position until things are more secure and does not want her name appearing on invoices and letter heads for the moment. However she will help with the record keeping and administration. Regardless of the form of organization the principles of maintaining accounting records and producing management information remain the same.

Key words

Practice questions

1 What is meant by the term 'limited liability'? Why would John and Azina not obtain the full benefit of limited liability if they set up as a company?
2 What three documents must be produced during the formation of a joint-stock company? Describe the purpose of each.
3 State if the shares below are being sold at a premium or at a discount.

Par value (£)	Selling price (£)	Premium/discount
1.00	1.20	
1.00	0.80	
0.25	1.10	
4.00	2.50	
3.00	1.00	
0.10	0.35	
100.00	110.00	

4 Is it true to say that shareholders in a large joint-stock company (the legal owners) have very little say in the management of the company?
5 Explain the crucial differences that exist between a debenture and an ordinary share (equity).

3 The system boundaries and data capture

Learning objectives

After reading this chapter you should:
- be aware of the input and output boundaries which define the AIS
- have an overview of the way in which the output boundary is established
- have an understanding of the conventions accountants employ to establish the input boundary
- have a practical understanding of the way in which data are captured
- appreciate the need for good design of the basic documentation for the AIS
- be aware of the need for internal control procedures
- understand how basic internal control procedures would apply in a small business.

Introduction

In Chapter 1 you were introduced to the accounting information system (AIS) as a subset of the management information system (MIS). As an open system the AIS needs:

1   input and output boundaries to define the data which it encompasses and
2   a means of classifying and processing the data so that the system will provide useful information.

The relevant part of the diagram from Chapter 1 which was used to represent the AIS is reproduced in Figure 3.1. The boundaries in the diagram are set by long established conventions or principles and this chapter will look at these in some detail and see how

Figure 3.1
The basic AIS system

they apply to the situation in the case study. The process involves the accounting technique of 'double entry' and will be considered in the next chapter.

We start with the output boundary. This might sound back to front but it is the output requirements which determine the input needed. Until you know what output you need from the AIS, you cannot decide what input will be relevant, just as until you know what cake you are going to bake you don't know what ingredients you need. In accounting, the output takes the form of information and to determine what information is needed we must first find out who will use it and why.

Some of the accounting terms introduced in this chapter have been codified in a draft *Statement of Principles* prepared for the accounting profession by an organization known as the Accounting Standards Board (ASB). This organization has the task of setting detailed standards for preparing output reports for the owners of companies. The *Statement of Principles* provides a reference point for basic definitions and they are introduced and used here as needed.

C A S E S T U D Y

THE RECORDING SYSTEM

Azina had a problem.

Initially the bookkeeping had seemed easy, but, as work came in, it became more and more difficult to answer the questions from customers and suppliers, not to mention John.

'I am sure we didn't order all the items on this invoice' she explained to John one afternoon, 'I can't even be certain that we received it all. As for the customers, as we are going to offer credit we need to have some means of checking their credit standing and monitoring their payment record.'

'You'll cope' comforted John absent-mindedly 'I don't suppose you've had time to work out those cash flow figures I need?'

Azina realized that if she was going to be able to answer these questions she would need to learn more about accountancy. Her local University offered a part-time degree in Accounting and Finance and Azina enrolled. More urgently she needed immediate practical advice. She rang Bill.

Bill was glad to act as advisor and wished that all his clients would take as keen an interest.

He discussed a number of issues with Azina and John about the planned operation of the business. These are outlined below:

A. Are you proposing to sell more than one line of goods? What would you see as the main classes of sales?

John considered these points and decided that in his own mind he categorized the sales in the following way:

- computers
- printers
- other.

B. Will you sell on cash terms, credit terms or both?

The business was going to involve a retail outlet with a showroom, and a mail order and direct sale service by John himself. They would be selling on cash and credit terms.

C. How many customer accounts do you think you are likely to operate?

This was guess work to John. He said 'As many as we can persuade to buy from us.' However he hoped it would be in the range of 40–50 within the first year and expand year by year after that.

D. Will you buy on credit terms, cash terms or both?

Through John's contacts he could get credit terms from most of the major suppliers which the business would use. However John did not rule out the prospect of buying elsewhere and for cash if he saw a good bargain.

E. How many suppliers?

Initially most of the supplies would be purchased from eight major suppliers.

F. What types of expenses will you incur?

The retail outlet and offices would need the usual housekeeping costs such as insurance, heat, light and energy, maintenance, telephone, cleaning. The intention was to launch the business with good advertising and possibly host some receptions to introduce clients to the service on offer. The expenses of running the office would need to be considered and they would need such items as desks, chairs, filing cabinets, stationery, fax machines, photocopiers, files, etc.

G. Will you pay some expenses in cash?

Generally speaking expenses would be paid through the bank but a petty cash float would be needed to meet small office payments e.g. the coffee and milk, some petrol and travelling expenses.

H. Are you going to employ people in your business?

John was quite clear that they intended to employ staff as the business grew. He had plans for a string of retail outlets, a telephone mail order service and . . . the possibilities seemed endless.

The answers to these questions give Bill an overview of the new business and from this he could begin to define the boundaries of the AIS which would be needed. The system must not only cope with initial requirements, it must be flexible enough to grow with the business should Bale and Company prove successful and John's ideas be fulfilled.

The output boundary

As we have seen, the output boundary determines the rest of the AIS. Once you know what you want from the system you can determine what needs to go in and how it should be processed. We start by looking at who the users might be and what information they need. In Chapter 1 we looked at the qualitative characteristics of information derived from the AIS. Here we take an overview of the nature of that information.

The users

The AIS provides accounting and economic information for those users who have a legitimate need for information whether they work for the organization as insiders, or trade with or invest in the organization as outsiders.

The *Statement of Principles* is concerned with 'outside' users. It states that the objective of the financial statements for these users is 'to provide information about the financial position, performance and financial adaptability of an enterprise that is useful to a wide range of users in making economic decisions'.

Who those users are will depend upon factors some of which are under the control of the owner but some of which are outside factors.

Controllable factors include:

1 *The size of the business*, e.g. if you employ people they have an interest in the accounts of the business and the more managers there are the more people who need information to do their work.
2 *The legal form chosen for the organization*, e.g. a sole trader has one owner/ manager to provide information to but a partnership will need to provide information for all the partners. A company will need to report to all the current shareholders and any future possible shareholders as well as making information available to the public at Companies House.
3 *Methods of finance*, e.g. if the money invested comes from the owners then only they will need information but if money is borrowed from banks or other lenders these institutions will also want reports on what is happening.
4 *Management structure*, e.g. if the owner employs a manager then both manager and owner will require information.

Factors outside the owner's control include:

1 taxation systems;
2 social pressures;
3 environmental concerns;
4 employment legislation;
5 public relations requirements.

The first thing to notice is that the factors will differ from organization to organization. As a result each organization must define its own output requirements and this will determine its own unique AIS.

The second point is that all these factors, whether controllable or not, can, and do, change. New tax laws or changes in sources of finance for the organization can change the range of users and their need for information. This means that any AIS must be designed to be flexible and adaptable.

So the AIS varies between organizations and over time. However there is a core of information which you would expect for all organizations and some standard rules and concepts which have general application. It is these which we will develop in this book.

Bale and Co. is a sole trader and initially has no employees. This is one of the simplest forms of organization but there is still a range of users who need information. These will include:

1 John and Azina themselves as owner/managers;
2 the bank manager;
3 trade suppliers who offer them goods on credit terms;
4 customers who rely on them to supply goods;

5   the Inland Revenue;
6   the Customs and Excise.

Information needs

John and Azina will need the most detailed information in order to make day-to-day management decisions. At the very least they will need to know:

1   who owes them money,
2   who they owe money to,
3   how much cash is in the bank,
4   what sales have been made and expenses incurred.

There is no standard format for the output of this information. Just as managers in any larger organization, John and Azina will decide on the information that they need and the frequency with which they need it. In a larger organization the accountant would design a suitable format for the presentation of information. Azina will design her own.

In their capacity as owners and investors, the Bales will want to measure their income and assess their current position. It can be useful to:

1   compare the results of the entity with other similar concerns to assess performance; or
2   establish the return that the business is making for its owners; or
3   decide whether the owners would make a better return by closing the entity down and investing their capital in more lucrative investments; or
4   approach new investors or banks to see if they would be prepared to invest in the business.

Providing reports for investors in a standard form makes them easier for users to read and compare with those from earlier periods or from other similar organizations. Familiarity with the order and style speeds up the processes of preparation and comprehension. It is less likely that information will be inadvertently overlooked and there will be time savings in preparation and use. Three basic reports that will be met regularly are:

1   the balance sheet;
2   the profit and loss account;
3   the cash flow statement.

The *balance sheet* tells you the position of the organization at the time it is drawn up. It details the items owned, the amounts owed and the extent of the investment in the business by its owners.

The *profit and loss account* calculates the earnings of the business over a stated period of time. It details the income and the expenses of the organization.

The *cash flow statement* tells you where the cash has come from and where it has gone over a period of time.

Banks, creditors and customers require less detailed information than the managers but will be interested in cash generated to pay interest and the ability of the business to repay the amounts outstanding. They might also be interested in the value of property or other assets which could be used as a form of security. The reports they receive will be summarized information. For example, they will be interested in the overall total of the money customers owe Bale and Co. whereas John and Azina will want to know the detail of who each customer is, how much they each owe and when they are likely to pay.

Other users will need specialist but standard information and reports. The Customs and Excise require regular reports for VAT which are filled in on standard forms and the AIS must be able to provide the figures needed for those forms. We will discuss VAT in more detail in Chapter 8 when Bale and Co. register for VAT. In summary they will require details of sales and purchases of goods and services, classified according to tax category.

Similarly the Inland Revenue will require standard information for income and capital gains tax purposes. Their requirements are similar to those of the owners of the business in that they will want to establish the income of the business. They also require considerable detail regarding assets sold and purchased by the business.

There is a legal requirement to keep records for both the Inland Revenue and the Customs and Excise in sufficient detail to determine the tax liability. The records must be kept for at least six years.

You can see that the AIS must provide a wide range of reports some using summaries of the information from the AIS and some needing the data in considerable detail. As managers need the most detailed information, their needs will have most influence on the design of the AIS. However the need to summarize information for some outsiders and to provide information for the tax authorities must be catered for in the design of the system.

Input boundary

If the reports provided as output from the system are to prove valuable they must contain information which meets the qualitative characteristics discussed in Chapter 1 and the needs of the users as we have identified them. It is the function of input boundaries to select data from the environment which will meet these characteristics, rejecting non-relevant or inaccurate information and ensuring the completeness and reliability of the data.

Accountants have established conventions to set limits to the information which is processed through the AIS so that a relevant, reliable and complete database is available. The two we consider here are:

1   the entity concept;
2   the cost principle.

Entity concept

The first principle to consider is the **entity concept**. You might think this is a matter of common sense but it is important and often overlooked in practice.

The system you are trying to design is intended to record the financial information relating to one organization or 'entity'. The system must not mix up the transactions from this entity with the financial records or affairs of the owners, managers or any other person or organization. The users of the output of the AIS require information relating to the particular concerns of the organization they are interested in. Anything else is irrelevant.

This means for example that when a new business starts out in life operating from its owner's home or using some of its owner's belongings such as a car or a computer it is important that it is established either that the business is charged for the use of those items or that they are formally transferred to the ownership of the business.

The aim is to record the costs and benefits from the operation of the entity itself. The entity concept requires that the organization answers the following questions:

1 What is the entity?
2 What does it own?
3 What does it owe and to whom?

Activity

1 For each of the following transactions decide whether they are transactions of the business which should be recorded in the books of Bale and Co.
   (i)   The cost of the car Azina uses to drive to and from work.
   (ii) The electricity bill for the office.
   (iii) The electricity bill for their private address.
   (iv) The costs of the car that John uses for work and for driving to the golf club.
   (v)   The telephone bill of Azina and John for their private line.
   Would your answer be different if:
       (a) You knew that the line had been used to arrange the purchase of the business premises, establish the first customers and make the first purchases before the business line was installed at the business address?
       (b) John continues to use the private line for business purposes when he works from home outside normal office hours?

The cost principle

The **cost principle** relates to the fact that accountants report information on the financial operations of the business and therefore only record information which can be measured in money terms. This sets practical limits to the scope of the AIS but some important matters regarding the organization will be left out. For example, the value of well-motivated and highly trained staff or useful business contacts are not recorded. Contacts and staff do not belong to the entity. The cost of staff salaries and wages for the work done for the business will be recorded and the sales generated from the contacts but no attempt will be made to value the people or knowledge concerned. Legal contracts will only be recorded by the financial system when they are considered to have a financial effect, i.e. when the business incurs an expense or gain from their operation (Table 3.1).

Naturally the business will need to keep records of contracts entered into and staff

Table 3.1 Examples of the application of the cost principle

Don't record	Do record
Employment contract for new employee	Salary payments under the contract
Contract to supply goods to a client for the next ten years	Sales of items made under the contract with customer
Rental agreement to sublet part of the business premises	Rent receivable under the subletting agreement

contracts. They will form part of the overall management information system but are not part of the AIS.

Data capture

The case study of Bale and Co. illustrates that information becomes available from a wide range of sources. If the AIS is to provide reliable information then the information set which it contains must be complete and accurate. This information set or data can be captured from a number of sources. Traditionally it would take the form of pieces of paper but these days it could include such means as the Internet, bar coding or electronic data interchange (EDI). For the moment we will concentrate on the more traditional situation in the case study.

Input data will be received by the Bales in various forms but mainly through the post or fax or by hand and in the form of pieces of paper. There will be catalogues and advertising brochures, junk mail and bills to pay, orders from customers and bank statements, delivery notes explaining what is in the boxes which have just arrived and with any luck some cheques from satisfied customers. To make matters worse John and Azina will be generating a lot of paperwork for themselves. Every time a sale is made they will make out an invoice for the customer and keep a copy for themselves. They will have copies of the orders they send to suppliers for goods they want to buy. If they pay bills they will have the cheque book counterfoils. The list appears endless.

All these pieces of paper need to be carefully and speedily sorted, controlled, classified and filed. The data they contain are the basis of the information system. If any are missing the AIS loses its reliability. As the post is opened it should be sorted. It is a good idea to date stamp the papers so that there is a record of the day it was received.

At this initial stage the Bales' information can be classified under the following broad activities:

1   *Purchasing* – this includes information relating to the purchase of goods for resale and for use within the business such as office furniture and equipment; services and business expenses such as telephone, insurance and electricity.
2   *Selling* – this includes copies of sales invoices some of which will be for customers paying in cash and some for customers who have been given credit.
3   *Bank and cash* – cash and bank receipts and payments.
4   *Other* – this might include details of loan contracts, wages and drawings by John and Azina.

As the business grows, further categories will be needed e.g. wages and salaries or records of stock in hand, but for the moment we will concentrate on the categories needed to start. Having discarded the junk mail, an initial sort of the paperwork into these categories will be sufficient.

Purchasing

The process involved in purchasing is illustrated in Figure 3.2. Just as any private individual wanting to buy something, John and Azina will need to find out who the different suppliers are by comparing quality and price before they decide to make a purchase (A). The Bales might find it useful to store any catalogues, price lists etc. that they receive for reference. Once the decision is made, they need to place an order and

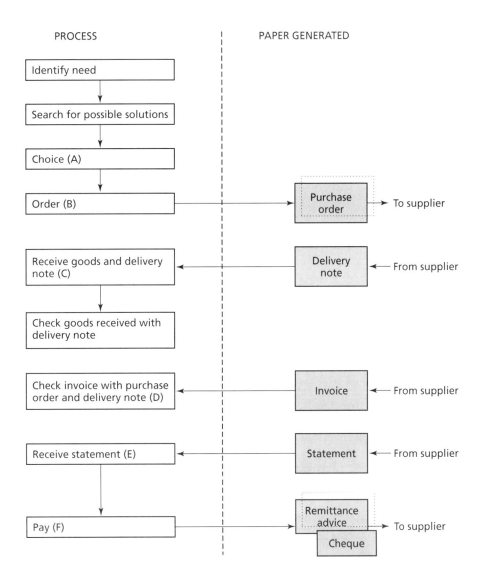

Figure 3.2
Overview of the purchasing system

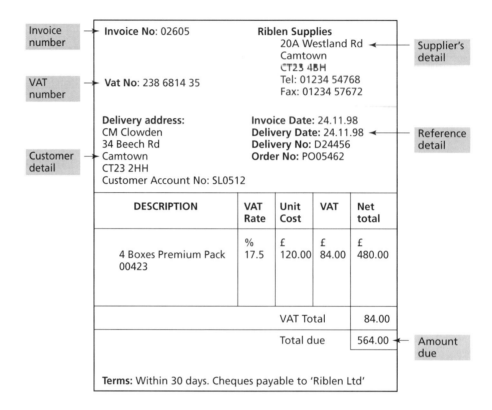

Figure 3.3
Example of an
invoice

while it could be done by phone it is safer to send a hard copy to specify quantity, style, colour, quality and price (B). When the goods are eventually received they will probably come with another piece of paper known as the delivery note confirming what should be included with the delivery (C). Eventually an invoice will be received from the supplier detailing the amount payable and explaining when it is due (D). If the amount is not paid it will appear on a statement from the supplier, usually sent monthly giving details of all unpaid invoices (E). Finally the Bales will pay the amount due sending the cheque with another piece of paper known as a remittance advice which just tells the supplier which invoices the accompanying cheque covers (F).

As far as the capture of data is concerned the crucial information is that found on the **invoice**. It is this document which is used as the source for entering information into the system. A typical invoice is shown in Figure 3.3. Look at the information that it contains.

Note the following information on the **invoice**:

1   Invoices are sequentially numbered for ease of reference so that any missing ones can be detected.
2   The supplier's name and business address, telephone and fax number are the means of communicating identity and contact point. Sometimes a contact name is given.
3   The VAT registration number must be given if the supplier is a registered trader and charges VAT. VAT will be considered in more detail in Chapter 8.
4   Details of the organization to which the goods have been delivered will be shown.

The date of the invoice may differ from the date of the delivery but the invoice should detail dates of supply as well as the quantity and quality of goods or services charged for and the price. Purchase order and delivery note numbers should be referred to.

5   Terms for settlement should be included i.e. when the supplier expects payment and how payment should be made together with details of any discounts available.

6   The total due including any VAT, giving the VAT rate used.

All this information and any calculations should be checked *before* the invoice is processed. The idea is to enter accurate and reliable information to the system to preserve its **integrity**.

The invoice forms the primary document from which information is posted to the system. This recording in the system is known as **posting**. When accountants talk about **posting** invoices they are referring to entering the information in the AIS.

All this assumes that what is delivered is in good order, has not been damaged in transit and is what was required. Sometimes things go wrong and some of the delivery is rejected. In this case special care needs to be taken to make sure that the rejected items are not paid for. The items themselves should be returned to the supplier with an explanation but the supplier will probably have already issued an invoice which includes the items returned. It will then be important to request confirmation that they will not expect it to be paid. Usually this confirmation will take the form of a piece of paper known as a credit note. This will need to be entered in the recording system in the same way as the invoice. Effectively it cancels out the amount due on the invoice.

It is useful to keep a separate record of the purchase returns. Obviously to have to return goods and chase up credit notes takes time and should be avoided if possible. Looking through the record of goods which have been returned might enable you to identify that a particular supplier is a regular problem. You could, therefore, switch orders to another more reliable supplier. On the other hand it might be that you need to be more careful in specifying what you require on the original order forms. Whatever the reason it makes sense for the business to identify the problems and take steps to prevent them happening again.

For returned goods, the credit note forms the primary document for posting information to the AIS. It will include all the information found on the invoice but will cancel payment rather than request it.

Selling

In the selling section the Bales will need to provide their own customers with the same type of information that they receive from their suppliers i.e. delivery notes, invoices and statements and sometimes credit notes. The design of these needs to be carefully considered to make sure that all relevant information is included and a copy should be retained for the Bales' own records.

Activity

2   Draft a sales invoice for the Bales to contain all the information that they would need. Remember that the design is important as these documents are the main

source of communication with the customer and need to give a suitable impression.

Bank and cash

Bank and cash will generate its own pile of papers. As far as the bank is concerned, the records should be fairly easy to keep. All payments from the bank should be identifiable from cheque counterfoils or payment records, and all receipts from paying-in records stamped by the bank. These records will be the primary data for posting details to the AIS.

The business will need to arrange with its bank for frequent bank statements to be supplied. This allows the business records to be checked against the bank records without too much delay and any differences can be sorted out before there is time to forget what the transactions involved.

Cash is more difficult. All cash received from sales should be banked intact without taking money out to pay for odd business expenses. That way all cash banked will be sales. If petty cash is needed it should be withdrawn as a separate item from the bank so that there is a record of exactly how much has been taken. It is easy to forget to write down what has been spent or to lose the receipt. Petty cash tends to be used for small payments such as parking tickets, parcel post, petrol, etc. some of which you will have no written record for. When you total all these small items together you come to a much larger figure and it is important to keep control over it. The primary documents will be the record of the withdrawals from the bank and the odd invoices and hand written explanations of where the money has gone.

This is probably the most difficult area to control. The items seem too small to worry about individually and yet can add up to large sums in total.

Control

Procedures and lines of responsibility must be established to control and safeguard the data as soon as it becomes available. These are known as internal **control procedures**. They become more complex as the business grows but even the smallest organization needs to establish suitable measures. Internal controls are classified under the following headings:

1   *Organizational* – these controls look at the plan of the organization, showing the duties, responsibilities and lines of authority for all employees. In other words it must be established who is responsible for each job and who has the authority to sanction transactions. In Bale and Co. while only Azina and John work for the organization such structures are minimal. Provided they both know the system and agree on who is responsible for the AIS, then no further organizational controls are necessary. However if they decided to bring in a temporary or part-time helper, then they would need to establish immediately the exact duties of the employee. Who is the employee answerable to – John or Azina? Can the employee open up credit accounts for new customers? Can they issue credit notes? Are they responsible for cashing up the till? Do they have access to the financial records? Do they open the post or handle cheques received from credit customers?

2   *Segregation of duties* – if employees are involved then it becomes possible to ensure that more than one person is responsible for each job. Effectively this provides a check on each other's work, so minimizing the risk of error, mistake or fraud. If someone can only *take* money, but not alter the records to show that the money is no longer owed to the business, then it is likely that the theft will be discovered. If someone can handle the cash *and* alter the records by the amount owed, then the theft is more difficult to detect.

3   *Physical* – these controls are established to make sure that the goods and assets of the business are properly safeguarded by reducing access. The Bales will need to display the goods available for sale but they need to ensure that this does not mean they are easy to steal. Information is an asset which is often forgotten, yet for many businesses it is even more crucial than the tangible assets. You can replace stock, but your market and customer information is irreplaceable.

4   *Authorization and approval* – all transactions require approval and each employee should know the limits to the transactions and amounts which they have authority to approve and those which require further approval.

5   *Arithmetical and accounting* – these controls operate to ensure that the data are complete and accurate. They involve pre-numbering invoices so that they can be and are checked to establish that all are accounted for; cash received should be listed as soon as received and banked as a whole so that the totals can be traced into the bank and none are missed.

6   *Personnel* – it is important to ensure that staff have sufficient skills and training to carry out their tasks.

7   *Supervision and management* – responsible officials should supervise the correct operation of the established system.

Summary

The output reports produced by the AIS are determined by user need. These users and their needs vary between organizations and over time as the organizations themselves and the environment in which they operate changes. The output reports must contain relevant and reliable information, the data must be complete and accurate if they are to meet user needs. Accountants have developed conventions which enable them to select the necessary data. The two main conventions which were considered are the entity concept and the cost principle. Once selected, the data must be properly controlled and protected to ensure that the database from which the reports are drawn has integrity. Similarly the classification and processing of the information within the AIS must be carried out in a controlled and systematic manner and be adaptable to changes in user need. The problems of classification and processing are the subject of the next chapter.

Key words

control procedures p. 42 • cost principle p.37 • entity concept p. 36 • integrity p. 41 • Invoices p. 40 • posting p. 41

Practice questions

1   The following notes describe the procedures which the Bales might adopt for the purchasing section of their business.

When goods are delivered they usually arrive with a delivery note detailing the goods being sent. John likes to check that the note agrees with the goods actually received and that they are in good condition before he moves them to the lock-up storeroom at the back of the shop. If he is happy that the goods are up to standard and they are what was ordered according to the purchase order, he initials the delivery note and puts it in Azina's in-tray. If no note is received he writes the details on a slip of paper so that she knows the goods are in stock.

The invoice will arrive soon afterwards and will be date stamped and numbered by Azina as she opens the post. Azina matches it with the notes from John and checks the price and calculations before she files both invoice and note in a temporary folder of approved invoices. Each week she counts up the invoices in the file received and totals the amounts due under them before entering them all in the records. The totals and number help her to check that she has not missed any or posted the wrong number by mistake. Then she files the invoices in a permanent file.

At the end of the month many suppliers issue statements of the records in their own system to remind their customers that amounts are due for payment and to ensure that customer and supplier agree on the amounts involved. Azina checks that the statement agrees with her own records and rings her contact name for the supplier if there is any problem. John thinks that these procedures are a bit too bureaucratic but Azina insists that if she doesn't follow a system she gets confused and things take longer to sort out. The business is growing fast. Her college course stresses the need for careful procedures and if, as they hope, they employ a part-time assistant to help in the office, they need to have a system in place.

Required
Identify the controls in the procedures. What type of control are they?

2   What is meant by the term 'internal controls'? Why is it important to have good internal control procedures in an organization?

3   Large food retailers have a problem with shop lifting, with making sure that all goods are paid for and controlling large numbers of part-time staff.

Required
Think of a large supermarket with which you are familiar. Identify and describe at least one control from each category of internal controls which the retailer should use to safeguard its assets and information.

4
   (i)   Define in your own words the terms 'entity concept' and 'cost principle'.
   (ii) Rose runs a flower arranging business from her home. She uses the study as her office but it is also used by the rest of the household on occasion for homework and household accounts. She undertook the following transactions:
       (a)   purchased flowers from wholesalers
       (b)   paid water bill for the house

(c) purchased van used mainly for delivery but occasionally for private use
(d) purchase special shrubs (and used plants from the garden) to provide greenery for the arrangements she sells
(e) signed a two-year contract with a local building society to supply floral arrangements for their offices
(f) sent one of her arrangements to a personal friend as a birthday present

Required
Which of the transactions should form part of the AIS and which not? Give your reasons.

Appendix 3A – The accounting profession in the UK

This appendix tells you about the accounting profession in the UK and how it is regulated. You can work through the text without this information but if you are serious about studying accounting it helps to have an overview of the different organizations that are involved and what their different roles are.

The professional bodies

Anyone can call themselves an 'accountant'. The title is not protected and unqualified people can and do describe themselves in this way. However, in the UK, professionally qualified accountants are members of one or more professional accounting bodies. The six main accounting bodies are as follows:

1 The Chartered Association of Certified Accountants (ACCA)
2 The Chartered Institute of Management Accountants (CIMA)
3 The Institute of Chartered Accountants in England and Wales (ICAEW)
4 The Institute of Chartered Accountants in Scotland (ICAS)
5 The Institute of Chartered Accountants in Ireland (ICAI)
6 The Chartered Institute of Public Finance Accountants (CIPFA)

There is common ground between the work of all the bodies and membership of each depends on passing a series of professional examinations and undertaking a period of practical training. Traditionally the CIPFA accountants trained in and specialized in the needs of the public sector such as local government and health authorities. The CIMA accountants specialized in working within organizations as part of the management team. ICAEW, ICAS and ICAI trained in professional practice offices, offering accountancy, consultancy, audit and tax advice to other organizations. The three 'Chartered Institutes' cover similar work but in different geographical areas. ACCA members cover similar ground in their professional examinations to the members of the chartered institutes but can train within organizations, in the way that CIMA members do, as well as in professional practice. Several attempts have been made to rationalize the number of bodies but this has not yet proved successful.

There are many issues on which the accounting profession needs to have one voice particularly when negotiating with the government or laying down professional guidelines. For this reason there are a number of organizations on which some or all of the

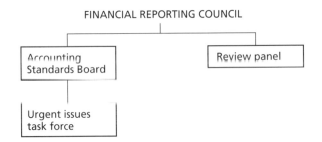

Figure 3.4
Organization of
the Financial
Reporting Council

bodies has representatives to deal with common problems e.g. the Consultative Committee of Accounting Bodies (CCAB).

The regulators

Companies have to produce financial information for their investors and in most cases they have that information audited by an independent professional.

The financial information which companies are required to produce is set out in the Companies Act 1985 but this gives only an outline. A separate organization known as the Financial Reporting Council has been set up to deal with the problem in more detail. It operates through a number of subsidiary companies (Figure 3.4).

The Accounting Standards Board (ASB) operates as a committee set up under the Companies Act and includes people other than accountants e.g. finance directors, members of the stock exchange. It researches problems of reporting financial information and issues standards known as Financial Reporting Standards or FRSs (earlier known as SSAPs) which need to be complied with. The ASB has also issued a document known as *The Statement of Principles* which tries to set down in one document the framework which accountants have developed to prepare accounting reports. It contains definitions of concepts used by all accountants.

Any problems with a company's reports can be taken to the Review Panel for an assessment of whether they comply with the regulations in issue. If in the opinion of the Panel they do not comply the company will be asked to change the reports.

The Urgent Issues Task Force (UITF) is a subsidiary of the ASB and works on specific problems which have come to light and on which there appears to be no direct ruling. The UITF makes a quick decision, referring to such rules as may be available for similar items. The UITF can make decisions far more quickly than the ASB, issuing a ruling within weeks where an FRS may take several years to develop.

The auditing of the external financial reports produced from the AIS is regulated by an organization known as the Auditing Practices Board (APB). It lays down standards for auditing work in a similar way to the standards produced by the ASB.

The work of these organizations is referred to where relevant throughout the text. You will find reference to them in the financial columns of the press and you should take the opportunity to read any such comments. It will give you an increased understanding of the role and standing of the profession.

4 Recording, classifying and processing data

Learning objectives

After reading this chapter you should:
- understand the role and structure of the nominal ledger within the AIS and the accounting records which it holds
- be aware of the different categories of accounts
- be able to use the concept of double entry bookkeeping to record basic transactions
- appreciate the need for control accounts and be able to operate them
- appreciate the purpose and limitations of the trial balance
- understand the purpose of a journal
- be able to use the accounting records from the nominal ledger to calculate profit and prepare a simple balance sheet.

Introduction

In the last chapter John and Azina set up a system to collect and sort all the information that arrived for the business. From that pile, they selected the particular information which was going to be relevant for the AIS. This information for the first month of trading by the Bales is summarized in the case study at the end of this chapter. They now need to record that information in such a way that the AIS can easily find the figures they need to manage the business and to supply all the other interested users as well.

First we will look inside the AIS and see what the individual records which make it up should look like. We can then see how those records are organized and stored within the AIS in a structured way so that the information can be found and extracted easily. Good organization should also help to make the recording process as efficient as possible while still being accurate and complete.

Having decided on the structure, we can start recording the transactions for Azina and John. To do this we will need to introduce the principles of **double entry**, a system of bookkeeping which is common to accounting systems throughout the world.

Bale and Co. is now at the end of their first month of trading. A summary of the transactions which it has undertaken in this first month is given at the end of this chapter after the Practice questions. They have been classified as sales, purchases, bank and cash. Azina now needs to design a system to record them in a way which will enable the output reports to be produced.

Accounts

The AIS contains a large database of information known as the **nominal ledger** made up of individual records known as **accounts** (see Figure 4.1). Think of the nominal ledger as a draw in a filing cabinet. The draw contains a whole series of cards or accounts.

Each account stores the information relating to one aspect of the financial affairs of the business. For example, there will be a separate account for recording the amount spent on telephone bills, another for electricity, another for insurance and so on. Each account will have a name to reflect its contents and a code number to help identify it. It will store all the information on its particular aspect of the business giving the date and amount of every transaction which affects it. In a manual system they were drawn up in the form of a 'T' and so they are sometimes known as T accounts. An example of a T account is given in Figure 4.2.

You can see the way in which the account records the date, detail and amount for each transaction and also a reference. This reference allows you to trace all the relevant documents about an item if the need arises. The account tells us that the business paid from its bank account three separate bills for office stationery on 31 May, 31 July and 30 September coming to a total of £1270.47. On 30 June a repayment of £34.22 was received and was banked in the business account. In total office stationery has cost the business £1236.25 i.e. £1270.47 less £34.22.

In practice you will find that very few businesses keep their accounts like this today

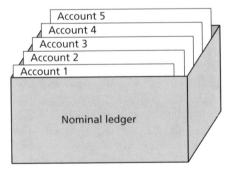

Figure 4.1
Nominal ledger

ACCOUNT NAME: Office Stationery				CODE: 6002			
Date	*Detail*	*Ref*	*£*	*Date*	*Detail*	*Ref*	*£*
31.5	Bank Payments	54	424.22	30.6	Bank receipts	67	34.22
31.7	Bank Payments	197	521.63				
30.9	Bank Payments	271	324.62				

Figure 4.2
Example of a
T account

because very few systems are kept manually. However, although the format may look a bit different, accounts in non-manual systems contain the same information as that in the T account and the old style T accounts are often used to solve problems or to work out how to correct a mistake in the AIS. You will find that the accountant with a problem will sketch out a number of T accounts on a rough piece of paper to work out where the entries should have been made and what entries need to be made to correct things. They are a handy way of checking that you understand what is happening. We will use them to explain the principles of what we are doing before looking at the way in which we achieve that result with a modern computerized system. We will keep coming back to them in later chapters of the book to explain the principles of new ideas. They are a useful way of visualizing what is going on within the AIS.

You can open as many T accounts as you need but you should bear in mind the following guidelines:

1 *Too many* – If you open too many accounts you will have so much detail that you cannot find any information. For example you could record all office stationery purchased in one account. However if you need information on which office is using the most or how much paper is being used in the photocopying machine then you will need to have separate accounts for each office and for photocopying paper. However if you start to keep a separate account for each type of stationery, e.g. each size of envelope that is used, you will find that you have many bits of information that are of little use and yet cannot easily find the information that you do need, i.e. how much the office spends on stationery.

2 *Too few* – If you open too few accounts you will still not be able to find the information that is needed, this time because it is too summarized. Looking at an example, if all office costs such as stationery, telephone, postage, and fax are kept together in one account then you will easily pick up the costs of running the office but you will not be able to find out how the costs are made up and where savings could be made.

3 *Flexibility* – Each organization needs to decide for itself the amount of detail that it requires from its AIS in order to fulfil its users' needs. You must remember as well that the needs will change over time as new activities are started; the business grows or contracts; or the managers discover the need for more information on a particular matter. The business can open up new accounts as the need arises; the list of accounts is not fixed for all time.

Nominal ledger

The accounts need to be kept in some order if any sense is to be made of the information they contain. As we have seen they are kept in the file known as the **nominal ledger** (NL).

Within that file they are organized by type. Accountants recognize the following five main types or elements:

1   assets
2   liabilities
3   owner's capital
4   income
5   expense

We will look at each element in turn.

Assets

Assets are things which the organization owns and which have some positive value either now or in the future. Assets do not have to be tangible things that you can see and touch. They include legal rights to some benefit. For example they might include cash and bank balances; amounts owed by customers; goods available for sale; as well as the property from which the business works. Accountants classify assets as either current or fixed. Fixed assets are assets which were bought to be used within the business such as the buildings that it operates from and the equipment and vehicles which it uses. Current assets are the assets which the business trades with including goods which it bought to sell to its customers, money owed by customers and cash and bank balances. Note that it is the purpose for which the asset was purchased which matters not the nature of the asset. If a business buys and sells cars then the cars will be a current asset.

Activities

1   Imagine you are in the shop belonging to Bale and Co. It looks much like any computer hardware and software store that you may be familiar with.
    Required
    (a)   What 'assets' might you find in the shop?
    (b)   Can you name at least five different assets that a shop of this sort will have?
    (c)   Are they fixed or current?
2   Ahmed started in business as a newsagent on 1 April. The following information has been extracted from the business records of Ahmed at 30 April.

	£
Bank deposit account	3 100
Loan from mother	10 000
Telephone bill	200
Rent paid	300
Shop premises purchased	35 000
Goods on display in shop at 30 April (at cost)	1 800
Sales of goods during April	1 500
Amount owed by customer at 30 April	1 500
Amount owed to supplier at 30 April	1 000

Money invested by owner	30 000
Cost of goods sold	800

Required

Which of the items represents an asset in Ahmed's business? Are they fixed or current assets?

Liabilities

These are amounts which the business owes to other people. They will include loans, amounts owed to suppliers and bank overdrafts. They are classified according to how soon the amount will have to be paid. If the payment has to be made within the next twelve months they are known as *current liabilities*. If they are due to be paid after twelve months they will be known as *long-term liabilities*.

Activity

3   Look at the list of items for Ahmed's shop given above.
    Required
    (a)   What liabilities does Ahmed have?
    (b)   Can you find one long-term liability and one short-term liability?

Owner's capital

This is the investment that the owner has made in the business. It will include the money put in when the business started and anything invested since, less any money taken out. If the business is successful and makes money this increases the amount of the owner's capital in the business. Conversely if the business loses money then the owner's capital decreases because their investment is worth less. Whether the business makes money or loses it depends on the income and expenses.

Activity

4   Look at the transactions for Ahmed.
    Required
    How much capital did Ahmed himself invest in the business?

Income

This will record anything that the business earns, for example, by selling goods or services, renting out some of the assets that it owns or interest on money deposited in a bank. Bale and Co. earns income from its sales to customers, either for credit or for cash.

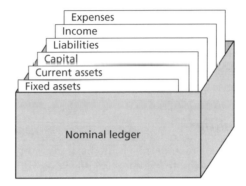

Figure 4.3
The classified
nominal ledger

Expenses

This will include the cost of any running expense of the business such as light and heat, postage and stationery, telephone and insurance. Sometimes it is difficult to distinguish between an asset and an expense. They both involve the business spending money, but an expense is used up as it is recorded where as an asset will continue to benefit the business in the future.

Think of the money spent on electricity. By the time you get the bill you will have used up the electricity. You have to pay for it but you have already had the benefit of using it and it will not benefit you in the future. You will need to pay another bill next quarter. Compare this with the cost of putting in a new electric heating system. Again you will be presented with a bill but this bill is paying for the use of the heating system which will be used in the future and so is recorded as an asset until it wears out.

The accounts which the business has opened will be filed in the nominal ledger classified under the five headings we have identified. Figure 4.3 illustrates this structure.

Activity

5   Look at the list of transactions for Ahmed for April.
    Required
    Identify the expenses incurred.

If you had any difficulty answering the exercises in this section you should find the solution in the next section.

Links between the categories

The information stored in the accounts can be organized into reports to meet the needs of the particular users of the AIS.

Calculating profit

At regular intervals, the accounts in the income and expense categories will be used to calculate whether the business has made a profit or a loss by its operations. If the total of the amounts in the income accounts is greater than the total on the expenses then the business has made a profit. This profit or loss belongs to the owners of the business and can be included with the amount originally invested by the owners in the capital section. The amount that the owners have invested in the business has increased. If the expenses are greater than the income the business has made a loss and the owners investment has gone down.

$$\text{Profit (loss)} = \text{Income} - \text{Expenses}$$

Note that the loss is put in brackets. For some reason accountants use brackets around a figure instead of a '−' sign to indicate a negative figure. If you see a number surrounded by brackets in a set of accounts assume it means minus.

The profit or loss has to be calculated for a particular period in time. The business may last for many years. It is of very little use to be told that in the last twenty years the business has made sales of £5 million, say, with expenses of £4 million. The owners and investors want to know whether the business is making sales and profits now. So we need to keep the records in such a way that the profit for each period can be calculated separately and then transferred to the owners capital.

To do this, the figures for income and expenses are accumulated in their accounts over a period of time – a month or a year perhaps. At the end of this time the income and expenses figures are all transferred to another account known as the **Profit and loss account** included under the owners capital category in the nominal ledger. The income and expense accounts are then reduced to zero and the next period's sales and expenses can start to be accumulated.

We will come back to the mechanics of this later when we look at the preparation of the statements in more detail. However you should understand that the income and expense accounts are summarized into the profit and loss account and that this new account is a part of the capital category, i.e. it forms part of the AIS.

Looking at the figures for Ahmed for April you should have the following figures.

		£	£
Income from sales			1 500
Expenses	Cost of sales	800	
	Telephone	200	
	Rent	300	
			1 300
Profit			200

The position statement

The profit or loss is part of the owners capital. Any income made by the business belongs to the owner who has the right to draw it out for personal use or to leave it to reinvest in the business. Any loss made is the responsibility of the owner and will reduce the amount the business is liable to the owner for. With the remaining categories of accounts, i.e. the assets and liabilities, it forms part of a simple report on the position of the business at any point of time.

The position statement or **balance sheet** as it is usually called, reflects the fact that what the business 'owns' must equal that which it 'owes'. We say it balances. The money to buy the assets that the business owns must have come from somewhere either from the owners or from money that has been borrowed. This is usually put in the form of another equation known as the **Accounting equation**.

$$\text{Assets} = \text{Capital} + \text{Liabilities}$$

or

$$A = C + L$$

Capital includes not just the original money invested in the business but also any profit left in the business from previous years.

A position statement could be drawn up for Ahmed from the information in the example above. It would look like this:

Ahmed Balance sheet at 30 April

Fixed assets	£	Capital	£
Premises	35 000	Invested	30 000
		Profit/(loss)	200
Current assets			
Owed by customer	1 500	Long-term liabilities	
Goods for sale	1 800	Loan	10 000
Bank	3 100	Current liabilities	
		Supplier	1 200
	41 400		41 400

The accounts in that statement include any account that has not been 'emptied' into the profit and loss account. The profit and loss account itself is included under capital. By recording the information under the five elements which make up these equations, it makes it much easier to calculate profit and draw up the balance sheets.

Coding

To help to find the accounts they are usually given a number or code as well as a name. The number gives an idea of the type of account (the first digit) and the order within that type (the last few digits). For example the code for a bank account might be as follows:

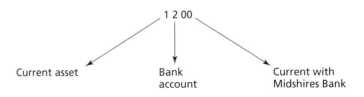

If the business had another bank account with another bank or perhaps a different type of account with the same bank it might be numbered 1201 or 1202. This is a bit like hotel room numbers where the first number indicates the floor of the building and the following numbers the order of the rooms on that floor. Unlike a hotel room however you need to leave gaps in the number system for the accounts. This will allow you to bring in new accounts if and when you need them. For instance, if the business opens a new account with the Southshires Bank it could use the code 1 2 05 to reflect that it is a current asset and a bank account but separate from the first account. Other accounts with the Midshires can be slotted in to the codes 1200 to 1204. The fact that they are filed together under code 1200 means that the owners can see quickly how much money they have available in total in the bank accounts and in which accounts it can be found. The next account in the NL file might start with 1300 leaving plenty of room from 1200 to 1299 for all the bank accounts that the business is likely to open in the future.

As the business expands this flexibility is important. Without it the new accounts would need to be added at the end of the list in random order which makes searching for information much more difficult. The organization of the accounts within the nominal ledger and the coding system used is known as the *chart of accounts*.

Concept of double entry

Now you have an overall view of the structure of the main ledger within the AIS we can look at the recording entries for the transactions in the case study.

The entries in the accounts are kept under a system known as **double entry**. This method is used throughout the world although it was originally devised in Italy some 500 years ago. The systems which use double entry may have become more sophisticated but the idea is the same. Basically the method reflects the fact that every transaction which the organization undertakes will affect two accounts. This must be so if the accounting equation $A = C + L$ is to stay in balance.

Consider an example. The business buys a new machine costing £10 000 on credit terms from the supplier. The system needs to record both:

1   the arrival of the new machine worth £10 000, and
2   the amount now owed to the supplier £10 000

The one transaction has two effects and each effect needs to be recorded. Two accounts are affected. In this case there will be an increase in an asset account and an increase in a liability account both for the same amount.

All transactions have this two sided effect which is why the system for recording them is known as 'double entry'. You can see the result of this double record by looking at the way in which transactions affect the accounts which form the balance sheet. Figure 4.4 shows the way in which the first few transactions from the case study would be reflected in the asset, liability and capital accounts for Bale and Co. As you can see, for each transaction two adjustments are necessary but each for an equal amount. The accounting equation still balances.

Each transaction is discussed in detail below.

Account	A	B	C	D	E	F	G	Total
	£	£	£	£	£	£	£	£
ASSETS								
Property			+100 000					100 000
Goods for sale				+9 472		−1 500		7 972
Bank	+50 000	+70 000	−100 000		+2 000		150	21 850
								129 822
CAPITAL	+50 000				+2 000	−1 500	−150	50 350
LIABILITIES								
Loan		+70 000						70 000
Supplier				+9 472				9 472
								129 822

Figure 4.4
The double effect
of transactions

Transaction A

The first transaction which Bale and Co. will need to record will be the transfer to the new business bank account of the £50 000 cash from the owners' own resources that is being invested in the business. This takes place on 1 November. The transaction creates a bank account with a balance of £50 000 but under the double entry principle the business also needs to record where the money comes from, i.e. the owners capital. So the system should show:

1   a new bank account with £50 000
2   an amount of £50 000 capital.

We need to open two accounts, one for the bank account and one for owners' capital.

Transaction B

A loan amounting to £70 000 is taken out to help finance the purchase of a property to house the shop and office. The loan will have the following effect:

1   an increase in the bank balance of £70 000
2   a loan owed to the bank £70 000.

Transaction C

The property costs £100 000. Again we need to put in both sides of the transaction, but this time both entries are on the same side of the balance sheet. This is because we have not raised any new money to make the purchase, we are just changing the make up of the assets owned by the business. The balance sheet needs to reflect:

1   the purchase of the new property at £100 000
2   the reduction of £100 000 in the bank account to pay for it.

Transaction D

On 5 November the Bales buy goods for resale costing £9472 on credit terms from a supplier. We need to record:

1   the stock of goods purchased as an asset of £9472
2   the amount owed to the supplier as a creditor under liabilities.

Transaction E

On 12 November some of the goods that have been purchased are sold for £2000 cash. This is a more complex transaction and can be divided into two parts. First we need to record the money received from the customer (transaction E) and then we need to record the goods going out (transaction F). The two entries required to record the money coming in will be:

1   increase the cash by £2000
2   increase sales and therefore the owners' capital by £2000.

Transaction F

This still leaves the goods which have been sold included under the stock of goods purchased asset in the balance sheet. The business needs to record these goods going out. Assume that the goods sold cost £1500. This would be recorded with the following entries:

1   reduce stock of goods for sale by £1500
2   increase expenses and therefore reduce owners' capital by £1500 for the goods which are no longer owned by the business.

Transaction G

Similarly if the business pays its bills these reflect a loss to the business and are shown as a reduction in the amount the business owes the owners. If Bale and Co. pay a telephone bill of £150 this will:

1   reduce the bank and cash by £150 and
2   increase expenses and reduce owners' capital by £150.

In summary the balance sheet at the end of all these transactions will look like this:

Balance sheet at 12 November

Fixed assets	£	Capital	£
Property	100 000	Capital	50 000
Current assets		Profit	350
Goods for sale	7 972	Long-term liability	
Bank and cash	21 850	Loan	70 000
		Current liability	
		Supplier	9 472
	£ 129 822		£129 822

Debits and credits

You should now appreciate that every transaction will have two effects. Two accounts need to be adjusted. Unfortunately as you can see it is not as easy as one account increasing and one decreasing. You might have an increase in an asset and an increase in a liability for example, or a decrease in both. So the two effects cannot be understood in terms of one '+' and one '−' for each transaction.

Accountants use the terms **debit** and **credit** to describe the two adjustments needed. Each transaction must consist of one debit item and one credit item of equal value. The terms debit (DR) and credit (CR) have come from the original Italian words for the double entry records. Some people like to think of them as meaning 'value in' i.e. debit, and 'value out' i.e. credit. In terms of the balance sheet we have been looking at, the assets are debit balances and the liabilities and capital are credit balances. An asset has value to the business. To increase an asset value you make a further debit record in the asset account. If the asset is sold or decreases in value you reduce its value in the account by making a credit entry or record. Liabilities represent value owed outside the business and any increase in the borrowings will require a credit entry to record it. If the business pays back the borrowing then the amount owed reduces and a debit entry is made in the liability account.

Asset accounts have more debits than credits and so accountants would say that they are debit balances. Similarly liability and capital accounts would have more credit entries than debits and would be credit balances.

Income and expense accounts reflect the fact that they represent the owners' income or losses and are increases or decreases in the amount the business owes the owner. Income such as sales would be recorded as a credit entry since it represents an increase in the amount owed to the owner. Expenses are recorded as debits because

Table 4.1 Summary of debit and credit entries

Type of account	Increase	Decrease
Assets	DR	CR
Liabilities	CR	DR
Income	CR	DR
Expense	DR	CR
Capital	CR	DR

they represent a reduction in the amount due to the owner. These entries are summarized in Table 4.1.

The best way to understand this is to work through an example. Think through the transactions for Bale and Co. again, but in terms of debits and credits.

Transaction A			£	£
Bank account	DR		50 000	
Capital account		CR		50 000

Transaction B				
Bank account	DR		70 000	
Loan account		CR		70 000

Transaction C				
Property account	DR		100 000	
Bank account		CR		100 000

Transaction D				
Goods for resale	DR		9 472	
Supplier		CR		9 472

Transaction E				
Bank account	DR		2 000	
Sales		CR		2 000

Transaction F				
Cost of sales	DR		1 500	
Goods for sale		CR		1 500

Transaction G				
Telephone	DR		150	
Bank account		CR		150

If you have any difficulty with these records go back to Figure 4.4 which shows the two effects of the transactions. Work out which type of accounts were changed and whether they increased or decreased. Then check in the table summarizing the debit and credit entries by type of account.

Format for accounts

Earlier in the chapter we looked at the format for an account in traditional T style (Figure 4.2). Debits are the records on the left hand side of the T account and credits are on the right hand side. There is no logic to this. It is just accepted practice. The horizontal balance sheet format that we have used is consistent with this and sometimes you will find it easier to remember the correct side for the entry by visualizing where it should be found in the balance sheet.

Account

Debits on the	Credits on the
left	right
ASSETS	LIABILITIES
EXPENSES	INCOME

DEBITS record increases in assets and expenses
CREDITS record increases in liabilities and income

You can see now that the account illustrated in Figure 4.2 reflects three debit entries and one credit. It is an expense account and as expected for an expense it has a debit balance. Most computer systems produce accounts in a slightly different format but with the same information. A typical layout is given in Figure 4.5.

Figure 4.5
Computerized
ledger account

Account Name: Office Stationery Code: 6002

Date	Detail	Ref	DR	CR	Balance
31.5	Bank Payments		424.22		
30.6	Bank Receipts		34.22		390.00
31.7	Bank Payments		521.63		911.63
31.8	Bank Payments		324.62		1236.25

The debit is still on the left and the credit on the right but this time the layout allows the running total or balance to be recorded after each transaction. The information is still the same. When solving problems and drafting the accounts by hand it is still normal practice to use T style accounts but you should be able to read the newer style because this is the format you will find presented by the computer.

The debit and credit transactions from our earlier example can now be recorded in the accounts.

Capital accounts

Capital accounts

	A	Bank	50 000

Profit and loss account

Long-term liability accounts

Loan account

B	Bank	70 000

Current liabilities

Suppliers account

D	Goods for sale	9 472

Fixed asset accounts

Property account

C	Bank	100 000			

Current asset accounts

Goods for sale

D	Supplier	9 472	F	Cost of sales	1 500

Bank account

A	Capital	50 000	C	Property	100 000
B	Loan	70 000	G	Telephone	150
E	Sales	2 000			

Income accounts

Sales

E	Bank	2 000

Expenses accounts

Cost of sales

F	Goods for sale	1 500		

Telephone

G	Bank	150		

Balancing accounts

To find the value for any account it needs to be 'balanced off'. In other words all the debit entries and all the credit entries are added up and the balancing figure found. The **balance** is either a debit balance or a credit balance depending on whether the debits are bigger than the credits or the other way around.

If there is only one figure in the account there is no need to find the balance and the figure is left untouched. For the first transactions for the Bales only the bank account and the goods for sale need balancing. These are shown below.

Bank account

A	Capital	50 000	C	Property	100 000
B	Loan	70 000	G	Telephone	150
E	Sales	2 000		Balance c/d	21 850
		122 000			122 000
	Balance b/d	21 850			

Goods for sale

D	Supplier	9 472	F	Cost of sales	1 500
				Balance c/d	7 972
		9 472			9 472
	Balance	b/d	7 972		

Note that 'c/d' stands for carried down and 'b/d' for brought down. The double entry is complete because the balance appears on both the debit and the credit side of the account.

Trial balance

Once the entries have been made and before any reports are extracted from the accounts, a **trial balance** is drawn up. This is just what it says it is – a try at balancing the figures before the profit is worked out and the balance sheet drawn up. If the double entry is correct, i.e. a debit entry for every credit entry and vice versa, then the total of the debit balances and the total of the credit balances in the NL should agree. If they do not, you know there is a problem somewhere. The trial balance after recording transactions A to F is set out below.

Trial balance at 12 November

	DR (£)	CR (£)
Capital		50 000
Profit		nil
Loan		70 000
Supplier		9 472
Property	100 000	
Bank	21 850	
Goods for sale	7 972	
Sales		2 000
Cost of sales	1 500	
Telephone	150	
	£131 472	£131 472

If you have just recorded several hundred transactions the fact that the trial balance balances is comforting. There is some likelihood that the balance sheet you prepare from the trial balance will balance. In a computerized system the trial balance will be made to balance arithmetically. Unfortunately it does not guarantee that the records are correct. There are a number of errors that might well have occurred but which do not show up as an imbalance, for example:

1   *Omission* – This happens where an item is missed entirely from the records so that neither the debit nor the credit entry appears.
2   *Commission* – This happens where one entry is put in the wrong account although on the correct side. For example it may be in the wrong expense account or the wrong bank account. The trial balance will still balance.
3   *Compensating errors* – These occur where one error is compensated for by another of exactly the same amount.
4   *Duplication* – This occurs where the record is entered twice.

Errors like these will only be discovered by chance.

Control accounts

In the AIS so far we have kept all the accounts in the NL. Some accounts will have more use than other accounts. We have already seen how many transactions are

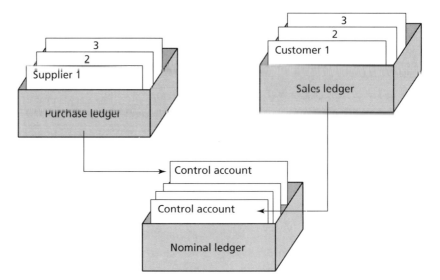

Figure 4.6
Control accounts

recorded in the bank account. In a business which offers credit to its customers and buys goods on credit terms from its suppliers the accounts which record the amounts owing and owed also get a lot of use. The records will need to show not just the total amounts but how much is owed to each supplier and how much is due from each customer. These personal accounts are usually recorded in separate subsidiary or memorandum ledgers with only the total figures for all suppliers and customers kept in the NL. These total accounts are called **control accounts**. The idea is that at any time the balance on the control account should be equal to the total of all the individual accounts which make it up. The illustration in Figure 4.6 should help you to understand how this works.

The system has a number of advantages. First it keeps the NL at a reasonable size. There might be hundreds or even thousands of individual personal accounts. Keeping all these in the NL would make it very difficult to work with. Second, you can allow assistants to work on the subsidiary ledgers without letting them have access to the figures in the NL. Many of the accounts in the NL hold information that the owners would not want other people to see and certainly would not wish them to be able to alter. With subsidiary ledgers it is possible for different staff to work on or have access to parts of the AIS while restricting access to the more private information.

We will look at the way in which this idea works by looking at the operation of the *sales ledger* for customer balances and its related control account known as the *debtors control account* in the NL. The system would be exactly the same for the *purchase ledger* for suppliers balances and the *creditors control account* in the NL. In practice the system is also used for other NL accounts where a detailed breakdown of the figures is needed, e.g. this might happen with fixed assets where the business owns a great number of similar items of machinery for which it keeps detailed information in subsidiary ledgers while keeping a control account in the NL. The system would be exactly the same.

The key point to remember is that every transaction which is entered in a subsidiary account must also be entered in the control account and on the same side. The double entry in the NL is kept up through the control account not the subsidiary ledger.

Bale and Co. make quite a number of sales on credit terms. In their first months trading they have opened up accounts for eight customers. These accounts are all kept in the subsidiary ledger in T account form. The NL will have the *debtors control account* to record the transactions with these customers in total.

Invoices issued to customers will be recorded on the debit side of the personal account for each customer and the total invoice figure will be recorded on the DR side of the control account (and the CR side of the sales account). Money received from customers will be entered as a CR entry in the personal accounts and the total figure as a CR in the control account (and as a DR in the bank account). Consider an illustration:

Invoices issued (£)		*Bank receipts* (£)	
Customer 1	2 353	Customer 4	345
Customer 5	3 667	Customer 3	124
Customer 3	1 020	Customer 1	1 440
Customer 4	422	Customer 5	2 451
Total	7 462	Total	4 360

Sales returns: Customer 5 returned goods worth £500.

Entering these transactions in the ledgers gives:

Nominal ledger

Debtors control account

Sales	7 462	Bank	4 360
		Returns	500
		Balance c/d	2 602
	7 462		7 462
Balance b/d	2 602		

Subsidiary ledger

Customer 1

Sales	2 353	Bank	1 440
		Balance	913
	2 353		2 353
Balance	913		

Customer 2

Customer 3

Sales	1 020	Bank	124
		Balance	896
	1 020		1 020
Balance	896		

Customer 4

Sales	422	Bank	345
		Balance	77
	422		422
Balance	77		

	Customer 5		
Sales	3 667	Bank	2 451
Returns	500	Balance	716
	3 667		3 667
Balance	716		

Customer 6

Customer 7

Customer 8

Periodically the balance on the control account has to be agreed with the total of the list of balances on the individual accounts in the subsidiary ledger. If they do not agree a reconciliation of the two figures is needed. The difference must be put right.

In our simple example the reconciliation would be a straightforward total of the balances in the sales ledger which should agree with the total in the control account:

		£
Customer	1	913
	2	–
	3	896
	4	77
	5	716
	6	–
	7	–
	8	–
Total		2 602
Debtors control account		2 602

In more complex examples errors can creep in and there will be differences which must be put right.

Sources of information

Chapter 3 looked at the process of collecting and sorting information to record in the system. It stressed the importance of making sure that the data were complete and accurate if the information which the AIS produces was to be of any use. The system is said to have 'integrity' if the records it contains are reliable. The recording process should include only those transactions which the collecting and selecting process described in the last chapter has produced, i.e. it should record:

1   sales invoices;
2   sales returns;
3   purchase invoices;
4   purchase returns;
5   bank payments;
6   bank receipts;
7   petty cash payments.

Anything which is not from these sources should not be entered in the recording system because it is not properly validated.

Sometimes it does become necessary to make adjustments to the figures in the NL for events which have not been captured by one of the above files. Perhaps some goods for sale have been damaged or stolen from the warehouse and the cost has to be taken out of the asset account and treated as a loss; or a debtor becomes bankrupt so the debt will not be paid and the amount owing has to be removed from the debtors figure. In these cases the transaction has to be recorded in a special book, known as a **journal**, set aside for the purpose before it can be processed. Entries in the journal should only be made by people who are very senior in the organization. The journal entry should show:

1   the date
2   the accounts affected
3   the amount to be entered
4   the reason for the entry
5   the signature of the authorizing person.

A journal entry would be used to transfer the balances on the income and expense T accounts to the profit and loss account to calculate the profit for the period. The journal might look like this:

Ref	Date	Detail	Code	Amount
Journal	5 th Nov.	Sales	DR	2 000
1		Profit and loss account	CR	2 000

Being the transfer of the income to the profit and loss account at the end of period

Authority _____

The journal is also used to correct any errors. If a mistake is made it should be put right by completing another entry through the journal to adjust the balances to what they should be.

In the case study at the end of the chapter you should set out a proper journal for all the adjustments which are not part of the primary data. At the end of the month the expense and income accounts should be closed off to the profit and loss account using another journal entry. Remember that they should be numbered consecutively and the journal reference number used in the record in the relevant accounts.

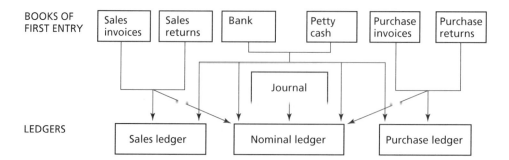

Figure 4.7
AIS for Bale and
Co.

Summary

This chapter has introduced the basic principle of double entry bookkeeping and the structure of the records within the AIS. These ideas form the basis for accounting systems whether they are kept manually or on a computer. Bale and Co. now have an AIS which is summarized in Figure 4.7.

   You should work through the examples at the end of this chapter and complete the case study before you try going any further. You might find that you have to come back to this chapter several times as you meet new ideas. Later chapters will often use T accounts to illustrate what is happening in the recording system so it is important to understand. As with any skill, practice is the way to become familiar with the ideas in this chapter.

Key words

account p. 48 • accounting equation p. 54 • balance p. 62 • balance sheet p. 54 • control account p. 64 • credit p. 58 • debit p. 58 • double entry pp. 47, 55 • journal p. 67 • nominal ledger pp. 48, 59 • profit and loss account p. 53 • trial balance p. 63

Practice questions

1   Which of the following items would be recorded as part of the accounting system for a retail shop?
   (i)   Rent of shop £2400 p.a.
   (ii)   Rent of flat over shop which is used by the owner as a main residence £2400
   (iii)   Bank charges on the owner's bank account £450
   (iv)   Telephone for the shop £800. Would the answer be different if the telephone was used for private as well as business use?
   (v)   Running expenses of the car used for business deliveries and also to take the children to school £2300 p.a.
   (vi)   An employment contract for an employee with specialist knowledge signed when the employee agreed to work for the business. No payment was made.
   (vii)   Salary for employee £20 000 p.a.
   (viii) A signed contract with a specialist supplier for one line of business to sell their products exclusively. It entitles the owner of the shop to discounts on

the cost of the goods purchased and the sole right to market the product within the area.

(ix) Payments for a holiday for the owner's family made through the business bank account

2 Using the accounting equation fill in the following:

Assets	3 500	Capital
Liabilities	1 000	
Capital	4 000	Liabilities
Assets	7 200	
Capital	4 000	Assets
Liabilities	200	
Fixed assets	6 000	Capital
Current assets	2 900	
Liabilities	1 700	
Capital	10 000	Current liabilities
Loan	1 500	
Current assets	4 800	
Fixed assets	7 300	

3 Describe transactions that would explain the changes in the following series of balance sheets:

A	Bank	<u>12 000</u>	Capital	<u>12 000</u>
B	Van	6 000	Capital	12 000
	Bank	6 000		
		<u>12 000</u>		<u>12 000</u>
C	Van	6 000	Capital	12 000
	Stock	2 000		
	Bank	<u>4 000</u>		
		<u>12 000</u>		<u>12 000</u>
D	Van	6 000	Capital	12 000
	Stock	1 000	Profit	500
	Bank	<u>5 500</u>		
		<u>12 500</u>		<u>12 500</u>
E	Van	6 000	Capital	12 000
	Stock	3 000	Profit	500
	Bank	<u>5 500</u>	Creditors	<u>2 000</u>
		<u>14 500</u>		<u>14 500</u>

F	Van	6 000	Capital	12 000
	Equipment	1 500	Profit	500
	Stock	3 000	Creditors	2 000
	Bank	4 000		
		14 500		14 500

G	Van	6 000	Capital	12 000
	Equipment	1 500	Profit	1 250
	Stock	1 500	Creditors	2 000
	Debtors	2 250		
	Bank	4 000		
		15 250		15 250

H	Van	6 000	Capital	12 000
	Equipment	1 500	Profit	1 000
	Stock	1 500	Creditors	2 000
	Debtors	2 250		
	Bank	3 750		
		15 000		15 000

4   Teek starts business with £5000 capital, paying this amount into a bank account
   (i)   Bought fittings £600, paying by cheque.
   (ii)   Bought goods on credit £2000.
   (iii) Bought van for £3000 paying cheque for £1000, the balance to be paid later.
   (iv)   Sold on credit for £800 goods which had cost £550.
   (v)   Paid creditors from transaction (ii) the full amount owing by cheque.
   (vi)   Purchased more goods £400, paying by cheque.
   (vii) Sold goods for cash receiving £300. They originally cost £200.
   (viii) Teek withdrew £150 in cash for her own personal use.
   Required
   (a)   Draft the initial balance sheet and then the changes that occur as each of the
          transactions takes place.
   (b)   Enter the transactions in T accounts.
   (c)   Prepare a trial balance.
   (d)   Calculate the profit and prepare a balance sheet.

5   Aileen starts in business as a supplier of specialist art supplies by mail order on 1
   May and makes the following transactions in the first few weeks:
   1 May   Opens a business bank account by depositing £15 000 of her own money.
   2 May   Buys a second hand van for £5000 paying by cheque drawn on the
           business account.
   3 May   Signs a rental agreement with the owners of a small office block to rent
           the ground floor for the next five years. Rental will be £2000 p.a.
   4 May   Buys equipment costing £3000 on credit terms from Office Supplies Ltd.
   5 May   Buys stock costing £4000 on credit from Helen's Trade Supplies Ltd.
   6 May   Organizes advertising in a trade magazine run by Trade Publications plc at
           a cost of £1500 on credit terms.

8 May Pays first rental instalment of £200 for the month with a cheque drawn on the business bank account.

12 May Sells stock which cost £2000 for £3500 in cash.

13 May Sells stock which cost £300 for £500 on credit to F. Godbeer.

14 May Pays for telephone installation £120.

15 May Pays advertising creditor Trade Publications plc in full and £2000 to Helen's Trade Supplies.

16 May Buys further stock on credit costing £10 000 from Helen's Trade Supplies Ltd.

17 May Draws £100 for her own use.

Required

(a) Draft the initial balance sheet and then the changes that occur as each of the transactions takes place.

(b) Enter the transactions in T accounts.

(c) Prepare a trial balance.

(d) Calculate the profit and prepare a balance sheet.

NOVEMBER TRANSACTIONS

The business started on 1 November when John and Azina signed the deeds to purchase a business premises with a small ground floor showroom and office unit above. The purchase price of £100 000 was financed with a deposit of £30 000 and a mortgage over 15 years from the bank. The current rate of interest was 10 per cent.

The November financial transactions are listed below under the following headings:

- Bank receipts
- Bank payments
- Petty cash transactions
- Credit sales
- Credit purchases
- Other

Bank receipts		£
1.11	Transfer of owners' cash	50 000.00
12.11	Sales – other	58.00
13.11	Sales – printers	456.30
17.11	Sales – printers	384.23
17.11	Sales – other	34.50
23.11	Sales – other	34.26
23.11	Customer 5	108.10
25.11	Sales – other	67.87
28.11	Customer 6	1 311.00
28.11	Sales – other	87.45
30.11	Sales – other	128.32
30.11	Customer 2	4 278.00
30.11	Customer 1	50.00

Bank payments

	Cheque No	£
1.11	001560 Deposit on premises	30 000.00
2.11	001561 Petty cash float	100.00
3.11	001562 BT telephone connections	150.00
3.11	001563 Insurance (for 12 months)	423.05
3.11	001564 Traders Second Hand Ltd – shop and office equipment	1 558.32
3.11	001565 J & W Promotions Ltd – advertising	1 200.00
4.11	001566 Evening standard – advert	80.00
12.11	001567 Petty cash	85.03
22.11	001568 Supplier 1	9 472.00
28.11	001569 Office Supplies Ltd	4 631.20
28.11	001570 Caring Carpets	1 280.60

Petty cash book

Receipts:

		£
2.11	Petty cash float	100.00
12.11	Bank	85.03

Payments:

1.11	Coffee, milk, tea etc.	4.53
2.11	Petrol	18.00
2.11	Postage	20.00
4.11	Stationery	4.50
9.11	Petrol	18.00
10.11	Postage	20.00
13.11	Milk	3.15
16.11	Petrol	18.00
17.11	Sundry stationery	2.25
18.11	Coffee	1.75
20.11	Sundry stationery	5.15
23.11	Petrol	18.00
24.11	Milk	3.15
28.11	Sundry cleaning materials	5.31

Credit purchases

		£
2.11	Caring Carpets (flooring for office and shop)	1 280.60
3.11	Office Supplies Ltd (desks, chairs, filing cabinets, in trays, etc.)	4 631.20
4.11	Publicity Printers Ltd – catalogue and promotional printing	1 534.00
4.11	Highwood Printer's – office stationery	232.00
5.11	SUPPLIER 1 invoice no 472	9 472.00

5.11	SUPPLIER 2 invoice no 69453	3 473.66
18.11	SUPPLIER 3 invoice no 4267	452.00
18.11	SUPPLIER 4 invoice no 634	650.00
18.11	SUPPLIER 1 invoice no 984	400.00
18.11	SUPPLIER 4 invoice no 45	387.00
22.11	SUPPLIER 3 invoice no 107	723.00
22.11	SUPPLIER 5 invoice no 942	615.00
28.11	SUPPLIER 2 invoice no 12874	62.50
28.11	SUPPLIER 4 invoice no 09564	33.00

Credit sales

Date	Invoice No.	Account No.	Type of sale	£
6.11	0001	1	O	71.30
6.11	0002	2	O	55.20
6.11	0003	3	P	226.55
8.11	0004	4	P	286.35
8.11	0005	5	O	108.10
9.11	0006	1	O	115.00
9.11	0007	6	C	1 311.00
9.11	0008	2	C	4 222.80
10.11	0009	4	P	575.00
11.11	0010	7	O	15.00
14.11	0011	5	P	230.00
16.11	0012	1	O	57.50
16.11	0013	4	O	11.50
17.11	0014	3	C	2 831.30
18.11	0015	1	O	103.50
22.11	0016	6	O	54.62
22.11	0017	2	P	286.35
23.11	0018	8	P	730.25
23.11	0019	7	P	853.30
24.11	0020	1	P	776.25
25.11	0021	2	O	345.00
28.11	0022	3	O	460.00
28.11	0023	7	O	115.00
28.11	0024	6	O	40.25
28.11	0025	5	O	23.00
28.11	0026	4	O	46.00
30.11	0027	1	O	14.95
30.11	0028	2	O	18.97

Sales codes: C = computers; P = printers; O = other

Other

1.11 Transfer of John's car into the business, value second-hand £6000.

1.11 Completed purchase of the premises 122 Birch Street, Heath Park, Cardiff. The mortgage of £70 000 having been arranged with the bank. Repayments of £700.00 per month by direct debit need to be arranged. This will go out of the account on the 25th of each calendar month. The payments represent a figure for interest of £585 and a repayment of capital of £115.

26.11 Returned goods purchased from supplier 5 for an invoiced cost of £85.00. The goods were not the items ordered.

30.11 John counted the stock remaining on hand at 30.11. It had a cost of £8246.00.

Required

Give names to the customers and suppliers.

Record the above transactions in accordance with the chart of accounts you devised earlier using a manual system. (For the moment ignore VAT and the stock count at the end of the month.)

Practice questions

6 How informative is the manual system? Can you answer the following questions without calculating further figures:
(i)   What did customer 2 owe on 22 November?
(ii)   What was the balance of the bank account on 22 November?

7 Is there a problem when customer 1 pays £50.00? Should Azina be concerned?

8 How should the purchase return be treated?

9 Should the creditors for fixed assets be kept separate from other creditors?

10 What procedures should be followed before a supplier invoice is paid?

Appendix 4A – Some definitions

The records should show:

1   What an entity owns, i.e. **assets**
2   What an entity owes, i.e. **liabilities**
3   What the owner has invested in the entity, i.e. **equity**
4   What the entity has earned, i.e. **gains or income**
5   What expense the entity has incurred, i.e. **losses or expenses**

In more formal terms the Statement of Principles has defined these ideas as basic **elements** which are needed to form statements about an organization's financial position, performance and financial adaptability.

1   **Asset** – right or other access to future economic benefits controlled by an entity as a result of past transactions
2   **Liability** – an entity's obligation to transfer economic benefits as a result of past transactions
3   **Equity** – ownership interest in the entity
4   **Gains and losses** – gains are increases in equity other than those relating to

contributions from owners, whereas losses are decreases in equity other than those relating to distributions to owners

5   **Contributions from and distributions to owners** – Contributions are increases in equity resulting from investments by owners in their capacity as owners, whereas distributions to owners are decreases in equity resulting from transfers to owners in their capacity as owners

The records in the AIS hold information on all these elements. The first three items – assets, liabilities and equity – form the balance sheet or position statement of an organization. The gains and losses are used in performance reports and the final element describes the relationship of the organization with its owners.

5 Computerized accounting – setting up the system

Learning objectives

After reading this chapter you should be able to:
- set up a backup procedure for a computer system
- manage the backup log and the media on which the backup has been taken
- create accounts in a computerized accounting system.

Introduction

In this chapter we shall build on Chapters 3 and 4 by working with an integrated computerized accounting system. Your working lives will, no doubt, see you managing, controlling and designing such systems, and their introduction at this early stage is seen as being important because we believe that the procedure of learning about recording classifying and processing accounting data is made more efficient by using software which will be similar to software that you will use in real life situations. The software is a vehicle for teaching you accounting but the knowledge gained of working with and controlling a commercial system is an important biproduct of this process.

We shall be using Sage Sterling Financial Controller software and therefore making specific reference to its procedures. All accounting software, however, is designed and constructed using the same broad accounting principles, consequently other accounting software can be used with this textbook.

CASE STUDY

Azina stood in front of her desk looking down at her brand new computer and printer. Fred Blackwell from Codas Business Systems Ltd had just left having set up all the hardware, installed the software and run some checks to ensure that everything was in working order.

Azina felt quite intimidated but was, as usual, determined to come to grips with the new system. She had been running the accounts quite successfully on a manual system but as the business grew she was finding it more and more difficult to keep up with the processing and the demand for information. John needed information on sales of specific items, while individual customers and suppliers wanted information about their accounts, and Azina wanted to know details of the bank balance. The production of the end of the month balance sheet and profit and loss account for November had taken an age.

If Azina had made an arithmetic error it only revealed itself during the end of the month reconciliations and it had taken her hours to track them down. Bill had always emphasized how important debtor control was 'Its no good thinking you're doing well Azina just because you are selling to your customers, you must ensure you can be paid, and paid regularly and on time'.

Bill had explained to Azina the importance of sending customers timely and accurate statements of their accounts but producing these manually took so much time. 'There must be an easier way than this, John' said Azina one evening having spent three hours going through each customer's account making sure that they had not exceeded their credit limit. 'Well,' said John 'we are in the computer business ourselves, we should set an example and run a computerized accounting system. We can supply the hardware ourselves and I'll contact Fred Blackwell from Codas Business System Ltd who are specialists in accounting software. I am sure that a computerized accounting system will be able to supply me with some useful sales information.'

Within a few days Fred called around to the office to discuss their requirements. Fred's company would supply and install the software and also provide Azina with some training. Following installation Azina would also be able to phone Codas on what they called their 'Hotline' if she experienced any difficulties during the day-to-day operation.

Before finally committing themselves Azina told Bill Davies what they were thinking of doing. Bill thought it was a great idea. 'I've been aware that you have been getting snowed under. Properly set up this new system should be able to provide you with a great deal more management information for less effort'.

'By the way Azina, make sure Fred explains to you the procedures for making the information secure'.

'What do you mean Bill? Do you think someone will want to steal the information?'

'Not necessarily the information, Azina' said Bill 'but certainly computer theft is on the increase and it would be terrible if someone took the computer with all your records on the hard disk. However it isn't just theft I'm worried about. It is interruptions to processing brought about by power failures, etc. I am sure Fred Blackwell will explain it all to you. If he doesn't mention it, remind him.'

Security

Data security is always important, but with a computer system it is even more so. Although extreme cases of fire and flood can destroy both manual and computerized records, quite simple events, such as a power failure which has no effect on a manual system, can destroy or make inaccessible data on a computer system.

Your programs and data will be held on a hard disk within your computer. The data are stored as electrical impulses which can only be accessed through the computer itself. Can you envisage the nightmare scenario if three days prior to the end of the financial year there is a power failure or general computer failure which make access to the data held impossible? You will have filed all the manual documents that generated each transaction, but it would be an enormous and almost impossible task to reconstruct the accounts – particularly in a short period of time.

Denied access to their accounts, most companies would now go out of business within 72 hours. They would not be able to process orders, send out statements, collect money, pay creditors, provide information to the Inland Revenue, Customs and Excise and shareholders.

Our dependence on computer systems and the vulnerability of the data held means that we must take data security very seriously even at this early stage. Its importance must be appreciated now, right at the outset and good habits developed. Recognizing this vulnerability, data on the hard disk should periodically be backed up externally and then in the event of a problem with the data on the hard disk the backup can be used to **restore data** to the position represented by the date of the backup.

For small companies floppy disks can be used as the **external backup** (external referring to the fact that the information is taken outside the computer) but for larger organisations which have many megabytes of information (e.g. 40 megabyte +) a tape backup will be used. These tapes are approximately the same size as a music cassette but can store huge volumes of information and the backup procedure is very quick. A floppy disk can only store 1.4 megabytes which means that if you have 7 megabytes of data you will require five disks for each security cycle (see the section Creating you accounts below) and therefore 15 disks for the full security cycle. Floppy disks by their very construction can be an unreliable backup media for large volumes of data and the management of large quantities of disks becomes a nightmare. As the volume of data grows, therefore, more reliable sources of backup, e.g. tape should be explored.

Grandfather–father–son

Traditionally the method for security backups used is the three cycle method known as grandfather – father – son.

Backups will be made on media that suits the volume of data within the system. On small systems floppy disks will be used, while on larger systems tapes will be used that can back up many hundreds of megabytes. Regardless of the size of the system and the media used the principle is always the same and is illustrated in Table 5.1.

At the end of processing on Monday, disk A will be used to back up the system. Following the backup, make an entry into the **backup log** (Figure 5.1). Keeping this log up to date is crucial because, in the event of you needing to restore data, you do not want to restore from the wrong disk. At the end of processing on Tuesday, disk B will be used and on Wednesday, disk C.

Table 5.1 Backup sequence for floppy disks

Day	Cycle
Monday	A
Tuesday	B
Wednesday	C
Thursday	A
Friday	B
Monday	C

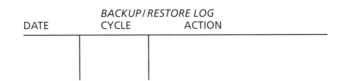

Figure 5.1
Backup log

Experience suggests that a three cycle backup gives sufficient security so that at the end of Thursday, disk A is recycled, followed by B on Friday, C on Monday and so on.

If first thing on Thursday morning a restore was found to be necessary you would go back to the most recent backup which was C. If something is wrong with disk C then you can fall back and use backup B and in the unlikely event that disk B was also corrupted you could use backup A.

Remember that restoring puts you in the position you were in when the backup was taken. So, for example, if a power failure occurred at 12 noon on Wednesday you would have to restore from disk B. This puts you in the position you were at, at 5 p.m. on Tuesday. All work that has been done since must be processed again, i.e. Wednesday morning 9 a.m. to 12 noon. This also shows how important document management is, so that documents can be retrieved from files where they have been suitably referenced and stored for re-inputting. In systems where extremely large volumes of data are processed, backups may be taken more frequently than once per day to minimize the re-inputting of documents in the event of a system failure. It is also recommended that backups are taken at times other than end of day processing and these occasions will be highlighted in the following chapters.

The need to restore, say, for example, after a power failure, is due to the fact that if processing were underway and files were open the processing would have been terminated with open files. The need to insure the integrity of the data has meant that the software has been designed to demand a restore when any such interruption occurs.

It could well be the case that an interruption took place during the posting of an invoice. At the crucial moment when the operator chooses to save the entry, the sales ledger record could be updated but before the double entry was completed in the nominal ledger the power failure occurred. The time scale for all this happening is fractions of a second but it is enough to question the completeness of the transactions and hence the integrity of the accounts. The same effect could be achieved by failing to back correctly out of the programme on completion of processing and just switching off the power. An orderly exit that closes all files is essential.

You will therefore require three formatted $3\frac{1}{2}$" floppy disks for your backups. One disk labelled 'Exercises' will be used for non-case study exercises and practice. For the case study a cycle of two has been shown to provide sufficient security. Label one disk A and the other B. These disks must be dedicated to your case study accounts work. No other data must be held on these disks. The commencement of the backup procedure clears the disk of all data. Unlike a company, *you* will be working in a computer laboratory where many people will use the same computer and software. Therefore your procedure will be:

1   At the end of each session take a backup copy, e.g. A, and update your log.

2 At the commencement of your next session restore from the relevant cycle, i.e. A, and continue processing.

3 When you complete that session take a backup on disk B and update your log.

4 At the commencement of your next session restore from disk B.

Security of the backups

Taking the backups and maintaining the log would be of no avail if you discovered they were damaged in some way and hence unreadable when you needed to use them. Take care therefore of your backups.

In a company the backups should be stored everyday in a fireproof safe. These are special safes that can withstand extreme temperatures. Many companies still keep their backups in standards safes in spite of repeated warnings that these safes, as strong as they look, will get extremely hot in a fire and will not be able to protect disks or tapes.

Periodically (monthly) an end of month backup should be taken off site for storage. These can be recycled in the same way as the daily backups and serve to provide additional security.

The software

Let us now turn our attention to the software to develop your accounting skills.

Sage Sterling Accountancy software is designed for the small to medium sized business that wants (or needs) to computerize its bookkeeping and accounting functions.

This is a truly integrated system: all ledgers and control accounts are automatically updated with only one keyboard entry. For example, posting a sales invoice will automatically:

1 update the sales ledger;
2 post VAT to the VAT account;
3 updates debtor control account;
4 posts to the correct nominal account;
5 posts the transaction to the audit trail, assigning an unique transaction number.

Compared to the manual system this process is far more efficient, faster and prone to less error. The relevant data, e.g. date, invoice number, narrative, net value and VAT value are entered only once. Once a posting has been made, say to the sales ledger, every other relevant account is updated automatically without further effort required. Also because data are entered once, there is no chance, as occurs in manual systems, of arithmetical errors being made or figures being transposed.

All accounting software works on the principle of 'double entry' and through the main ledgers, i.e. sales, purchase and nominal. Computer systems can increase efficiency and accuracy by sorting, organizing and storing data but the act of managing and controlling processing still depends upon understanding basic accounting principles and the relationship between various accounts and ledgers.

Chapters 3 and 4 introduced you to the main accounting principles and also to double entry and the ledgers. Before we can develop that theme you must set up your accounts in readiness to receive data from the case study. Figure 5.2 shows the

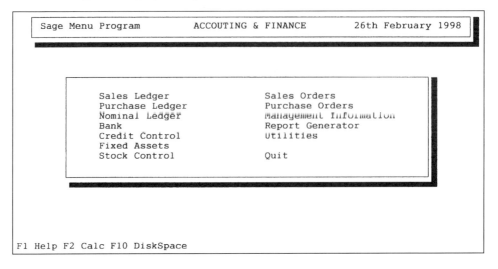

Figure 5.2
SAGE menu

main menu of Sage. By using the arrow keys the cursor (red bar) can be moved to the option of your choice and by pressing the enter key you make your selection. You will be concentrating on four options:

1   sales ledger;
2   purchase ledger;
3   nominal ledger;
4   utilities.

The software is extremely user friendly and you will soon learn to read the bottom of the screen where the program is constantly 'talking' to you.

It gives you options	–	Yes or No?
It tells you what to do	–	Enter date
		Switch on printer
		Printer not ready
Asks you questions	–	Do you wish to take a backup?
Makes you think twice	–	Are you sure?

There is a great consistency in the use of certain keystrokes and in the layout of the posting screens in the three ledgers which means that once you have mastered one ledger you have almost mastered them all. This is particularly the case with the sales ledger and the purchase ledger which are mirror images of each other.

Do not be fooled or overwhelmed by the technology. You are in charge. Chapters 3 and 4 explained that all entries into the accounts are prompted by transactions/ documents/requests for information. These tell you what to do, i.e. which ledger you should be in and which option to choose. The information to enter will be asked for by the program and found on the document. You will be surprised how quickly you become familiar with the menu options and sub-options.

At this stage your data files will be empty with the exception of some control accounts so it is advisable to take your first backup using disk A. Follow these steps to take a backup and restore. This will enable you to experiment with the system (setting up accounts, posting entries, etc.) then restore to this starting position when you are ready to set up all the accounts for the case study. Don't forget to update your backup log.

Creating your accounts

Sales ledger/purchase ledger

Select *Sales Ledger* from main menu and then select *Customer Details*. (Select *Supplier Details* from the *Purchase Ledger* menu to view, edit or add supplier account details). Your screen should look like Figure 5.3.

The information requested will be used by the program to help you manage the processing and also to provide you with management information, i.e. warnings, exceptions, statements, letters and reports. When you want to enter **customer details** Sage will prompt you to enter the following details:

1 *Account Reference*: This must be an unique reference and can be up to six characters in length including letters, numbers or a combination of both. (If you choose a purely numerical code then your first code number, No 1 must be entered 000001.)

   When you enter an account reference the system checks to see that this reference has not already been used. If it has the account details appear on the screen. If it is unused the program will ask you to confirm that you wish to create a new account by asking.

2 *Is This a New Account*: No/Yes. This procedure ensures that each account has its own unique reference number.

   Having indicated that you wish to create a new account you should enter the appropriate information in each of the following fields.

3 *Account Name*: Up to 25 characters.

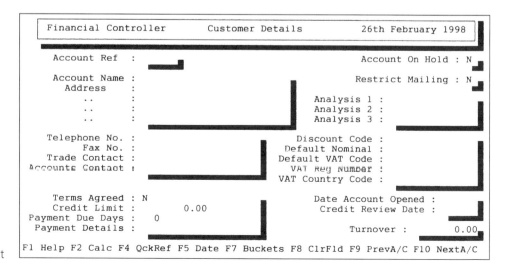

Figure 5.3
Creating a new customer account

```
┌──────────────────────────────────────────────────────────────────────┐
│ │Financial Controller      Customer Details      26th February 1998│ │
│ └──────────────────────────────────────────────────────────────────┘ │
│                                                                        │
│      Account Ref   :    ▉                     Account On Hold : N      │
│                                                                        │
│     Account Name   :                          Restrict Mailing : N     │
│        Address     :                                                   │
│           ..       :                          Analysis 1 :             │
│           ..       :                          Analysis 2 :             │
│           ..       :                          Analysis 3 :             │
│                                                                        │
│    Telephone No.   :                          Discount Code :          │
│         Fax No.    :                          Default Nominal :        │
│     Trade Contact  :                          Default VAT Code :       │
│  Accounts Contact  :                          VAT Reg Number :         │
│                                               VAT Country Code :       │
│                                                                        │
│     Terms Agreed   : N                        Date Account Opened :    │
│      Credit Limit  :        0.00              Credit Review Date :     │
│  Payment Due Days  :    0                                              │
│  Payment Details   :                          Turnover :       0.00    │
│ F1 Help F2 Calc F4 QckRef F5 Date F7 Buckets F8 ClrFld F9 PrevA/C F10 NextA/C │
└──────────────────────────────────────────────────────────────────────┘
```

4 *Address*: Up to 4 lines of 25 characters.

5 *Credit Limit*: By inserting a **Credit limit** the program checks the current balance on the account with the credit limit and gives a clear warning when the limit has been exceeded either on printed reports (Account History/Aged Debtor/Aged Creditor Reports) or on screen enquiries. The credit limit check is an important aid in debtor control and Chapter 9 will explain how this process is set up.

6 *Turnover*: This figure is automatically maintained by the program. Every invoice or credit note posted will change the total. Under a manual system simple questions such as 'How much have we sold to Ebson's this year to date?' or 'What is the total value of goods supplied by Mirage Computers Ltd?' can cause a considerable amount of work. This information tends to be required quickly because it is probably needed for negotiation on discounts. With a computer system, by selecting *Customer Details* followed by the account number your current screen will appear with the up to date figure.

7 *Telephone No*:

8 *Fax No*:

9 *Accounts Contact*: In addition to being printed on certain reports this information can also be required to help control debtors/creditors and contact the company concerned quickly in the case of queries.

The remaining fields will not be used at this stage. When all details have been entered press escape *ESC* and the system asks:

Do you want to: Post Edit Abandon

1 Select *Post* if details are correct and a new account will have been created ready to accept the posting of transactions.

2 Select *Edit* if any of the details are incorrect. You will be allowed to change them by using the arrow keys to move the cursor to the field that requires amendment.

3 Select *Abandon* if you decide to discard the record completely.

Do not be concerned if you post a record and then discover you have made a mistake. By selecting Customer Details and entering the account number the details entered will appear on the screen and you can make the necessary amendments. This would be the procedure if one of your customers/suppliers changed their address, telephone number, etc.

What you cannot do is change the account number. This is the unique identifier of the account. You can only change this by deleting the record but this must be done before any posting takes place. Once a transaction has been posted to an account it cannot be deleted even if the balance is zero. This is a control feature of the program and is important in ensuring the integrity of the total database. Audit and control would be impossible if records containing transactions could be deleted.

Nominal Ledger

Select *Nominal Ledger* from the main menu followed by *Nominal Account Structure* and the *Account Names*. Your screen should look like Figures 5.4 and 5.5.

In the same way as the customer and supplier codes, each code will uniquely

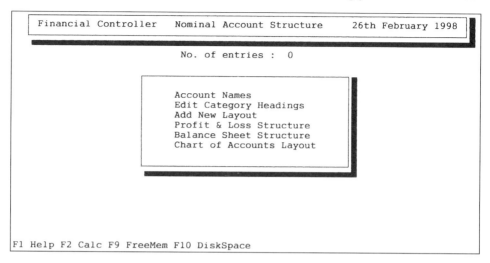

Figure 5.4
Nominal account
structure

identify only one account and the dialogue with the program will be same. Chapter 4 explained the importance and logic of coding accounts and each business should choose a coding system to suit its own circumstances. When you want to enter data into the **nominal account structure**, Sage will prompt you to enter the following details:

1   *Account Reference*: The system checks if the code has been used previously. If it has it displays those account details. You can make changes to existing accounts if necessary. If the code is not in use already, the system will ask you to confirm that you wish to create a new account.
2   *Is This a New Account*: No/Yes.
    If you are creating a new account answer *Yes* and the system now prompts you for the *Account Name*. You are allowed 25 characters for the account name.

We are not, at present, using the budget facility so press *ESC* and you will be asked:

Do you want to: Post Edit Abandon Delete

```
 Financial Controller        Account Names        26th February 1998

 Account Reference :                  Account Name :

                       Actuals                      Last Year
          B/fwd     :        0.00 Dr   Budget             0.00 Dr
     1 - October    :        0.00 Dr             0.00     0.00 Dr
     2 - November   :        0.00 Dr             0.00     0.00 Dr
     3 - December   :        0.00 Dr             0.00     0.00 Dr
     4 - January    :        0.00 Dr             0.00     0.00 Dr
     5 - February   :        0.00 Dr             0.00     0.00 Dr
     6 - March      :        0.00 Dr             0.00     0.00 Dr
     7 - April      :        0.00 Dr             0.00     0.00 Dr
     8 - May        :        0.00 Dr             0.00     0.00 Dr
     9 - June       :        0.00 Dr             0.00     0.00 Dr
    10 - July       :        0.00 Dr             0.00     0.00 Dr
    11 - August     :        0.00 Dr             0.00     0.00 Dr
    12 - September  :        0.00 Dr             0.00     0.00 Dr
         Future     :        0.00 Dr
         Totals     :        0.00 Dr             0.00     0.00 Dr

F1 Help F2 Calc F4 QckRef F7 Cr/Dr F8 ClrFld F9 PrevA/C F10 NextA/C
```

Figure 5.5
Creating a new
nominal ledger
account

These prompts are identical in meaning and operation to those in the sales and purchase ledgers. If you are sure the details you have entered are correct select **Post**. As in the other ledgers changes can be made to any of the details entered with the exception of the account reference and accounts can be deleted only if no transactions have been made to them.

Azina was very satisfied with her day's work. She had nearly completed setting up the ledgers on her new computerized system. The sales and purchase ledgers were complete and only about another five or six nominal codes remained to be entered.

Suddenly to Azina's amazement the computer screen went blank. She couldn't believe it. She sat there for a few seconds wondering why the computer screen had lost its power before she realized the lights had gone as well. She groaned. A power cut was all she needed, but it didn't last long and within minutes the power was restored. Azina re-entered the program. A message however flashed at the bottom of the screen:

PROCESSING INTERRUPTED – PLEASE RESTORE FROM LAST BACKUP

In spite of the training course and warnings from Bill she had become so engrossed with entering data that she had forgotten to take a backup. No transactions were being posted so it did not seem so important.

Azina phoned Bill and then the Codas Hotline but the message was the same, without a backup she was going to have to start again.

The parallel run

On the introduction of a computerized system it is essential that for two months a 'parallel run' takes place. By this is meant that the manual and computer systems are run together side by side.

This imposes an enormous strain on what is probably, a hard-pressed workforce but it is necessary at these early stages because:

1 the hardware may cause problems;
2 the software may cause problems;
3 operator error will take place;
4 new procedures will not be in place.

The two systems are run side by side and at the end of month one a comparison is made between the two sets of accounts. If a discrepancy exists no further processing can take place until it is detected and rectified. Reasons for the discrepancy must be established and action taken to prevent repetition.

The parallel run continues into the second month, at the end of which another comparison is made. Hopefully at this stage very few errors exist and the management and operators feel confident in 'cutting over' completely to the new computerized system.

You will follow this exact procedure by comparing the November manual accounts for your case study with the computerized accounts. If there are any errors these must be rectified before progressing to the December accounts. The same procedure will then be followed for December.

Summary

We have seen in this chapter how the pressures of producing management information from a manual system has persuaded Bale and Co. to invest in an integrated computerized system.

You have started to work on this system by setting up the chart of accounts in the nominal ledger and a list of customers and suppliers in the sales and purchase ledgers respectively. This setting up process is important in preparing the program to accept accounting information and also, from your point of view, to start learning how the program works and appreciating what is available within the program.

Time has been spent emphasizing the importance of security and backups and we hope you will never find yourself in the unfortunate position of Azina in the case study.

It is important that you spend time now familiarizing yourself with the menu layout and the functions we have used to date. Further opportunity exists for you to practice using your 'Exercises' disk in the end of chapter exercises.

Key words

backup log p. 79 • credit limit p 84. • customer details p. 83 • data security p. 78 • external backup p. 79 • main menu p. 82 • nominal account structure p. 85 • restore data p. 79

Practice questions

For these non-case study exercises you will need to use as a backup disk the one you marked 'exercises'.

Before you commence these exercises you must ensure there are no data present in the accounting system. If there are you will have to restore with a disk that contains blank files.

At whatever stage you reach in the exercise during your laboratory session (e.g. you may have completed question 1) before you leave the laboratory:

1 take a backup of your data using the disk marked 'exercises'.
2 when you return to the laboratory, restore your data using the disk marked 'exercises'.

Exercises related to the setting up of the sales and purchase ledgers:

1 Create the following customer accounts:

Account Reference	SL001	SL002	SL003
Account Name	Cardiff Timber Suppliers	Micham & Micham	Brian Werrett
Account Address	South Dock	High Street	The Haven
	Cardiff Docks	Bristol	Offa's Dyke
	Cardiff	BS22 4TK	Gwent
	CF21 4ZK		GG42 36T
Credit Limit	£10000	£12000	£8000
Telephone No	01222 421369	01722 493666	01495 621488
Fax No	01222 421370	01722 493680	01495 421495
Contact Name	Sandy Thomas	Bill Walker	Brian Werrett

2 On checking your work you discover that you need to make the following alterations:

(i) SL001 Change Credit Limit to £9000

(ii) SL002 Change post code to BS24 4TY

(iii) SL003 Change contact name to Julian Werrett

When making these changes select *Customer Details* and at the prompt for *Account Ref* press *F4*. This will list all the accounts that currently exist in the sales/purchase ledger. To select an account use the arrow keys to position the cursor and press enter. The F4 key is a very useful quick search facility that you will use frequently. When large volumes of data are held on the system you will know the name of the account you wish to access but not always its reference number. The F4 key will speed up access to the relevant account.

3 Print a list of the customers accounts you have created (names and addresses). Study the sales ledger menu and select the correct option and follow the prompts.

4 Create the following supplier accounts:

Account Reference	PL0001	PL0002	PL0003
Account Name	Mirage Computers	Office Equipment Ltd	BJ Ltd
Account Address	Mirage House	The Green	9 Tree Drive
	Singleton	42 Crawshay St	United St
	Swansea	Merthyr	Leeds
	S42 6DJ	M49 672	L49 6ZB
Credit Limit	£7,500	£6,000	£4,500
Telephone No	01972 635611	01624 532701	0142 973333
Fax No	01972 635600	01624 532704	0142 973333
Contact Name	Ellis Jenkins	Hugh Coombs	Helena Snee

5 On checking your work you discover that you need to make the following alterations:

(i) PL0001 Change post code to S42 8DJ

(ii) PL0002 Change Credit Limit to £6,500

(iii) PL0003 Delete account completely

6 Print a list of the customer accounts you have created (names and addresses).

Exercise relating to the setting up of the nominal ledger:

Required

7 Create the following nominal ledger accounts:

Account number	Account name
1001	Fixture and Fittings
1050	Building Society
1030	Computer Equipment
2150	Tax Due
4001	Sale of Computers
4002	Sale of Printers
4003	Sales other

4500	Sale Returns
5001	Purchase of Computers
5002	Purchase of Printers
5003	Purchase other
5500	Purchase Returns
6000	Rent
6010	Electricity
6200	Advertising
8000	Share Capital

8 Make the following changes:

   (i)   6000 Mortgage Interest
   (ii) 6200 Sales Promotion
   (iii) 1050 Building Society Investment
   (iv) 2150 VAT

 9 You have just created 16 nominal ledger accounts, state which ones are assets, liabilities, expenses or revenue.

10 Print a list of your nominal accounts.
At this point after taking a backup on the disk marked 'exercises' inform your lecturer that you are now ready to set up all the accounts for the case study.

11 Using the chart of account you designed for the manual system and the names of your customers and suppliers, create all the necessary accounts on your computer system in preparation for the posting of the November transactions.

   (i)   Set up the chart of accounts and print a list of the accounts.
   (ii) Set up the sales ledger accounts and print a list of all the accounts.
   (iii) Set up the purchase ledger accounts and print a list of all the accounts.
   (iv) The printouts should be filed in a special file that you will be maintaining for this case study. All printouts from the case study will be filed here, e.g. Daybooks, Audit Trail, Transaction History, Aged Debt Analysis, and you will need to give some thought as to the best way of managing these reports so that the information they contain can be accessed quickly and efficiently.

Finally remember to take backups and keep your log up to date.

6 Accounting entries

Learning objectives

After reading this chapter you should be able to:
- understand how entries into the computer system update the relevant accounts and complete the double entry
- use computerized integrated accounting systems to post
  - invoices
  - credit notes
  - receipts
  - payments
  - journals
- manage the flow of documents in the accounting system to ensure entries made are authorized and accurate.

Introduction

You should now have a good understanding of the relationship between the main ledgers and the double entry method of keeping records. In this chapter we shall build on that introduction and using the computerized system reinforce the principles of double entry bookkeeping, a sound understanding of which, is essential to managing an accounting information system. You will now be able to access the accounts you set up in Chapter 5 and complete the main posting routines, i.e.

1 sales invoices;
2 sales credit notes;
3 purchase invoices;
4 purchase credit notes;
5 sales receipts;
6 purchase payments;
7 nominal journals.

You must work towards a position where, for a given transaction, you can see in your 'minds eye' very clearly the accounts that will be affected. This is essential to ensure that the correct postings take place and also that errors, which will inevitably occur, can be rectified. The computer program will complete the double entry posting automatically (this will be explained below) but to manage an accounting information system effectively and to ensure that the correct controls are in place a thorough understanding of double entry within the computer is very important. Consequently within this chapter we shall ask you to make postings through the computer system but also to repeat those postings in double entry diagrams. Once you have understood this process all further postings will take place using only the computer system.

CASE STUDY

Jean Sutherland looked up from her notes, switched off the OHP and waited for the usual salvo of questions. Jean taught the Computerized Accounting module on which Azina had enrolled. It was an evening class and the enthusiasm of the students made the class very enjoyable.

Azina had followed the lesson closely and felt reasonably confident that she understood most of the points but she still had a nagging doubt in her mind as to which ledger to access when faced with a transaction. A student two rows in front of her thankfully had the same doubts and asked Jean could she go over the reasoning behind deciding on which ledger to use for posting a transaction. The student explained to Jean 'If I receive a cheque from a customer then I know that the bank account is in the nominal ledger and so my first reaction is to try and post it directly into the nominal'.

Jean had taught this module for a number of years and had heard this question many times before. She appreciated how at this stage it might all seem confusing.

'You're right,' said Jean 'The bank account is in the nominal ledger and the cheque will find its way into that account, but you must also remember that this cheque has come directly from a customer and as long as a customer or supplier is involved all transactions must be posted through the sales or purchase ledgers. The cheque will be posted to the bank account in the nominal ledger, but via the sales ledger'.

Which ledger?

Students initially experience some difficulty in deciding in which ledger to make an entry. Figure 6.1 shows, for each of the documents/transactions, in which ledger the transaction is initiated. The arrows indicate that information flows from the sales ledger and from purchase ledger into the nominal. Every transaction affects the nominal and this is where the double entry actually takes place. What you must clarify in your mind now is the starting point.

Faced with any transaction ask yourself the following questions:

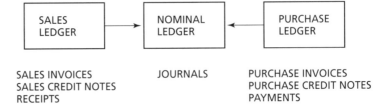

Figure 6.1
Selecting the right ledger

SALES LEDGER → NOMINAL LEDGER ← PURCHASE LEDGER

SALES INVOICES
SALES CREDIT NOTES
RECEIPTS

JOURNALS

PURCHASE INVOICES
PURCHASE CREDIT NOTES
PAYMENTS

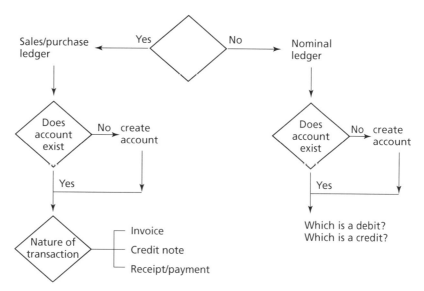

Figure 6.2
Does the
transaction affect
a customer or a
supplier?

1   *Does the transaction affect a customer (supplier)?* If the answer is 'yes' then you
    will need to make the transaction through the sales ledger (purchase ledger).
2   *Which accounts are affected?* One must be the customer (supplier) account in the
    sales (purchase) ledger and within the nominal ledger the debtor (creditor) con-
    trol account and the sales (purchases) account.
3   If the answer to question 1 is 'No' then entries will be made directly into the
    nominal ledger and you must:
    (a) name the accounts affected.
    (b) decide which one is to be debited.
    (c) decide which one is to be credited.

Figure 6.2 shows the decision process in diagrammatic form.
    To help us to check that the double entry has been made when we post various
transactions, we are going to use a special feature of the Sage Sterling programs known
as the Periscope. The Periscope allows enquiries to be made in one ledger whilst you
are working in another ledger. Without such a facility you would have to leave your
current ledger, return to the main menu, select the ledger in which you wish to make
an enquiry and then select the relevant option.
    Similarly, you may be posting a journal in the nominal ledger when you receive a
query concerning a customers account. The Periscope would allow you to access the
customers account through a 'pop up' menu without having to leave the nominal ledger.
    Periscope needs to be loaded before you access the Sage Sterling programs. At the
system prompt C: type in the following command:

View and then press *ENTER.*

You will be prompted to enter your password. The screen will inform you that the
Periscope utility has been successfully installed. You can then load Sage Sterling in the
normal way. At any point during processing you can call up the Periscope menu by
pressing the following key combinations:

ALT + ENTER

To remove the menu from the screen select the *Quit* option or press *ESC*.

Posting transactions to the computer

We shall now concentrate on dealing with the following transactions.

1   sales invoices;
2   sales credit notes;
3   sales receipts;
4   purchase invoices;
5   purchase credit notes;
6   purchase payments;
7   nominal journals.

The whole focus will be on understanding the relationship between the ledgers and on the process of double entry. Figure 1.6 in Chapter 1 showed the flow of input–process–output and how this structure affects the Accounting Information System. Posting transactions forms part of the input aspect of this process. The information contained on invoices, credit notes and cheques together with the design of the input screens on the computer dictate the data that will be captured. The design of your chart of accounts and the application of the accounting principles explained in Chapter 3 determine how the data will be processed.

Sales (purchase) invoices

Invoices issued to credit customers – **sales invoices** – will be posted against the customer account in the sales ledger. Select *Sales Ledger* from the main menu and choose *Batched Data Entry* and then *Sales Invoices*. Your screen will look like Figure 6.3. The program contains a number of important control features to minimize errors during data capture.

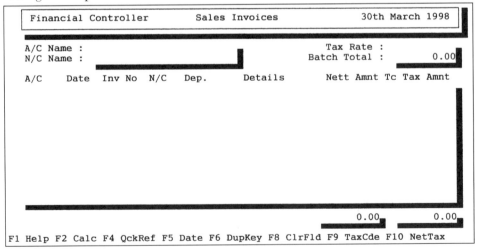

Figure 6.3
Batched data entry
for sales invoices

1   *A/C* – Sales ledger account number. If you do not know the number press F4 to obtain a list of all current sales ledger accounts. If the number you select exists, the name of the account will be displayed in the box named '*A/C Name*' if the account does not exist the program will prompt *Is This a New Account: No/Yes.* If the answer is yes you will be taken to the customer details screen to enable you to create the account.

2   *Date* – The date of the document and not the date on which the transaction is being posted.

3   *Invoice No* – Every invoice will be pre-numbered and the invoice number will need to be entered here.

4   *N/C* – Nominal code. Which nominal code do you wish to post to to complete the double entry? When this is entered the name of the account appears in the box named 'N/C Name'.

5   *Dep* – Department. We will not be using this field so press enter to skip this field. John and Azina's business is at the moment too small to be able to make use of this facility. Departments are used by the report generator to provide departmental analysis of your transactions. As Bale and Co. grows their demands for management information may see them activating and making use of this field.

6   *Details* – This is a 19 character field which allows you to enter some narrative that identifies this transaction. At a later date (possibly 6–8 months time) when you have an enquiry on this account the narrative field will help you to remember this transaction. During the case study make sure you make full use of this field.

7   *Net Amnt* – The value of the goods sold net of VAT (Value Added Tax). VAT will be explained in Chapter 8. At the moment Bale and Co. are not registered for VAT.

8   *Tax* – Tax Code. There will be a number of VAT codes. For the moment enter 'To' and the box named 'Tax Rates' will show a rate of 0.000.

9   *Tax Amnt* – Amount of VAT charged on this invoice.

Another important control feature is the top right hand box named 'Batch Total' which allows you to exercise **batch control**. On each screen you can post up to 12 invoices. The Batch Total facility can be used to control and check the accuracy of your input. For example, you may have three invoices to post which have the following values £1200, £740 and £625. A pre-posting batch total gives you £2565. Input each invoice and before accepting them for posting check the computer batch total with your pre-posting total. If the totals agree accept the three invoices for posting. If there is a discrepancy carefully check the details of each invoice against what you have input against each field. The full use of this facility will be explained in more detail below.

   Figures 6.4 and 6.5 show an invoice being posted to Cardiff Timber Supplies for £1000 following the delivery of a Viglen 486PC. This is an example of a **sales invoice**. By completing the information in Figure 6.5 the following has taken place:

1   By inputting the reference number SL0001 you have indicated which sales ledger account is to be accessed.

2   Whatever amount is posted to account SL0001 will automatically be posted to the debtor control account. Chapter 4 explained why every entry in the sales (purchase) ledger will be repeated in the debtor (creditor) control account. How this occurs automatically in a computer system is explained in Appendix 6A of this chapter.

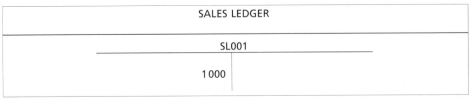

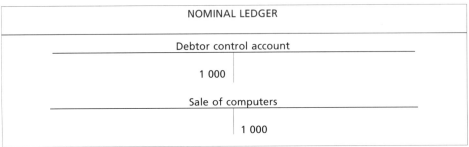

Figure 6.4
Double entry
record for sales
invoice

3   Inputting nominal code 4000 informed the program which account would be used
    to complete the double entry.

Sales (purchase) credit notes

Sometimes, when a customer receives goods it is possible that:

1   the goods were never ordered;
2   they arrive damaged;
3   more have been delivered than were ordered;
4   the wrong goods have been delivered.

An invoice would have been raised and then posted to the customers account as in the
previous section. The account however is now showing a false position regarding the

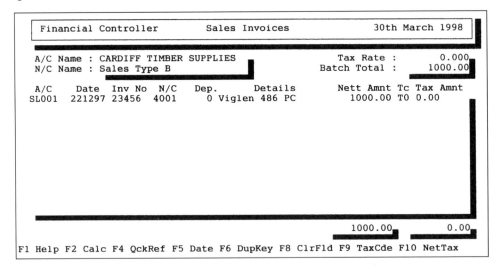

Figure 6.5
Posting a sales
invoice

indebtedness of the customer which must be rectified. You cannot remove it from the records. The document exists, it has been issued and posted. What is done in these circumstances is that a document called a *credit note* is raised which cancels out or reduces the original charge.

The nominal ledger accounts that these are posted to have already been set up by you in Chapter 5. Sales returns (4500) and purchase returns (5500). Note once again the logic in the coding of accounts. Although you have created just one sales returns and purchase returns accounts, if you wished to obtain more management information you could set up a returns account for each main category of your sales and purchases e.g. sales returns computers; sales returns printers, etc.

Figure 6.6 shows the posting screen for a **sales credit note** and the accounts that are affected by the posting. On receipt of a credit note the sequence of questions in Fig 6.2 should go through your mind. Because it is your business that is issuing the credit note the customers account will be credited, the debtors control account is also credited and the sales returns account debited. The posting screen is identical to the posting screen for sales invoices with the exception that the invoice number is replaced by the credit note number. Note once again the logic in the coding of the accounts.

Figure 6.6 shows a **sales credit note** that has been issued to Cardiff Timber Supplies Ltd because the computer that had been ordered was found to be damaged upon delivery. Following discussions with Cardiff Timber Supplies Ltd they agreed to keep the computer providing they received an allowance of £100 for the damaged casing.

By completing the information in Figure 6.6 the following has taken place:

1   By inputting the reference number SL0001 you have indicated which sales ledger account is to be accessed.
2   Whatever amount is posted to account SL0001 will also be automatically posted to the debtor control account.
3   Inputting nominal code 4500 informed the program which account would be used to complete the double entry.

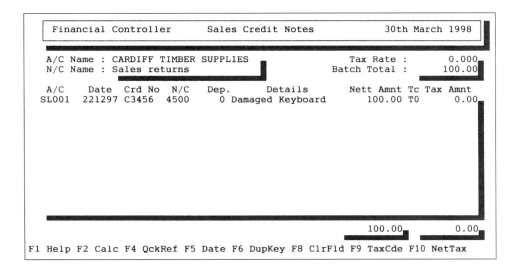

Figure 6.6
Posting a sales
credit note

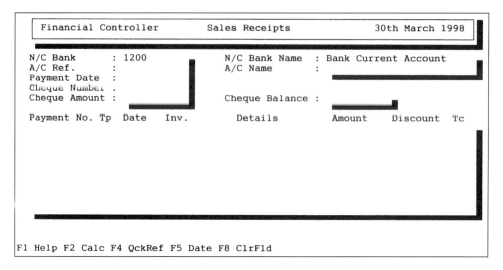

Figure 6.7
Sales receipts
screen

Sales receipts/purchase payments

These transactions represent the receipt of cheques from credit customers and the payment of cheques to credit suppliers. As credit customers and credit suppliers are directly affected the transaction will be posted directly through the sales and purchase ledgers.

Select from the *Bank Menu, Sales Receipts (Purchase Payments)* and your screen will look like Figure 6.7.

A cheque received from Cardiff Timber Supplies Ltd for £75 would be entered as shown in Figure 6.8.

1   *N/C Bank* – This field will show the default bank account code. If you have other bank accounts set up, you may change the code.
2   *N/C Bank Name* – This appears on inputting your bank account code and is a control on the accuracy of posting.

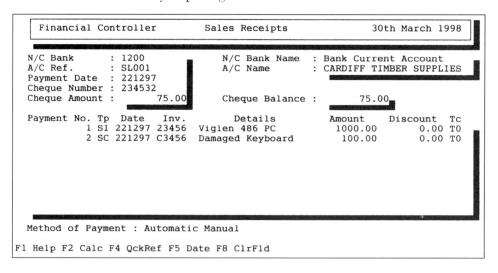

Figure 6.8
Posting sales
receipts

3 *A/C Ref* (customer or supplier account) – Enter the reference to identify the customer (supplier) and check the *A/C Name* field to ensure that the correct account is being accessed.
4 *Payment Date* – Enter the date of payment.
5 *Cheque Number* – Enter the cheque number.
6 *Cheque Amount* – Enter the total value of the cheque.
7 *Cheque Balance* – This field initially shows the full cheque amount. As you allocate the cheque to invoices this balance reduces accordingly.

The word 'allocate' was used above and it refers to the process of matching receipts (payments) against invoices. Clients will pay you for specific invoices or in some cases part of invoices (when some goods in a delivery have been damaged). A cheque received can cover a number of invoices and you will want to know which invoices are being paid because it will not necessarily be the oldest invoices on the account. The cheque will normally be accompanied by a *remittance advice* which will list the invoices being paid. This document can be used therefore to allocate payment against specific invoices.

The allocation process is enhanced enormously by keeping accounts on a computerized system. This process is straightforward and once allocations have been made reports can be generated which automatically highlight outstanding invoices. To produce such information from a manual system involves a considerable effort.

Having entered the payment or receipt details, the screen lists up to the first nine outstanding transactions relating to the customer or supplier accounts. At the bottom of the screen the following prompt is displayed.

Method of Payment: AUTOMATIC MANUAL

Choose *Manual* (Appendix 6B explains in full the various option choices of this receipts/payment routine). Use the arrow keys to move the cursor to the invoice that is being paid and press *ENTER*. The following prompt will be displayed:

Type of Payment: FULL PART DISCOUNT CANCEL

Choose *Full*. If you are sure that you have completed the entries correctly press *ESC* and the following prompt will be displayed:

Do you want to: POST EDIT ABANDON REMITTANCE?

Select *Post* to save the receipt (payment) and update the ledgers.
If you are satisfied that your journal is correct select *Post*.

Journal entries

Journal entries are perhaps the easiest of the transactions to understand and take place primarily within the nominal ledger. Examples of some transactions that would require a journal entry are as follows:

1 an owner transfers a personal bank account to the business bank account;
2 correction of errors e.g. sales of computers account has been credited with £2000 but this should have been posted to sales of printers account;
3 transfers from bank account to petty cash account;

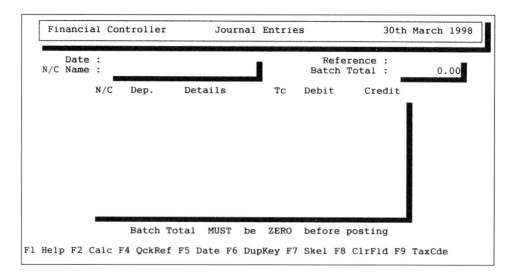

Figure 6.9
Example of a
journal
document

4   stock adjustments (Chapter 7);
5   accruals and prepayments (Chapter 11);
6   depreciation (Chapter 12).

Journal entries must be entered with the same respect afforded to invoices, credit
notes and cheques. The business should have pre-printed pre-numbered journal
stationery which becomes the input document (Figure 6.9). Any adjustments, entries
or error corrections made should only be attempted following the correct completion
of a journal which has been authorized. Following entry into the system the journal
document should be filed for future reference.

Select *Nominal Ledger* from the *Main Menu* and *Journal Entries*. The screen will
appear as in Figure 6.10. Note the message at the bottom of the screen: *Batch total
must be zero before posting*. This means that every debit must be matched with a
credit. Remember that the journal can only alter accounts in the nominal ledger. It

Figure 6.10
Journal entry
screen

cannot alter anything in the sales or purchase ledgers. Enter the nominal code for the account to be debited, the detail, tax code and amount of the debit. Then repeat for the credit entry. Press *ESC* and if you are sure the figures are correct select *Post*.

Activity

1   The accountant has discovered that an electricity bill of £700 has been posted to the advertising account by mistake.
    Required
    Draft a journal entry in good form to correct the error. Post to the system. Check the nominal accounts concerned to check that the entry has worked.

Managing the process

In the previous sections to this chapter we have dealt with the main posting routines inputting data into the accounts. In the examples and exercises small volumes of data were processed but it must be appreciated that in practice data volumes and the flow of documentation can be extremely large and for security, efficiency and accuracy systems must exist to manage this flow.

Computerized accounting systems, as we have seen contain many control features that prevent errors or reduce the chances of errors being made. In spite of these control features methods must be introduced and implemented to manage large volumes of documentation.

Each morning every business will receive a substantial amount of mail containing, letters, cheques, purchase invoices, statements and purchase orders and each day it will itself be sending out a similar variety of documentation. Below we will be making suggestions as to what systems can be implemented and you will be expected to utilize such procedures when you are working on the exercises and the case study.

Chapter 4 referred to the use of day books which are an essential part of controlling the inputting of data in a manual system. The integrated nature of computerized systems means that day books can be dispensed with because as we have seen, entries into the sales and purchase ledgers are automatically posted to the nominal ledger. This process in itself eliminates many errors that would be found in a manual system, e.g. arithmetic errors, transposition of figures, etc. and together with input prompts, e.g. *Customer Code = Account Name* and batch totals should reduce many inputting errors.

Control still needs to be exercised, however, in managing the flow and processing of documentation. Day books are printed from the computer system but these are available after inputting and not prior to inputting as is the case with a manual system.

Sales invoice/credit notes

These will be pre-printed and pre-numbered. Custody of the documents is important as is the retention of spoiled documents. If invoices and credit notes are produced automatically by the computer every invoice/credit note run is likely to result in a number of spoiled documents. These must be retained and filed to ensure the

Sales Invoice	Sales Credit	Purchase invoice	Purchase credit

Tick as appropriate

PREPARED BY: _____

Nominal Code	DATE	DETAILS	NET	TAX	GROSS

Figure 6.11
Example of a
batch control slip

completeness of the audit trail. Blank forms falling into the wrong hands creates a potential for fraud to take place.

Documents should be inputted in batches of probably no more than 20 documents per batch and a batch total calculated prior to inputting. Most computer systems automatically keep a running total of the batch, so that as the last document is processed one can check that the keyed in details correspond to the pre-total.

An example of a **batch control** slip is shown in Figure 6.11. Once processing is complete the completed batches can be filed in batch/numerical order for future reference. For our exercises and case study it is recommended that batch sizes of a maximum of six transactions should be used.

Purchase invoice/credit notes

These will arrive by post each morning and a system must be in place that opens, sorts and distributes all documents ensuring effective control at all stages. All documents entering the business should be registered as proof of arrival and the time, date and destination during distribution noted. In sophisticated Management Information Systems this process is computerized.

Purchase invoices and credit notes will be arriving from many different suppliers all using their own unique numbering systems (alpha, numeric, alpha-numeric). To improve control it is recommended that each document is given an internal number which will run sequentially (in the same way as sales invoices and credit notes).

Figure 6.12
Example of a
control stamp
used for incoming
invoices

ABC LTD	
DATE	26.3.98
NO	5623
NL CODE	7200
APPROVED	JRD

Each invoice or credit note, when it arrives in the processing department, will be stamped and relevant information inserted prior to posting. An example of such a stamp is shown in Figure 6.12.

1   No. – The sequence number which will become the document's unique identifier. Documents will be filed in this number order.
2   NL Code – The nominal ledger code to which this invoice/credit note will be posted. When ready for inputting documents should be batched in the same way as explained above for sales invoices and credit notes.

Cheques paid/cheques received

Of all the source documents, cheques represent the areas of highest risk in terms of potential abuse brought about by poor management control. Cheque books should be locked away together with pre-printed cheque stationery and no blank cheques should be available that are already signed. We shall return to this issue of payment management in Chapter 9. For the moment we can note that pre-printed cheque stationery appears to be treated with far less respect than the traditional cheque book. During a cheque run on the computer it is inevitable that cheques will be spoilt because, for example, of non-alignment of the printer or the tractor feed becoming jammed. In many businesses you can see these cheques being ripped off the continuation stationery and thrown in the waste bin. It must be emphasized that all spoilt cheques must be retained and filed. All cheques, used and spoilt, must be accounted for.

Journals

These will be used for posting opening balances, making direct postings in the nominal ledger and correcting errors. As with the other documents mentioned they will be pre-printed and pre-numbered and should be authorized, processed and filed in the same way. During the case study all journal entries should be accompanied by a written journal.

Till rolls

In some businesses cash sales are made via a till. At the end of the day the **till roll** is used to reconcile the cash balance in the till and as an input document updating the relevant accounts. As no credit customers are involved this entry would be made directly into the nominal ledger using a journal.

Activities

Test your understanding of the control features by answering the following questions:
2   What sort of errors, that can be common in a manual system, are eliminated by an integrated accounting system?
3   Why are day books available after inputting in an integrated system rather than before processing as in a manual system.

4   Why should batches not exceed 20 documents?
5   Design a journal document which will be available pre-printed and pre-numbered.

Summary

You should now understand all the documents that are used in an accounting system and also through which ledgers to post these documents. It must be emphasized that no posting takes place in an accounting system unless a document exists to support that entry. You must feel confident when the accounts are being audited that you can prove, by production of an authorized document, why every entry has taken place.

Sales and purchase invoices, credit notes, cheque stubs and bank statements will in most cases be retained and filed but the same care must be taken for error correction and adjustments through journals. In your working lives you will be managing accounting systems and this is why we have emphasized the process of managing documentation and implementing controls at all levels of processing. Take special note, therefore, of document control, numbering, batch control and the overall **system controls** that are built into the computerized system e.g. **field control** (date, number of digits), that the account number brings up the account name for confirmation, etc.

To reinforce the principle of double entry and the relationship between the ledgers we have asked you, for each exercise, to complete T accounts and to post to the accounting system. This will be vital in helping you to visualize what is happening in the computer system. This will be important when you are supervising others in helping rectify errors.

Key words

batch control pp. 95, 102 • field control p. 104 • journal entries p. 99 • purchase credit note p. 97 • purchase invoice p. 95 • sales credit note p. 97 • sales invoices p. 94 • system control p. 104 • till roll p. 103

Practice questions

1   Jean Sutherland had devised an exercise to test the students understanding of which ledger to access and how the double entry is completed. The exercise, although manual, is very similar to the way in which the computer works.
Transactions:

   (i)   Invoice of £50 to SL0001 for 3 boxes of floppy disks.
   (ii)   Transfer £100 from bank to petty cash.
   (iii)   Invoice of £150 to SL0002 for 2 printers.
   (iv)   Purchase of 10 IBM 486 PCs at £600 each from PL0001.
   (v)   Purchase of 20 boxes of floppy disks at £10 each from PL0002.
   (vi)   Cheque received from SL0001 for £50.
   (vii)   Cheque received from SL0002 for £150.
   (viii)   Make a payment of £3000 to PL0001.
   (ix)   Purchase of 5 printers at £80 each from PL0001.

(x)	Make payment of £200 to PL0002.
(xi)	Credit note received from PL0001 for £1 500 for damaged goods.
(xii)	Invoice of £1200 to SL0003.
(xiii)	Invoice of £2000 to SL0001.
(xiv)	Invoice of £3500 to SL0001.
(xv)	Credit note sent to SL0003 for £700.
(xvi)	Direct payment of £300 from bank for insurance.
(xvii)	Purchase of stationery for £35 from petty cash.
(xviii)	Purchase milk and coffee from petty cash £11.
(xix)	Transfer £60 from bank to petty cash.
(xx)	Payment of £1000 to PL0001.
(xxi)	£2000 cheque received from SL0001.
(xxii)	£2000 cheque received from SL0002.
(xxiii)	£500 cheque received from SL0003.
(xxiv)	Sales invoice to SL0001 for £1000.
(xxv)	Sales invoice to SL0003 for £3000.
(xxvi)	Purchase invoice from PL0001 for £1700.
(xxvii)	Purchase invoice from PL0002 for £750.
(xxviii)	Make a payment of £1300 to PL0001.
(xxix)	Make a payment of £750 to PL0002.
(xxx)	Transfer £75 from bank to petty cash.

Required

For each transaction listed ask yourself the questions shown in Figure 6.2 and then write your answer out as illustrated in Figure 6.13. Transaction one is done for you as an illustration.

Transaction No 1:

(a) The transaction is a sales invoice, therefore the sales ledger is involved.
(b) Account SL0001 will be debited with the value of the invoice i.e. D £50.
(c) The debtor control account in the nominal ledger must also be debited with the value of the transaction i.e. D £50.
(d) The other half of the double entry in the nominal journal is to credit a sales account i.e. 4002. C £50.

SALES LEDGER	PURCHASE LEDGER	NOMINAL LEDGER						
		Debtors Control	Creditors Control	Bank	Sales	Purchase	Exp	Other
SL001 DR £50		DR £50			4002 CR £50			

Figure 6.13 Analyzing transactions for posting

106   *Accounting entries*

You have already set up all the codes you need to use. Following each transaction ensure that the nominal ledger remains in balance i.e. the value of the debit entry is equal to the value of the credit entry.

2 **A** Post the following invoices. Due to the fact that we have limited space to record detail, reference each transaction using the transaction number given in column one. Ensure that the total value of debtors is equal to the value shown in the debtor control account and that the nominal ledger is in balance.

Trans	Customer	Date	Inv No	Goods	Net Amt (£)
1	SL0001	010695	45678	P	350.00
2	SL0002	020695	45679	P	470.00
3	SL0003	030695	45680	C	200.00
4	SL0003	030695	45681	O	78.00

P = Printer; C = Computer; O = Other.

Make a suitable narrative for the 'Details' field. You have already created the nominal ledger accounts in which to post sales. Before posting using Figures 6.14 and 6.15:

 (i) Fill out the invoice screen (Figure 6.14)
 (ii) Complete the double entry posting (Figure 6.15)
 B Within the sales ledger examine each account you have posted to by using the menu option *Transaction History.*
 C Within the sales ledger examine the nominal ledger accounts that have been posted to using the Periscope facility.
 D The purchase ledger is a mirror image of the sales ledger. It holds the records of credit suppliers and by looking at the menus of both sales and purchase ledgers you will see that the functions and options within each menu are

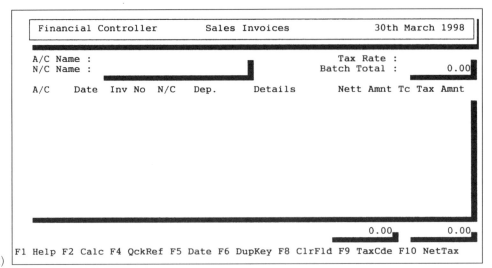

Figure 6.14
Screen for sales invoice exercise (Practice question 2)

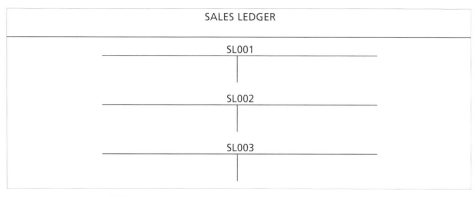

Figure 6.15
T accounts for
sales invoice
exercise (Practice
question 2)

identical. All postings within the purchase ledger however will be opposite to a similar posting in the sales ledger. For example an invoice posted in the purchase ledger would:

(i) credit the supplier account;
(ii) credit the creditor control account in the nominal ledger;
(iii) debit the purchases account in the nominal ledger.

Use Figures 6.16 and 6.17 to post the following invoices ensuring that the total value of creditors is equal to the value shown in the creditors control account and that the nominal ledger is in balance.

Trans	Supplier	Invoice No:	Date	Goods	Net Amount (£)
5	PL0001	62347	020695	C	6 000.00
6	PL0002	914628	030695	P	3 000.00
7	PL0003	62501	050695	O	1 500.00

E   Post the invoices through the purchase ledger on the computer.
F   Within the purchase ledger examine each account you have posted to by using the menu option *Transaction History*.
G   Within the purchase ledger examine each nominal ledger account you have posted to using the Periscope facility.

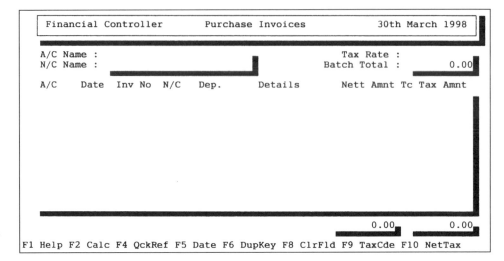

Figure 6.16
Screen for
purchase invoice
exercise (Practice
question 2)

3   A   Post the following credit notes

Trans	Customer	Date	CN Note	Goods	Net Amt (£)
9	SL0002	100695	62341	P	70.00
10	SL0003	120695	62342	C	60.00
11	SL0003	140695	62343	O	78.00

Make a suitable narrative for the 'Details' field using the following codes:
P = Printer; C = Computer; O = Other.

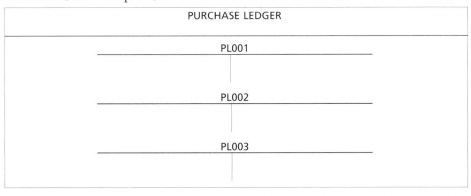

Figure 6.17
T accounts for
purchase invoice
exercise (Practice
question 2)

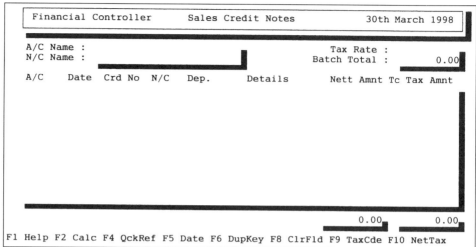

Figure 6.18
Screen for sales credit note exercise (Practice question 3)

Before posting using Figures 6.18 and 6.19:

(i)   Fill out the sales credit screen (Figure 6.18);

(ii)   Complete the double entry posting (Figure 6.19).

Check and make sure that the total value of your debtors is the same as the balance showing on the debtor control account.

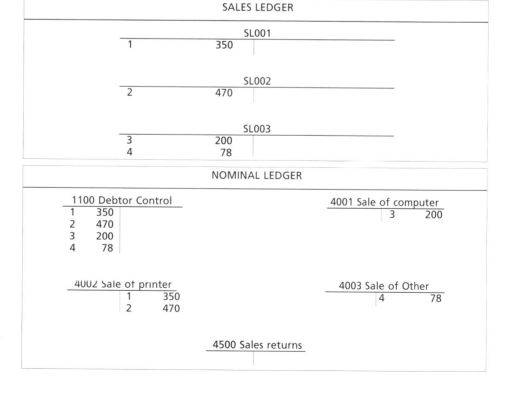

Figure 6.19
T accounts for sales credit notes exercise (Practice question 3)

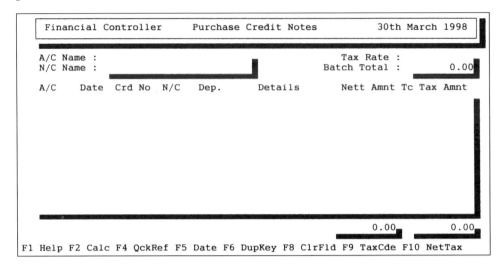

Figure 6.20
Screen for
purchase credit
note exercise
(Practice
question 3)

B   Within the sales ledger examine each account you have posted to by using the
menu option *Transaction History.*
C   Within the sales ledger examine the nominal ledger accounts that have been
posted to by using the Periscope facility.
D   Using Figures 6.20 and 6.21 post the following purchase credit notes, completing the double entry.

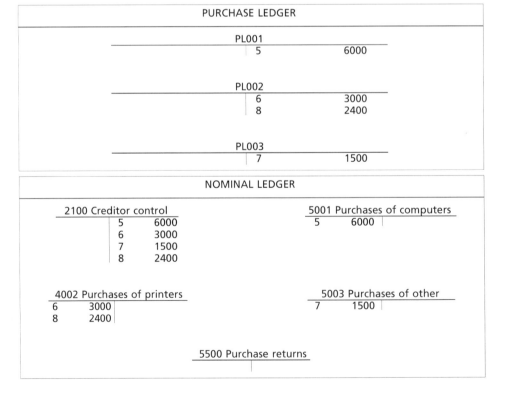

Figure 6.21
T accounts for
purchase credit
notes exercise
(Practice
question 3)

Trans No	Supplier	CN No	Date	Goods	Net Amt (£)
12	PL0001	62531	180695	C	2 000
13	PL0002	78682	190695	P	1 000

E   Check and make sure that the total value of your creditors is the same as the balance showing on the creditor's control account.

F   Post the transactions in D above into your computer system.

G   Within the purchase ledger examine each account you have posted to by using the menu option *Transaction History.*

H   Within the purchase ledger examine the nominal ledger accounts that have been posted to using the Periscope facility.

I   Post the credit notes on your computer system.

J   Within the purchase ledger examine each account you have posted to by using the menu option *Transaction History.*

K   Within the purchase ledger examine the nominal ledger accounts that have been posted to by using the Periscope facility.

4   **A**   Post the following receipts in a manual system and then on to your computer system:

Trans No	Date	Customer	Amount (£)
14	190795	SL0001	350
15	200795	SL0002	400
16	210795	SL0003	140

B   Within the sales ledger examine each account you have posted to by using the menu option *Transaction History.*

C   Within the sales ledger examine the nominal ledger accounts that have been posted to using the Periscope facility.

D   Post the following payments in a manual T system and then into your computer system.

Trans No	Date	Supplier	Amount (£)
17	050895	PL0001	4 000
18	060895	PL0002	3 000
19	070895	PL0003	1 500

E   Within the purchase ledger examine each account you have posted to using the menu option *Transaction History.*

F   Within the purchase ledger examine the nominal ledger accounts that have been posted to using the Periscope facility.

G   Ensure that within both sales and purchase ledgers the value of the individual debtors and creditors equals the value of the debtor and creditor control accounts.

Appendix 6A – Control accounts

Computerized accounting systems are designed and written to work using the logic of double entry. For the program to perform this task however it must be given certain information during the installation and setting up of the software.

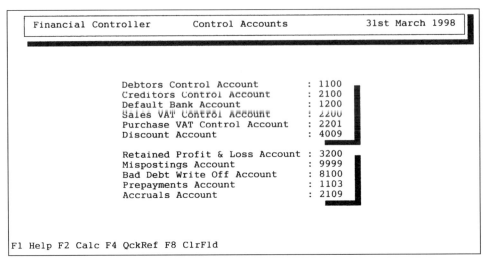

Figure 6.22
List of control accounts on SAGE system

When posting an invoice for example, as illustrated in Figure 6.5, the program will:

1 debit the customers account;
2 automatically debit the debtor control account;
3 credit the named nominal account;
4 automatically credit the VAT account.

Some of these lines are established when the program is written ((i) and (iii)) and the others during program set up ((ii) and (iv)).

From the main menu select *Utilities* and from *Utilities* select *Control Accounts*. Your screen will appear as in Figure 6.22. By directing the program to work in this way you reduce the number of entries required during data capture and also reduce the opportunity for errors being made during data capture.

Debtors Control Account	1100
Creditors Control Account	2100
Default Bank Account	1200
Cash Account	1230
Sales VAT Control Account	2200
Purchase VAT Control Account	2201
Discount Account	4009
Retained Profit & Loss Account	3200
Mispostings Account	9999
Bad Debt Write Off Account	8100
Prepayments Account	1103
Accruals Account	2109

Debtors control account

This is the account to which double entry postings are made when transactions are added to the sales ledger. For example, when you post an invoice, the total value of the invoice is debited to the debtors control account, while the sales analysis account is credited with the net goods value and the tax control account is credited with the VAT amount.

Creditors control account

This is the account to which double entry postings are made when the transactions are added to the purchase ledger. For example, when a purchase invoice is posted, the creditors control account is credited with the total amount, while the purchase analysis account is debited with the net goods value and the tax control account is debited with the VAT amount.

Default bank account

The default bank account offered when payments and receipts are posted is the one specified here. You can set up as many bank control accounts as you wish in the nominal ledger, but typically, you would specify the default as being the account in which most of your business transactions are drawn or deposited (such as a current account). The program will only accept a code for a nominal ledger account already identified as a bank account. This is done when the nominal account record is set up by pressing F3 before the record is saved (see also the description of setting up bank accounts in Chapter 4).

Cash account

This is the account used for petty cash postings made in the nominal ledger. It will be debited when receipts are posted and credited when payments are made.

Sales and purchases VAT control accounts

These are the accounts to which the value of any VAT is posted when transactions are entered in the sales or purchase ledgers. For sales VAT (outputs), the sales VAT control account is credited for invoices and debited for credit notes, and for purchase VAT (inputs), the purchase VAT control account is debited for invoices and credited for credit notes.

Discount accounts

These are the accounts to which the value of any discounts is posted when receipts or payments are entered in the sales or purchase ledgers. The accounts are debited for sales discount allowed or credited for purchase discount taken.

Retained profit and loss accounts

This account accumulates the net balance of all profit and loss accounts and represents the net profit (or loss) shown at the end of the profit and loss report. It is the account to which all profit and loss items are posted at the year end by the *Year End* option.

Mispostings accounts

This is the control account used to record the double entry against the appropriate bank account for the value of cheques cancelled through the *Refunds* function in either the sales or purchase ledgers. The balance on this account should always be zero.

Bad debt write off account

This is the control account to which the value of bad debts written off is posted when the *Bad Debt Write Off* or *Write Off Account* functions in the sales or purchase ledgers are used.

Prepayments account/accruals account

These are the control accounts used when prepayments and accruals are posted through the nominal ledger. Press the *ESC* key when you have finished making changes to the control accounts entries to return to the *Utilities* sub-menu.

Appendix 6B – Allocation of receipts, payments and credit notes

Why allocate?

Allocating payments and receipts to invoices helps you double-check which invoices are being paid and make sure the amounts involved are correct. This is particularly important where discounts are involved or part payments are being made because you can see at a glance if the payment or receipt doesn't match up.

Automatic versus manual

There are two methods of allocation offered – automatic and manual. The automatic process simply matches the payment or receipt amount to as many transactions as possible, starting with the first transaction listed. Payments or receipts are matched to invoices in full as far as possible.

If the amount is not enough to pay all outstanding transactions, the automatic process will pay as many as possible until the full payment or receipt amount is used up. If the amount doesn't add up to an exact number of invoices, either an invoice will be part allocated or, if the payment or receipt amount is more than the value of the invoices to be paid, a balance will be posted on account.

The automatic allocation process ignores credit notes and cannot cater for discounts taken, nor will it include any payments on account, but you can adjust the automatic allocations if necessary using the manual allocation process. With the manual allocation process, you identify the invoices being paid and choose one of the allocation, options: *Full*, *Part* or *Discount*. The part allocation option allows you to enter the amount being allocated and the discount option allows you to enter the value of discount taken.

Whichever allocation method you choose, you are not restricted to allocating one payment or receipt to one or more invoices. You can also choose to allocate any other cheques that were posted on account previously as well as any credit notes that may be on the account. In effect, you can allocate anything that may be applicable.

How to post payments and receipts

Choose either the *Receipts* option from the sales ledger menu or the *Payments* option from the purchase ledger menu. The program will display a blank screen ready for entry of the details which are described in the following paragraphs. An example of a completed receipt details screen is shown later.

The following function keys are available to assist processing:

F1 to display a help screen
F2 to pop-up the calculator
F4 to display a list of customers, suppliers, departments or nominal accounts
F5 to insert today's date in the date field
F8 to clear the contents of a field.

N/C Bank (Nominal bank account)

This field will display the default bank account code defined as set up in the control accounts utilities. Unless you change the installation settings, this will be '1200 Bank Current Account'.

If you have other bank accounts set up, you may change the code or press F4 to display the other bank accounts available. To accept the default displayed, simply press *ENTER*. The name of the bank account chosen is displayed in the *N/C Bank Name* field.

A/C Ref (Customer or supplier account)

Enter the reference to identify the customer or supplier account to which the payment or receipt is to be posted. You can press F4 to display a list of accounts from which to select. The name of the account chosen is displayed in the *A/C Name* field.

Payment date

Enter the date of payment. If it coincides with today's date you can press F5 to insert the date automatically.

Cheque number

Enter the cheque number or any payment reference that you want stored with the transaction. You can enter up to six digits. If you wish to carry out the allocation process without posting a payment or receipt, leave this and the cheque amount field blank.

Cheque amount

Enter the total value of the cheque up to £999,999.99. If the value is higher than this split the payment over two postings. When posting a payment or receipt that is to be allocated to one or more outstanding invoices, you can amend the cheque amount after the list of outstanding transactions has been displayed. This effectively means that you can leave the *Cheque Amount* field blank initially, and complete it after viewing the values outstanding transactions displayed for the account. This enables you to allocate and post a receipt against an invoice which you know is being paid in full, but you are not sure of the cheque value until you have viewed the invoice total. When the list of outstanding transactions is displayed you can cursor back up to the cheque amount, having chosen *Automatic* or *Manual* from the allocation options, and change the value accordingly.

Cheque balance

This field initially shows the full cheque amount. As you allocate the cheque to invoices, this balance reduces accordingly. If you pick up any payments on account or credit notes during the allocation procedure, this balance will be increased by the corresponding amount. Any balance left showing in this field when you complete the allocation procedure will be posted as a payment on account with the reference and date as entered for the cheque.

Having entered the payment or receipt details, the screen lists up to the first nine outstanding transactions relating to the customer or supplier account. If there are more than nine transactions outstanding on an account you can scroll the display using the cursor control keys, *HOME, END, PAGE UP* and *PAGE DOWN* after you have chosen the manual allocation method described later.

For each outstanding transaction on the account, the following is shown:

1   *Payment* – this field will be used to display the type of allocation done (i.e. *Full, Part* or *Discount*);
2   *No* – this is the transaction number (for the audit trail) automatically assigned by the program;
3   *Tp* – a code which identifies the type of transaction. It will be one of the following:
   SI   sales invoice
   SC   sales credit note
   SA   sales payment on account
   PI   purchase invoice
   PC   purchase credit note
   PA   purchase payment on account
4   *Date* – the date of the transaction;
5   *Inv* – the reference, such as an invoice number, associated with the transaction;
6   *Details* – the description associated with the transaction;

7   *Amount* – the amount outstanding; inclusive of VAT (and after any part allocations have been deducted);

8   *Discount* – the amount of any discount taken against an invoice;

9   *To* – the tax code associated with the transaction.

At the bottom left of the screen, the following prompt is displayed:

Method of payment: AUTOMATIC MANUAL

This allows you to select the allocation method as described earlier. The procedures are explained below:

Automatic allocation

As described earlier, if you select this option, the system will start with the first outstanding invoice listed and allocate the cheque balance as far as possible to as many invoices as possible. Invoices that can be allocated in full are marked as *Full* in the payment column. All of the cheque balance will be allocated unless it exceeds the total value of invoices, in which case the remaining balance will be posted as a payment on account.

A part allocated transaction is marked as *Part* in the payment column. No credit notes are processed by the automatic allocation procedure – this must be done manually.

Once all automatic allocations are completed as far as possible, the program goes into manual allocation mode. You can then make any adjustments to the allocations if this is necessary, following the instructions in the paragraphs on manual allocation. If all allocations made are satisfactory, press the *ESC* key and follow the instructions in the paragraphs on saving the payment or receipt and/or allocations.

Manual allocation

If you choose the manual allocation option, or if you wish to make manual adjustments after the automatic allocation procedure, you can select the transactions that are to be allocated by using the cursor up and down keys or mouse to highlight the transaction concerned. Press the *ENTER* key or click on the left mouse button when you have selected a transaction and the following prompt will be displayed:

Type of payment: FULL PART DISCOUNT CANCEL

The choices are described in the following paragraphs according to circumstances.

When an invoice is paid in full

If the cheque amount enables an invoice to be paid in full and there is no discount involved nor any credit notes to take into account, select the *Full* option. The word *Full* will be displayed in the payment column and the amount column will be zero, indicating that nothing remains outstanding against the invoice. The *Cheque Balance* field is reduced by the amount of the invoice.

When only part of an invoice is paid

If only part of an invoice is being paid, choose the *Part* option. The program will prompt you to enter the amount of the part payment. The word *Part* will be displayed in the payment column and the amount field will display the balance of the invoice remaining after part payment. The cheque balance will be reduced by the amount of the part payment. Alternatively, if the cheque value is less than the invoice value, select the *Full* option and the invoice is automatically part paid.

When discount is taken

If a customer has taken discount allowed or you have taken discount given by a supplier against the invoice, choose the *Discount* option. The program will display a default value for the discount calculated on the basis of the difference between the cheque amount and the value of the invoice being discounted. You can accept this recommended discount amount or amend it as required and it will be deducted from the invoice amount before allocating the payment or receipt. The tax code for the discount will default to *T9*.

The word *Disc* is displayed in the payment column, the amount field is reduced to zero, the discount field displays the value of discount taken and the cheque balance is reduced by the discounted invoice amount.

Matching credit notes with invoices

If there is a credit note on the account that needs to be offset against an invoice that is being paid, move the cursor to the credit note transaction and press *ENTER* or click on the credit note transaction with the mouse. Choose the *Full* allocation option which picks up the value of the credit note and adds it to the cheque balance field. You can allocate the payment or receipt and credit note value combined to one or more invoices as described earlier. (If you are using the VAT cash accounting scheme, make sure invoices and credit notes have the same tax code). If you want to match a credit note to an invoice independently to entering a payment or receipt, use a cheque value of zero.

Allocating payments on account

If there is payment on account already shown in the list of transactions that you wish to allocate, either on its own or together with a new cheque, move the cursor to the payment on account and press *ENTER* or point to the transaction and click the left mouse button. Choose the *Full* allocation option which picks up the value of the payment on account and adds it to the cheque balance field. You can then allocate this to one or more invoices as described earlier. If you want to match a payment on account to an invoice independently to entering a payment or receipt, use a cheque value of zero.

Undoing an allocation

If you want to remove an allocation, for example if you have made a mistake in the allocations or because you want to adjust an automatic allocation, move the cursor to the transaction and press *ENTER* or click the left mouse button. Choose the *Cancel* allocation option which reverses the allocation made and adjusts the cheque balance field accordingly. You can then reallocate as necessary. (Note that this must be done *before* posting the details to the ledger; you cannot undo an allocation that has already been posted.)

Saving payment or receipt and/or allocation postings

You can choose to save the payment or receipt and/or allocations at any time. If a cheque balance remains when you choose to post, a payment on account will be recorded, as described below.

Press the *ESC* key, or click the right mouse button, and the screen will display the following prompt:

Do you want to: POST EDIT ABANDON REMITTANCE

1   *Post* – Select this option to save the payment or receipt and/or allocations and update the ledgers as described later. The screen is cleared and you are returned to the N/C Bank field to process another cheque and/or allocation. If no further cheques or allocations are to be entered, press *ESC*, or click the right mouse button, to return to the sales or purchase ledger menu.
2   *Edit* – To continue the allocation procedure, select this option. The cursor will be returned to the position it was in when you pressed *ESC* or clicked the right mouse button.
3   *Abandon* – To abandon the cheque posting and/or allocations altogether, select this option and the program will clear the screen ready for the entry of another cheque and/or allocation. If no further cheques or allocations are to be entered, press *ESC* to return to the sales or purchase ledger menu.
4   *Remittance* – This option is only applicable to purchase ledger and enables you to print a remittance advice note which details the payments made.

Payments on account

Whenever you choose to post a payment or allocations while a cheque balance remains on the screen, the system will assume that you want to post the remainder as a payment on account that may be allocated at a later date. The following prompt is displayed:

Do you want to: POST-UNALLOCATED-AMOUNT EDIT ABANDON

1   *Post Unallocated Amount* – The ledgers will be updated with the posting.
2   *Edit* – Choose this option if you wish to continue allocating the over-payment, rather than posting it as a payment on account.
3   *Abandon* – Choose this if you wish to abandon the cheque and/or allocations altogether. The screen will be cleared so you can enter another cheque. If no more cheques are to be posted, press the *ESC* key, or click the right mouse button, to return to the sales or purchase ledger menu.

If the cheque balance exceeds the cheque amount

If the figure in the cheque balance field is greater than the cheque amount field at the end of your allocations, the program will display the following warning alongside the *Post, Edit* and *Abandon* options:

WARNING! Cheque Balance > Cheque Amount

If you still decide to post the cheque and allocations the payment on account prompts will be displayed as described above.

7 Stock adjustments and a simple profit and loss account

Learning objectives

After reading this chapter you should be able to:
- draft a simple income and position statement in vertical format
- understand the difference between periodic and continuous recording of stock
- count and value the stock at the period end
- understand the need for a period end routine.

Introduction

So far we have looked at a system which records stock as it is purchased and sales as the amount received or receivable from customers. No record has been made of the amount of the stock purchased which has been taken by the customers. This chapter looks at two ways in which this recording can be done in practice, known as the periodic and continuous methods of stock recording. Having recorded the stock figure, we can draw up a simple income statement to calculate profit, and a balance sheet or position statement. There are traditional layouts for these statements and we introduce these here.

CASE STUDY

At the end of November, Azina and John were keen to see how things were going. They had transferred their records to the new Sage system and wanted to reassure themselves that the results were the same as those shown in the manual records. Azina was sure that they should be able to measure the income for the first month and while they knew that it was far too early to judge the success of the business, it would be good to know that they were making some progress.

However Azina had identified a problem. She realized that when they bought goods for sale they were debited to the purchases account and credited to cash or creditors at the price paid. When they were sold, she recorded the price the customer was charged as a credit to sales and the amount the customer paid or owed in cash or debtors. Now she had come to the end of the first month it had dawned on her that she had not recorded which of the goods purchased had been sold. If she wanted to know the profit that was made on a sale she needed to know what each sale had cost. She was concerned that it was the result of the records being kept wrongly.

John told her not to worry. All he had to do was go and check in the stock room and he could tell her what item had gone to which customer and what was left. Azina was not sure that this was the best way to go about it. If business picked up it would not be possible to identify each item sold with the original record of the purchase in order to work out profit.

Methods of stock recording

There are two main approaches to working out the value of stock that is sold and the stock that is left in hand. The first requires each item sold to be separately identified. The second involves physically counting the stock which is left in hand. Both methods are acceptable and we look at both here.

Continuous stock recording

Continuous stock recording is the method in which each sale has to be identified at the time it is sold and the cost of the item recorded as being sold in an expense account known as cost of sales. Taking as an example an item costing £2500 cash in March, being sold in April for £3000 cash. First record the purchase and sale in the normal way:

Journal A		£	£
Purchases of stock	DR	2 500	
Bank	CR		2 500
Being purchase of goods for resale			

Journal B		£	£
Cash at bank	DR	3 000	
Sales	CR		3 000
Being sale of goods for cash			

However under this system we need to record the movement of goods out to the customer as well as the sale. A transfer from the purchases of stock account (an asset account) to a **cost of sales** account (an expense account) is needed.

Journal C		£	£
Cost of sales	DR	2 500	
Purchases of stock	CR		2 500
Being the cost of the current sale transferred to cost of sales			

At any point in time, this leaves the purchases of stock account with the balance of purchases of stock which have not yet been sold. This is the figure needed in the position statement as an asset. The balance on the cost of sales account will be the figure needed as an expense in the income statement.

Purchase of stock

March	Bank (A)	2 500	March	Cost of sales (C)	2 500

Cost of sales

April	Purchase of stock (C)	2 500			

Sales

			April	Bank (B)	3 000

Bank

April	Sales (B)	3 000	March	Purchases (A)	2 500

Until the last decade this method was not practical for the majority of businesses. You can imagine being in a queue in a shop waiting while each item in each customer's basket has to be identified and the purchase invoice found to see when it was bought and what it cost. The only businesses where this was viable were those such as specialist antique shops or art galleries where each item is unique and of considerable value. The quantity of sales would be small although the profit per item might be large.

Recently the same method has become possible for other businesses with point-of-sale technology. You will see these in most retail stores from national chain stores to corner shops. The bar code reader used by the check-out assistant does more than calculate the customer's bill. The item being sold is identified and, as the invoice for the customer is printed, so the stock record is updated, transferring the item from stock to cost of sales.

The advantages of the system are that the owner knows exactly what is in stock at any time and which lines are selling. With this information the stock ordering system can be efficiently controlled. In the more sophisticated systems the ordering is done automatically on-line, with suppliers linked to the system as well. The whole system can reduce the amount of stock the business needs to hold so saving costs.

Periodic stock recording

In **periodic stock recording** there is no attempt to keep an up to date figure for the amount of stock in hand except at set moments in time. The system records the sales and purchases as you have done in the last few chapters. When the time comes to work out the profit or loss on sales, the stock in hand is physically counted. With this information it is possible to estimate the cost of the items sold. For example, consider a shop selling bicycles. which starts with 20 bikes costing £200.00 each on 1 April. The shop purchases another 50 bicycles at £200.00 each during April. At the end of the month you count the number left and find that there are 25 in the shop. You can make a good guess that you sold 45 bicycles, i.e.

			£
Take the stock in hand at start	20 at	200	4 000
Add purchases in period	50 at	200	10 000
Available for sale	70		14 000
Remaining stock at month end	25 at	200	5 000
Therefore cost of sales	45 at	200	9 000

This logic gives the standard formula for working out cost of sales in the periodic method of stock recording:

Cost of sales = Opening stock + purchases − closing stock

In this case the records in the nominal ledger will show just the purchases and sales until the decision is made to count the stock. At this point it is possible to enter the stock in hand into the records and calculate the profit made. Taking our bicycle example, the records will show an opening balance at 1 April of stock in hand of £4000. Purchases during the month will be £10 000. At the end of April the stock is counted and valued at £5000 and it is this valuation which needs to be entered in the records by means of a journal. At the same time, a journal is needed to close off the opening stock figure to the profit and loss account as this stock is no longer in hand. There are different ways of achieving this and we look at two of them here. The end result is the same whichever method you use.

Method 1
Some systems open a cost of sales account and transfer the opening stock to the cost of sales.

Journal D		£	£
Purchases	DR	10 000	
Bank	CR		10 000

Being the purchase of goods for resale

Journal E		£	£
Cost of sales	DR	4 000	
Stock in hand	CR		4 000

Being the transfer of the stock in hand at the beginning of the month to cost of sales

Journal F		£	£
Cost of sales	DR	10 000	
Purchases	CR		10 000

Being the transfer of the items bought for resale during the month to cost of sales

Journal G

		£	£
Stock in hand	DR	5 000	
Cost of sales	CR		5 000

Being the stock counted as being left unsold at the month end transferred from the cost of sales to the asset account stock in hand

Journal H

		£	£
Profit and loss account	DR	9 000	
Cost of sales	CR		9 000

Being the transfer of the cost of sales for the month to the profit and loss account

These journals are recorded in the T accounts below.

Cost of sales

30 April Stock (E)	4 000	30 April Stock (G)	5 000
30 April Purchases (F)	10 000	30 April Profit and loss (H)	9 000
	14 000		14 000

Purchases

1 April Bank (D)	10 000	30 April Cost of sales (F)	10 000

Stock in hand

1 April Balance b/d	4 000	30 April Cost of sales (E)	4 000
30 April Stock (G)	5 000		

You can see in this example that the purchases account is transferred to the cost of sales account and the balance on the cost of sales account is cleared to the profit and loss account to start the new month afresh. The stock account shows the balance in hand at the start of the new month. The stock account would need to be in the current assets section but the cost of sales would be amongst the expenses in the chart of accounts.

Method 2

A similar result can be achieved by using the change in the stock figure. In this method, the difference between the opening and **closing stock** figures is transferred by journal to top up the stock account in the current assets and shown as a change in the stock account in the expenses section of the chart. The change in stock figure is then cleared to the profit and loss account automatically. In this case stock will be brought forward and purchases for the month will be recorded in the same way as for method 1. However the purchases will be transferred straight to the profit and loss account and the cost of sales automatically worked out there.

Journal J		£	£
Stock in hand	DR	1 000	
Change in stock	CR		1 000

Being the increase in stock in hand in the month

Journal K		£	£
Change in stock	DR	1 000	
Profit and loss account	CR		1 000

Being the change in the stock credited to the profit and loss account for the month

Journal L		£	£
Profit and loss	DR	10 000	
Purchases	CR		10 000

Purchases

1 April Bank	10 000	30 April Profit and loss (L)	10 000

Change in stock account

30 April Profit and loss (K)	1 000	30 April Stock (J)	1 000

Stock in hand

1 April Balance b/d	4 000	30 April Balance c/d	5 000
30 April Change in stock (J)	1 000		
	5 000		5 000
1 May Balance b/d	5 000		

In this method, the purchases for the month are transferred directly to the profit and loss account. The cost of sales is calculated in the profit and loss account itself and not in the ledger.

Stock counts

The physical **stock count** is a routine procedure for all businesses which hold stock. Even if the continuous method for recording the cost of sales is used, it is important to check from time to time that the records in the system agree with the stock which is held in reality. There are several reasons why they might differ. In addition to simple error, stock gets stolen or damaged. Some of it becomes out of date through fashion or technological change. The physical stock take is a time when the records can be checked, and the stock examined systematically to make sure that it is all in a good state of repair and still marketable. This is the time to decide whether some should be scrapped or sold at a discount to clear it. Storing, caring for and insuring stock is an expensive business and needs to be kept to a minimum if the business is to prosper. There are stock control systems available to help this process. The records in the nominal ledger then take on the features of a control account. The individual lines of stock will be recorded in a separate ledger with details of purchase prices, dates and location. In this chapter we are concerned with the records as they effect the nominal ledger and we will not go in detail into the control of stock.

The physical count should be handled systematically. The time and procedures should be organized beforehand. If a lot of people are needed to complete the task then they will all need to be instructed on the method and procedures involved. The important thing is that all stock is counted but no stock is counted more than once. In all but the smallest business it is good practice for the count to be undertaken by someone who is not involved in the day-to-day control of the stock. This acts as a control on stock being stolen by employees. If possible no stock should be moved during the stock taking process. It is not unknown for stock to be carried from one area to another behind the counting teams' backs to cover for items which have been stolen.

Special numbered stock sheets should be used so that no sheets can go missing. Each sheet needs to enter sufficient detail of the goods counted and the quantities for the items to be valued later. A note of any stock which is damaged or deteriorating over time needs to be made so that the value can be adjusted if necessary.

Stock valuation

Valuation is more difficult than physically counting. Quantities are a matter of fact; value is a matter of judgement. The accounting rule is that stocks should be shown at:

the lower of cost and net realizable value.

Net realizable value means the amount the stock could be sold for less any costs of getting it to a state and position where it can be sold. In other words, the stock should normally be shown at cost. If however it is likely that the amount it can be sold for is less than the cost, then the value needs to be dropped accordingly. The stock should not be shown as worth more than it can be realized for. Obviously for most stock, as the point of buying the stock is to sell it at a profit, the net realizable value will be higher than the cost. However, wear and tear, fashion, technology or changing safety rules can all lead to some stock falling in value.

It is important when judging whether stock is below its cost in value terms to judge each line of stock separately, not just look at the total figure. An example will show you why.

Activity

1   Take a business with five types of stock in hand at the year end. The cost and net realizable value of each is given below, together with the total cost and total net realizable value figures.

Type	Cost (£)	Net realizable value (£)
A	4 800	7 200
B	6 300	9 500
C	5 300	3 200
D	4 300	5 200
E	5 200	6 700
	25 900	31 800

Required
What value would you place on the stock in hand?

If the value of the stock in hand is based on either the total of the cost or the total of the net realizable values then the stock will be valued at £25 900. This disguises the fact that one line of stock is not going to be sold at a profit. Looking at each line individually, the value used should be £4800 + 6300 + 3200 + 4300 + 5200 = £23 800. It is this lower figure which is required.

Cost can also be difficult to establish where prices are changing.

Activity

2   Going back to our bicycle example; assume that the bicycles purchased in the month had cost £230 each instead of the £200 that the ones in stock had cost.

Required
What price would we use to value the 45 bicycles sold in the month and the 25 left in hand at the end of the month?

Stock in hand at start	20 at	£200	£4 000
Add purchases in period	50 at	230	11 500
Available for sale	70		
Stock at month end	25 at	?	?
Cost of goods sold	45 at	?	?

Unless each bicycle has been identified, there is no right answer. An assumption has to be made. Accountants would choose one standard approach from a number of possible approaches. We look at three common approaches below. However having chosen to use a particular approach in one period, the same approach must be adopted in following periods for consistency. If this were not so the results from period to period could not be compared.

LIFO

LIFO stands for Last In First Out. Using this method assumes that the first stock to be sold is the latest stock that was received. In our example this would mean that the cost of sales would be assumed to be at £230 each, but the stock in hand would include the stock brought forward at the lower price and the increase at the new price.

Stock in hand at start	20 at	£200	£4 000
Add purchases in period	50 at	230	11 500
Available for sale	70		15 500
Stock at month end	20 at	200	
	5 at	230	5 150
Cost of goods sold	45 at	230	10 350

FIFO

FIFO stands for First In First Out. In this method the first stock to be sold is assumed to be the stock purchased first. In this case the items in stock at the end of the period are valued at the latest prices with the earlier prices being charged against profit as cost of sales.

Stock in hand at start	20 at	£200	£4 000
Add purchases in period	50 at	230	11 500
Available for sale	70		15 500
Stock at month end	25 at	230	5 750
Cost of goods sold	20 at	200	
	25 at	230	9 750

AVCO

AVCO stands for **AV**erage **CO**st. In this method the stock is valued at the average price weighted according to the number purchased at that price. The result will be between the extremes of the LIFO and FIFO methods, but the price used is not necessarily one which has ever been charged in reality.

Stock in hand at start	20 at	£200	£4 000
Add Purchases in period	50 at	230	11 500
Available for sale	70	221.42	15 500
Stock at month end	25 at	221.42	5 536
Cost of goods sold	45 at	221.42	9 964

Activity

3 The calculations of cost of sales and closing stock is different for each method. Assume that the sales all took place at £350.
   Required
   What will be the profit under each method of stock valuation?
   Which method do you think is most realistic?

In the UK, the FIFO method is the one usually found; in other countries LIFO is popular. When prices are changing significantly, such as in times of high inflation, the method employed can make quite a difference to reported profit and to the values in the balance sheet. So if prices rise, the value of the stock in the balance sheet becomes increasingly out of date under the LIFO method but the profit figure is a more realistic figure for the difference between the original cost and the sale price that can now be achieved. On the other hand, FIFO gives a more realistic balance sheet figure, but shows a much higher profit.

The important point is that the method is applied consistently. In that case the reader of the accounts can identify the trends and make allowances for the methods chosen.

Activity

4   In the case study, John has now counted the stock at the end of November and valued it at £8246.
Required
Create the new accounts in the chart to record the stock in hand at the end of the month and make the necessary journal entries.

Simple draft income statement and balance sheet

With the stock counted and a method of valuation selected, a simple income statement and balance sheet can be drawn up from the trial balance.

Income statement or profit and loss account

The income statement compares the income for the period with the expenses incurred. This should not be confused with the profit and loss account in the chart of accounts. The profit in the chart is a running total and summarizes all the income and expenses to come to one balancing figure. As such it is not very informative. It is difficult to see where expenses were incurred or income earned. As it is a running total the figures do not distinguish the results for this period from those of earlier periods. For this reason it is helpful to redraft the figures included in that account into an income statement which should be more informative. This is usually drafted in vertical format as demonstrated in Figure 7.1. A vertical format allows several periods' results to be put alongside each other for ease of comparison. There are four sections: the trading account; the profit and loss account; return to lenders; and the appropriation account.

Note that the headings are not included in the final account. They are there to demonstrate to you the sections that make up a typical profit and loss statement. The first thing to notice is the heading at the top. It is important that the statement is headed up properly. Without the heading it is impossible to know who the information is for or the period it relates to.

The trading account indicates the sales less the cost of sales to give a subtotal for gross profit. This figure is to a large extent governed by the owners' decisions on prices. If they decide to price their goods for sale at cost plus 30 per cent then the gross profit will reflect that percentage. The margin chosen and achieved has to be large enough to cover the rest of the expenses of running the firm and a return to the lenders and owners.

```
Bale and Co.
Profit and loss account for the period ended

Trading account                                                    £        £
                          Sales                                             x
                          Less cost of sales                                x
                          Gross profit                                      x

Profit and loss account
                          Less expenses                        x
                                                               x
                                                               x
                                                                            x
                          Operating profit                                  x

Return to lenders
                          Less interest                                     x
                          Profit for the year attributable to owners        x

Appropriation account
                          Less drawings                                     x
                          Retained profit for the year                      x
```

Figure 7.1
Proforma profit
and loss account
in vertical format

The second section shows the deduction of the overhead and running expense such as advertising, telephone, rent and maintenance. The owner needs to control these although they cannot be reduced to zero.

Interest in the third section is shown separately to the other expenses. This is because the amount of interest will depend upon the way in which the business is financed and not on the way it operates. Giving a total for profit before this figure allows the owner to compare their results with those of another organization even if it is financed differently.

Finally the appropriation section indicates what happens to the profit once it has been earned.

Activity

5 Print off the trial balance for Bale and Co. for November and draft an income statement in vertical format with four sections as shown in the proforma.

The balance sheet

The balance sheet or position statement is used to present the remaining balances at the end of the period. A vertical format is useful to display the position at the end of this period with those of earlier periods.

Again the statement falls into a number of sections indicated for you in the draft format in Figure 7.2.

Note the way in which numbers are listed in one column and then the total is sent to

```
Bale and Co.
Balance sheet at
                                                         £          £
Fixed assets
                     Property                     X
                     Equipment                    X
                     Vehicles                      X
                     Etc.                          X
                                                              X
Current assets
                     Stock                        X
                     Debtors                      X
                     Cash and bank                 X
                                                   X
Less: Current liabilities
                     Trade creditors        X
                     Bank overdraft         X
                                                   X
Net current assets/working capital                           X

Total assets less current liabilities                        X
Less: Long-term liabilities                                  X
                                                              X
Financed by
Owners capital
                     Invested                     X
                     Retained profit to date       X
                                                              X
```

Figure 7.2
Proforma balance
sheet in vertical
format

the next column. The idea is that the figures in the inner columns show the detail making up the important figures in the outer column. So, for example, the different types of fixed assets would be listed in the inner column and then the grand total is thrown out to the outer column.

Reading down the balance sheet, it starts by showing the assets into which the business has invested its resources. These consist of fixed assets and working capital, also known as net current assets. Working capital is the money needed to finance the everyday operations of the business, such as buying stock and waiting to be paid but, at the same time, takes into account the fact that some of the stock can be bought on trade credit. The amount the business needs to invest will depend upon the amount of credit it gives to customers, the amount of credit it can get from its suppliers and the amount of stock it needs to hold. The figures for these items are usually put together as working capital because they form a cycle of cash flowing into and out of the business, e.g. into stock, out of stock but waiting for the customer to pay, paying suppliers and buying more stock and so on. The balance sheet just stops this process for a moment.

The fixed assets and working capital need to be financed and the rest of the balance sheet indicates where the resources have come from. First the money borrowed from lenders is deducted from the assets to show the amount financed by the owners.

6 Draft the balance sheet for Bale and Co. for November in vertical format.

Summary

This chapter has looked at the need to record the stock figures and methods for calculating the cost of sales. In the case study we will use the periodic method. Unless specialist point of sale software is available the continuous method is impractical. This means that every time John and Azina need to look at their statements, the stock will need to be counted. This can be costly in time and resources and as a result some businesses make an estimate of the stock in hand for routine management reports, only taking a complete physical count once a year. The benefits of the more accurate figures and the strong stock control procedures are outweighed by the cost of obtaining the information.

The recording process does not continue indefinitely. When you need information you have to stop recording and total the items in the income and expense records. When the next period starts you will want to record just the new period's figures and not muddle these up with the previous time period's transactions. In a manual system the records have to be stopped and the balances calculated. Income and expense balances are then 'emptied' by transfer to the profit and loss before the next period's transactions can be recorded. Some older software also requires a formal period end routine to do this. The Sage system is organized slightly differently: the information is stored by date and the system can select the data for a particular month and Sage will draw up statements for that period.

We will return to this procedure and look at the Sage templates for profit and loss accounts and balance sheets in Chapter 13. The intervening chapters will look in more detail at the end of period adjustments that are needed to produce more sophisticated results.

Key words

average cost p. 129 • closing stock p. 125 • cost of sales p. 122 • continuous stock recording p. 122 • FIFO p. 129 • LIFO p. 128 • periodic stock recording p. 123 • stock count p. 126

1 John Bale purchased and sold the following units of one line of stock. All the units are identical.

Purchases

Date	Quantity	Price per unit (£)	Total (£)
5 Nov	500	3.00	1 500.00
19 Nov	300	3.10	930.00
21 Nov	250	3.15	787.50
27 Nov	400	3.20	1 280.00

Sales

Date	Quantity
6 Nov	100
7 Nov	50
8 Nov	50
9 Nov	40
10 Nov	30
11 Nov	20
16 Nov	70
18 Nov	80
20 Nov	90
23 Nov	75
28 Nov	80

Required
(i) Value the stock in hand at 30 November and the cost of sales in November using each of the following methods for valuing stocks:
(a) FIFO
(b) LIFO
(c) AVCO
(ii) Comment on the advantages and disadvantages of each method.

2 Palo Ltd has put the following values on the stock in hand at the end of the period:

	Cost (£)	Net realizable value (£)
Cloth A	4 567	8 764
Cloth B	8 650	12 400
Trimmings	2 450	1 200
Lining cloth	4 750	6 300
Total	20 417	28 664

The company proposes to use the figure of £20 417 in the statements as it is the lower of cost and net realizable value.

Required
Comment on the stock value used by Palo Ltd calculating the figure you would include.

3 Compare the relative advantages and disadvantages of using the continuous and the periodic methods of stock recording.

4 What valuation would you include in the financial statements for the following items of stock:
(i) Ten printers were purchased for £4200 list price less a trade discount of 4 per cent. Delivery costs amounted to £85. The invoice was paid early to obtain an early payment discount of 2 per cent.
(ii) Due to a change in health and safety legislation, electrical toys purchased at a cost of £500 each now need to have alterations made at a cost of £75 per toy before they can be sold at a discount market for an estimated £550 each.

8 Value Added Tax

Learning objectives

After reading this chapter you should be able to:
- post invoices, credit notes and journals and account for VAT
- complete the quarterly VAT return which must be submitted to HM Customs and Excise
- understand the different categories of VAT and how they apply to various business organizations
- prepare for a successful periodic inspection by HM Customs and Excise Officers.

Introduction

This chapter introduces you to VAT (Value Added Tax) and will explore the practical problem of setting up a system and accounting for VAT to HM Customs and Excise. The concept of VAT and an organization's role in collecting VAT is quite straightforward and should not present you with any difficulties. Registered organizations must charge VAT (at specified rates) to the people they trade with. This VAT is not revenue for them, it belongs to the government. They hold it temporarily before paying it to the government. They will also be charged VAT on their purchases but this VAT is not an expense, only the net cost of the product or service supplied is an expense. Before paying VAT to the government they are allowed to offset the VAT they have paid against the VAT they have collected.

If we take one transaction as an example. Bale and Co. purchase a printer for £100 net and will be invoiced and will pay the supplier £117.50 (£100 net + £17.50 VAT). They then sell this printer from £235 (£200 net and £35.00 VAT). Their position following this transaction is summarized in Figure 8.1. The £17.50 will be paid to the government. Occasionally at the end of a period the VAT collected will be less than that paid and in this case the organization will receive a payment from the government.

When many thousands of transactions are involved a system must exist to ensure that VAT is properly accounted for. In this chapter we shall provide answers to the following questions:

Figure 8.1
Purchase and
sale of printer

Purchase & Sale of Printer			
Revenue	200.00	35.00	Output Tax
Cost	100.00	17.50	Input Tax
Profit	100.00	17.50	Tax Liability

1   Who should register for VAT?
2   How to register for VAT.
3   Are there different rates of VAT?
4   Document design to capture VAT information.
5   What accounts will need to be set up?
6   How to post transactions.
7   How to make a quarterly return.
8   Preparing for a visit by VAT inspectors.

**C
A
S
E

S
T
U
D
Y**

Azina came home from college one afternoon looking worried. She had listened to some students talking to their tutor about VAT and the penalties for not keeping proper records. ' We cannot afford to get it wrong,' she tells John.

'I am sure that Bill would have warned us if there was a problem,' he reassures her 'but it would be just as well to ask him.'

Bill has already thought about VAT and with his advice John and Azina registered with the Customs and Excise. Azina is concerned that the record keeping will be difficult and time consuming but Bill explains that most of the information will automatically be recorded by the accounting software package that they are using. However he warns her that if she is uncertain how an item is categorized for VAT purposes she must ask. Getting it wrong is expensive because Customs and Excise operate mandatory penalties. The business registered from 1 December. The transactions for December are included at the end of this chapter after the practice questions.

What is VAT?

Value Added Tax is a tax on most 'business' transactions which take place in the UK or the Isle of Mann. For example, if I supply 1 tin of paint to a customer the net price (price without VAT) may be £10.00, but I must also charge the customer £1.75 VAT. The customer pays me £11.75. £10 is part of my revenue but the £1.75 belongs to the government and will eventually have to be paid to them.

For VAT purposes 'business' has a very wide meaning and can include activities on which no profit is made. The following are examples of business transactions:

1   sale of new and used goods, including hire purchase sales;
2   rental and hiring of goods;
3   private use of business stock;
4   admission to premises;
5   facilities provided by clubs;
6   supplies made through agents;
7   supplies made by self-employed persons.

Transactions which are liable to VAT are called taxable supplies. Those which are not liable to VAT are called exempt supplies.

What are taxable supplies?

In the last sections the term 'taxable supplies' was used. **Taxable supplies** are business transactions on which VAT is chargeable. The value of these supplies is called your **taxable turnover** and is the total of the net value of your sales. In our example in Figure 8.1, the sale of the printer, the taxable turnover would be £200.

From the date on which you are first required to be registered you must charge VAT on all taxable supplies you make, either at the standard rate which is $17\frac{1}{2}$ per cent or the zero rate which is nil. If you expect your taxable turnover to exceed £49 000 (from December 1997) in the coming 12 months or at the end of any month the total value of the taxable supplies you have made in the past 12 months has exceeded £49 000, you must register for VAT. The limit of £49 000 is constantly being raised to keep pace with inflation and business activity.

To apply for **registration** you must complete form VAT1 and send it to Customs and Excise. If the person to be registered is part of a partnership you will also need a form VAT2. Both forms can be obtained from your local VAT office. After checking the details on your form VAT1 you will be sent an advice of registration which will provide you with your VAT registration number and show your date of registration. A certification of registration, showing your full registration details, will be sent to you shortly afterwards. The registration number must be shown clearly on all invoices and credit notes issued by your company, and the VAT charged must be shown as a separate item on the invoices. There are three rates of VAT currently in use: the **standard rate** of $17\frac{1}{2}$ per cent, the **zero rate** which is nil and a lower rate of 8 per cent. The lower rate is used only for domestic, charitable and residential fuel and power.

Zero rated supplies include the following:

1   most food (but not catering which includes meals in restaurants, cafes, etc. and hot take-away food and drink);
2   books and newspapers;
3   sales, long leases and the construction of new houses and some other new buildings (but not work to existing buildings);
4   young children's clothing and footwear;
5   export of goods;
6   dispensing of prescriptions and the supply of many aids for handicapped persons;
7   mobile homes and houseboats.

Almost everything else that does not appear in the above points would be supplied and charged at the standard rate. We say almost because there is a category of supplies termed as exempt supplies.

Exempt supplies

Exempt supplies are business transactions on which VAT is not chargeable. Exempt supplies are not taxable supplies and do not form part of your taxable turnover. Exempt supplies include:

1   most sales, leases and lettings of land and buildings;
2   insurance;
3   betting, gaming and lotteries;
4   provision of credit;
5   certain education and training;
6   services of doctors, dentists, opticians, etc.;
7   certain supplies by undertakers;
8   entry to certain sports competitions.

Exempt supplies, therefore, cannot charge VAT and the value of exempt supplies is not included as part of your taxable turnover. Consequently you cannot reclaim the VAT you are charged, which means that the VAT you are charged on your inputs becomes part of your business expense.

Data capture – the tax invoice

Figure 8.2 shows a tax invoice for Bale and Co. which contains all of the information necessary to satisfy your own accounting needs and the requirements of the Customs and Excise. This is a very important document the design of which has, to a large extent, been dictated by the strict requirements of the Customs and Excise. Each field is required for standard accounting data that can be further analysed and also to validate the quarterly return that is made to the Customs and Excise.

Whenever you supply standard rated goods or services to another registered person, you must give them a document showing certain information about what you are supplying. This document is a **tax invoice**. Your customers, if registered for VAT, may

Sales Invoice No: 174				VAT Regd. No 987 6543 21
From: FOUNDATION TRADING (UK) LTD BOWMAN STREET CHESTER				
To: A. N. OTHER LTD 57 NORTH ROAD, LONDON N12 5NA				
Sales: Time of supply 16/01/98				Date of issue: 19/01/98
Quantity	Description and Price	Amount exclusive of VAT	VAT Rate	VAT Net
6 4 6	RADIOS, SW15 @ £25.20 RECORD PLAYERS @ £23.60 LAMPS T77 @ £15.55 DELIVERY (STRICTLY NET)	151.20 94.40 93.30 338.90 9.00	 17.5 17.5	 56.34* 1.57
Terms: Cash discount of 5% if paid withing 30 days VAT TOTAL	347.90 57.91 405.81			57.91
* Calculated on the discount price				

Figure 8.2
Tax invoice

be able to reclaim the VAT you have charged them and the tax invoice is proof of such a charge. Similarly, you can only get back VAT you have been charged by your suppliers if you have tax invoices from them.

Records are, therefore, very important. You must keep copies of the invoices you send to your customers as proof of the VAT you are charging (**output tax**) and also copies of the invoices you receive from suppliers as proof of the VAT you are paying (**input tax**).

Bale and Co.'s invoice contains all the relevant information:

1   An identifying number. Invoices will be pre-printed and pre-numbered. All invoices must be accounted for, thereby ensuring that damage or spoilt invoices are retained.
2   Name, address and VAT registration number.
3   Time of supply. This is also referred to as the **tax point** and is the time when the supply of goods and services is treated as taking place. You must account for VAT in the tax period in which the tax point occurs at the rate in force at the time.
4   Date of issue.
5   Customer's name and address.
6   Type of supply (e.g. sale or rental).
7   A description which identifies the goods or services supplied. For each description you must then show the quantity, charge made excluding VAT and rate of VAT.
8   If a number of items are being shown on one invoice then you must also show the total charge made excluding VAT, each rate of VAT, total VAT payable and finally any rate of cash discount offered.

You will receive a variety of invoices from all of your suppliers. They will be of a different shape, size and colour, some very plain and some quite exotic containing all the colours of the rainbow. Their common feature, however, is that they will contain the information described above. Credit notes will, of course, use the same fields of information.

Accounting for VAT

Up to now when you have posted invoices and credit notes VAT has been ignored although a field has existed on the posting screen and tax code T9 has been input representing zero rated supplies. If we now introduce VAT we must ensure that an account exists in the nominal ledger to which the VAT can be posted. It is preferable to open two accounts, one for VAT on sales (output tax) and one for VAT on purchases (input tax).

Remember that every time you set up a new nominal code you must find a place for it in either the balance sheet or the profit and loss account. In this case it is possible for the VAT to be a current asset (when you are entitled to a refund from the government) or a current liability (when you owe them VAT). You must, therefore, direct both VAT accounts into a line in both current assets and current liabilities and, depending upon the balance, the computer program will decide where to place the balance (see Appendix 6A for details on setting VAT rates).

If we take our previous example of the sale of a tin of paint, the posting screen and the effect it has on the double entry in the nominal ledger are shown in Figure 8.3:

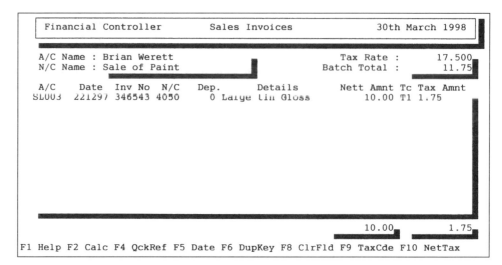

Figure 8.3
Posting a sales invoice

1   By inserting the accounts code SL003 you have indicated which sales ledger account is to be debited.
2   Whatever amount is posted to SL003 will automatically be posted to the debtor control account.
3   Inputting account 4050 indicates which nominal account will be credited with the *net* amount.
4   Inputting T1 places the VAT amount in the VAT on sales account (2200) and also updates the VAT analysis, i.e. increases your taxable turnover by £10.00 and your output tax at standard rate of VAT by £1.75.

By inputting T1 (or some other relevant code) the program will automatically calculate the VAT, in this case at $17\frac{1}{2}$ per cent. Remember, however, that you are posting details from a tax invoice, where the total VAT may not be $17\frac{1}{2}$ per cent of the net value (either because you are selling a mixed combination of standard and zero rated items or because a mistake has been made). You must always post what is on the document.

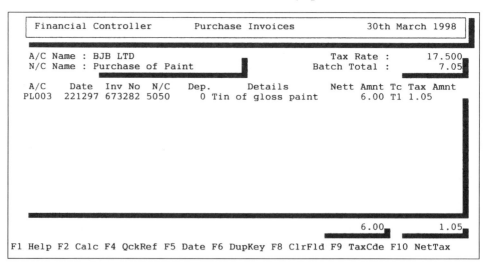

Figure 8.4
Posting a purchase invoice

If, on the purchases side, you have purchased a tin of paint for £6.00 net there will also be VAT charged of £1.05, making a total invoice value of £7.05. When this invoice is posted through the purchase ledger the posting screen in Figure 8.4 has the following effect on the double entry in the nominal ledger:

1   By inserting the account code PL001 you have indicated which purchase ledger account will be credited.
2   Whatever amount is posted to PL001 will automatically be posted to the creditor control account.
3   Inputting code 5050 indicates which nominal account will be debited with the *net* amount.
4   Inputting T1 places the VAT amount in the VAT on purchases account (2201) and also updates the VAT analysis, i.e. increases your total value of purchases by £6.00 and your input tax at the standard rate of £1.05.

The two transactions we have just looked at describe how the input tax and the output tax are accounted for. The case study and the real world are only different in that more transactions are involved. As long as a system is in place to account for the input tax and the output tax, VAT should not represent a problem.

VAT does not affect your profit and loss account, the balance of the input and output tax will appear in the balance sheet as an asset or a liability and all the information will exist to quickly complete the quarterly VAT return.

VAT quarterly returns

Normally you will receive a VAT return every three months, i.e. for you to complete a **quarterly return**. The information requested by the form is shown in Figure 8.5 and your system should, as explained above, already contain all the necessary information. By selecting *VAT Return Analysis* from the nominal ledger menu (Figure 8.6) all the figures required are automatically provided. In the case of our two transactions, the relevant information is shown in Figure 8.5 and our VAT liability would be £0.70 (i.e.

VAT return analysis for the period 010180 to 311299			P
VAT due in this period on Sales	1	1	75
VAT due in this period on EC acquisitions	2	0	00
Total VAT Due	3	1	75
VAT reclaimed in this period on Purchases	4	1	05
Net VAT to be paid or reclaimed by you	5	0	70
Total value of sales, excluding VAT	6	10	00
Total value of purchases, excluding VAT	7	6	00
Total value of all supplies to EC member states	8	0	00
Total value of acquisitions from EC member states	9	0	00
F1 Help F2 Calc			

Figure 8.5
VAT return analysis

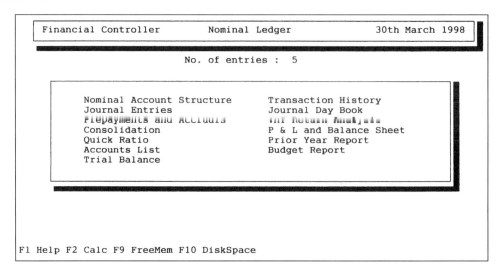

```
┌──────────────────────────────────────────────────────────────┐
│ Financial Controller        Nominal Ledger        30th March 1998 │
├──────────────────────────────────────────────────────────────┤
│                    No. of entries :  5                         │
│  ┌──────────────────────────────────────────────────────┐     │
│  │   Nominal Account Structure    Transaction History    │     │
│  │   Journal Entries              Journal Day Book       │     │
│  │   Prepayments and Accruals     VAT Return Analysis    │     │
│  │   Consolidation                P & L and Balance Sheet│     │
│  │   Quick Ratio                  Prior Year Report      │     │
│  │   Accounts List                Budget Report          │     │
│  │   Trial Balance                                       │     │
│  └──────────────────────────────────────────────────────┘     │
│                                                                │
│ F1 Help F2 Calc F9 FreeMem F10 DiskSpace                       │
└──────────────────────────────────────────────────────────────┘
```

Figure 8.6
Nominal ledger
menu

£1.75 − £1.05). The official VAT return (Form VAT100) is completed and returned to the Customs and Excise together with a cheque for £0.70. To complete the accounting, complete a journal showing the cheque of £0.70 being paid from the bank current account.

Figure 8.7 shows a journal which contains four lines. *Line 1* and *Line 2* move the £1.05 from account 2201 to 2200. *Line 3* and *Line 4* show a payment being made from the bank (credit account 1200) and being debited into account 2200. Accounts 2200 and 2201 now have a zero balance and are ready for the postings for the next quarter. Figure 8.8 illustrates the effect in the nominal ledger.

Your VAT return will contain a **due date** indicating when the form must be returned. Failure to complete and return the form on time is penalized.

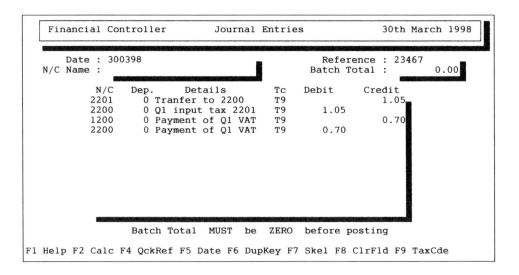

```
┌──────────────────────────────────────────────────────────────┐
│ Financial Controller        Journal Entries       30th March 1998 │
├──────────────────────────────────────────────────────────────┤
│   Date : 300398                    Reference : 23467           │
│ N/C Name :                         Batch Total :       0.00    │
│                                                                │
│     N/C   Dep.    Details      Tc   Debit      Credit          │
│     2201    0 Tranfer to 2200  T9               1.05           │
│     2200    0 Q1 input tax 2201 T9  1.05                       │
│     1200    0 Payment of Q1 VAT T9              0.70           │
│     2200    0 Payment of Q1 VAT T9  0.70                       │
│                                                                │
│        Batch Total  MUST  be  ZERO  before posting             │
│ F1 Help F2 Calc F4 QckRef F5 Date F6 DupKey F7 Skel F8 ClrFld F9 TaxCde │
└──────────────────────────────────────────────────────────────┘
```

Figure 8.7
Journal

Figure 8.8
Illustration of the double entry record of the journal transactions

Visit by VAT officers

Once you have registered for VAT you will be visited from time to time by an officer of Customs and Excise. These visits are made to ensure that the correct amount of VAT is being accounted for and an examination of your system will very quickly reveal to them whether or not this is happening. Take the visit as an opportunity to ask about anything you are unsure of or to ask advice.

By the time the first visit is made you will have already submitted a number of quarterly VAT returns. The officer will examine your business records and activities and check your completed quarterly return with the documentation you have available. For example, if you claim that you have paid £12 500 of VAT on your purchases (input tax) the officer will want to see documentary evidence (tax invoices) that supports the £12 500.

The more efficient your system and the way you operate it, e.g. daybooks printed from the computer matching the batches of invoices filed in chronological order, the more confidence he will have in the figures you present. A well-organized system will minimize the length of the visit as questions can be answered quickly, documentary evidence easily produced and all figures justified. The officer will want to look at the way your business operates, including how you record the goods you receive and supply and how you deal with cash coming in and going out. They can ask to see balance sheets, profit and loss accounts, bank statements, relevant correspondence as well as tax invoices. There is an obligation for all businesses to retain their records for six years.

Summary

You should now appreciate that the concept of VAT and accounting for it is quite straightforward. It is only straightforward, however, if you have set up a system to capture efficiently and correctly all the relevant data and to file in a logical way all the relevant documentation that will be required to support the figures you use in the quarterly return.

Your tax invoice must be designed to capture all necessary data and comply with the requirements of the Customs and Excise. Your accounts must contain at least one and possibly two accounts to which VAT is posted.

If this system is adhered to, the completion of the quarterly return becomes a very simple exercise and periodic visits from the officers of the Customs and Excise will run very smoothly.

A final reminder: VAT is neither an expense nor a revenue. Depending on the balance of input and output tax it will be a current asset or a current liability and, therefore, will appear in the balance sheet.

Key words

Practice questions

1 Test your understanding of the chapter by answering the following questions:
  (i) Is VAT an expense?
  (ii) What are 'taxable supplies'?
  (iii) How many rates of VAT are currently used?
  (iv) Distinguish between zero rated VAT and exempt supplies.
  (v) What is a 'tax point'?
  (vi) Which of the following would qualify as taxable supplies or exempt supplies:
    (a) sale of insurance
    (b) sale of computers and printers
    (c) services provided by an accountant
    (d) sale of warm take-away food
    (e) sale of baby clothes
    (f) services provided by a solicitor
    (g) sale of tickets to enter a cinema
    (h) rental of power tools for DIY
    (i) services provided by a dentist
    (j) sale of newspapers.

2 All the figures below relate to taxable supplies.
  (i) £10.50
  (ii) £115.00
  (iii) £5.00
  (iv) £236.00
  Required
  If the figure shown is net (without VAT) how much VAT would have to be charged (assume a standard rate of VAT)?

3 All the figures below relate to taxable supplies.
  (i) £117.50
  (ii) £27.40
  (iii) £94.20
  (iv) £2465.50
  Required
  If the figure shown is gross (inclusive of VAT) what is the VAT charged and the net value of the supplies (assume a standard rate of VAT)?

4 How frequently must you complete a VAT return?

5

	Q1	Q2
Total value of sales and all other outputs excluding VAT	142 367.00	125 750.00
VAT reclaimed in this period on purchases and other inputs	14 946.00	11 237.00
Total value of purchases and all other inputs including VAT	85 420.00	64 213.00
VAT due in this period on sales and other outputs	24 914.00	22 006.00

Required
From the above information calculate a company's tax liability in each quarter.

6 What is the significance of the 'due date' on your VAT return?

7 What records can VAT officers demand to see?

8 For how long must a business retain its records?

9 If you have 'bad debts' can you adjust your VAT liability (output tax) to reflect that you will never be able to collect this money?

C A S E   S T U D Y

DECEMBER TRANSACTIONS

Date | Transaction

1 December (A) The following invoices were received from suppliers:

Invoice	Supplier	Net	VAT	Gross
AOO158	Supplier 1	10 426.00	1 824.55	12 250.55
0689	Supplier 4	599.00	104.82	703.82

(B) Azina sent the following invoices to customers:

0029	Customer 2	C	8 947.00	1 565.73	10 512.73
0030	Customer 9	P	1 250.00	218.75	1 468.75

(C) The following amount was received from cash sales of disks, ink jet cartridges and filter screens £428.75

(D) Azina paid the following invoice with cheque no. 001571
            Vehicle insurance   £424.00

(E) John transfers computer hardware worth £2483.00 (not including VAT) purchased for stock to the office for use within the business.

2 December (A) Azina took the opportunity to pay a few invoices:

001572	Drawings	£200.00
001573	Highwood printers	232.00
001574	Supplier 1	400.00
001575	Supplier 2	3 536.16

(B) John came in with a petrol receipt for £18.00 (including VAT) having filled up the tank on his way to see a potential customer in Bristol. He reimbursed himself from the petty cash.

6 December (A) Invoice no. 9884S was received for goods delivered by supplier 3 for £6166.40 gross i.e. £5248.00 net and £918.40 VAT.

(B) Invoice no. 0031 was sent to Customer 1 for disks and software worth £526.00 net; VAT £92.05; Total due £618.05.

7 December	(A) Cash amounting to £942.20 was received from the sale of printers.
	(B) The milkman called with the week's milk bill amounting to £3.54 (zero rated). Azina paid him from the petty cash.
8 December	(A) Invoice no. 0032 was issued for a credit sale of a computer to Customer 3 for £1970.00 net with VAT of £344.75 making £2314.75 owing in total.
	(B) A cheque for £297.30 was received from Customer 1.
9 December	(A) Azina wrote cheques for the following amounts:

001576	Drawings	£200.00
001577	Insurance – professional liability	625.00
001578	Petty cas	96.30

(B) The following amounts were reimbursed from the petty cash:
Petrol (includes VAT)   £18.00
Postage   20.00

13 December	(A) Customer 7 bought disks and filter screens at a total cost of £290.43 including £43.23 VAT on credit terms.
	(B) Cleaning materials for the shop were purchased through petty cash at a cost of £9.56 gross (i.e. including VAT).
14 December	(A) An invoice was received from Supplier 6 for goods worth £428.00 net of VAT.
15 December	(A) Invoice no. 0034 was issued to customer 5 for printers, net price £424.00 (VAT £74.20).
	(B) An amount of £21.42 was received from a cash sale of disks and banked.
	(C) The following amounts were received from credit customers and banked:

Customer 2	£ 650.32
Customer 3	2 831.30
Customer 4	861.35

| 16 December | (A) Cheques were drawn on the business bank account as follows: |

001579	Drawings	£ 200.00
001580	Publicity printers	1 534.00
001581	Supplier 3	1 175.00
001582	Supplier 4	1 070.00

(B) Petrol (including VAT) £18.00 and parking (exempt for VAT) £2.30 were reimbursed from petty cash.

| 20 December | (A) Invoice no. 44761 was received from supplier 3 for £3242.00 net (VAT £567.35). |

> (B) Invoice no. 0035 was issued to customer 6 for a computer costing
> £3247.00 net (VAT £568.23).

22 December   (A) Issued invoice no. 0036 to customer 4 for computer equipment
worth £4778.00 net (VAT £836.15).

> (B) Cash was received from sales in the shop £132.19

23 December   (A) Cheque payments were made as follows:

| 001583 | Supplier 1 | 12 250.55 |
| 001584 | Drawings | 200.00 |

> (B) Took £42.32 from petty cash to pay for a mince pie and wine
> evening.

Required

Post the transactions for December to the Sage system building on the transactions
from November and run off the trial balance. Back up the disks.

Appendix 8A – Setting VAT rates and VAT control accounts

The procedure described will vary between computer systems but by and large there
will be a considerable degree of similarity.

Setting VAT rates

Select *Utilities* and then the option *VAT Code Changes*. You will be presented with a
matrix that helps you define which rate you wish to use with each tax code. Figure 8.9
shows the matrix you are presented with in the Sage program which is very straightforward and self-explanatory.

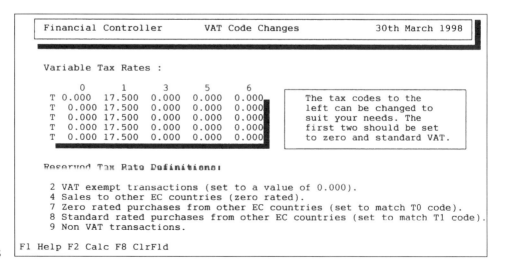

Figure 8.9
VAT code changes

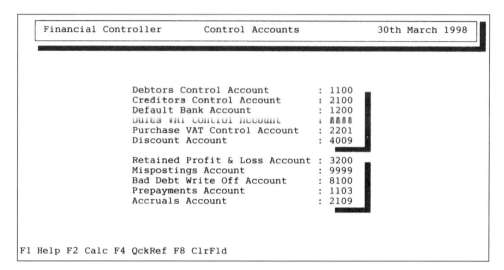

```
┌────────────────────────────────────────────────────────────────────────┐
│ Financial Controller        Control Accounts          30th March 1998    │
│ └────────────────────────────────────────────────────────────────────┐  │
│ ████████████████████████████████████████████████████████████████████ │  │
│                                                                          │
│                                                                          │
│                  Debtors Control Account       : 1100                    │
│                  Creditors Control Account      : 2100  █                │
│                  Default Bank Account           : 1200  █                │
│                  Sales VAT Control Account      : 2200  █                │
│                  Purchase VAT Control Account   : 2201  █                │
│                  Discount Account               : 4009  ▀                │
│                                                                          │
│                  Retained Profit & Loss Account : 3200  █                │
│                  Mispostings Account            : 9999  █                │
│                  Bad Debt Write Off Account     : 8100  █                │
│                  Prepayments Account            : 1103  █                │
│                  Accruals Account               : 2109  █                │
│                                                      ████████            │
│                                                                          │
│                                                                          │
│ F1 Help F2 Calc F4 QckRef F8 ClrFld                                      │
└────────────────────────────────────────────────────────────────────────┘
```

Figure 8.10
Control accounts

Setting VAT control accounts

Select *Utilities* and then *Control Accounts*. You will be presented with a screen as in Figure 8.10 which lists all the control accounts that will be required by the system during operation. Consult your chart of accounts to find the code number required and complete the table.

9 Managing the sales and purchase ledger

Learning objectives

After reading this chapter you should:
- be able to set credit limits for customers
- be able to utilize the aged debt analysis report to control credit and manage cash flow
- feel confident in helping to manage the sales ledger
- feel confident in helping to manage the purchase ledger
- be able to provide managers with information to help them achieve their objectives more efficiently and effectively
- contribute to improving the cash flow of your company.

Introduction

The majority of business is conducted using credit. Customers expect to receive credit and if you wish to do business then you must offer credit. The sales ledger, as you know, is the ledger that contains the accounts of your debtors, and within a manual accounting system, extracting effective management information and managing your debtors requires a considerable effort. Even with such an effort what could be achieved manually was limited.

Managing the sales ledger effectively is crucial because it provides the main inflow of cash into the company. Cash is the lifeblood of the company and if the flow of cash is not managed and controlled the company is in danger of going bankrupt. It is a well known fact that the majority of companies which go bankrupt are profitable, but through poor management of stock levels, and particularly of debtors, they run out of cash. Their bank loses confidence in them, refuses to support them any further and bankruptcy results.

Computerized accounting systems provides you with the opportunity of managing the sales ledger far more effectively, and the computer's ability to extract and manipulate information makes this management of the sales ledger far more efficient. Not all good management practice is computer dependent. Computers can help, but there is no substitute to good practice, common sense and knowledge of your particular business.

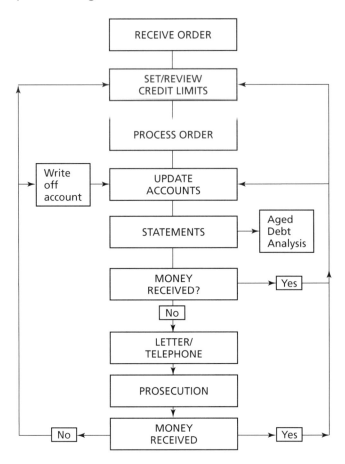

Figure 9.1
Managing the
sales ledger

This chapter will examine all aspects of managing the sales ledger from approving credit limits to sending out statements. Figure 9.1 takes you through the process step by step showing how experience is fed back into the credit limits to add to and refine your initial judgements.

John couldn't believe what he had just heard. He was having a drink with Brain Poole, a salesman for Twyford Computers Ltd and Brian had just casually mentioned that one of Bale and Co.'s customers had gone into liquidation.

'Do they owe you money John?' asked Brian.

'Yes, unfortunately' said John, 'how about you?' 'No, they used to be a good customer of ours,' said Brian, 'but about three months ago I heard they were going through a bad patch and asked the accounting department to check them out. As a result of that we refused to extend any further credit to them and would only conduct business for cash.'

'And that is when we picked them up as a customer.' said John. 'It had crossed my mind to wonder why they had come to us, because I knew they had been with you for years.'

C A S E   S T U D Y

'You must get into the habit of checking new customers out before granting them credit,' said Brian. 'We don't accept new customers until they've been thoroughly checked. We've had our fingers burned too many times in the past.'

On arriving home, John told Azina the bad news, only to discover she already knew.

'I received our bank statement this morning and their last cheque had bounced, so I phoned the bank and then them.'

'Do we check out all our customers Azina?'

'No, of course not. I don't have the time. The administration here has grown so fast that I am only just staying on top of it. Bill Davies tells me our computer program can help us control debtors by warning us if their credit limit has been exceeded and also by producing a report called an aged debt analysis.'

Setting credit limits

When you set up the accounts for your customers a field existed for inserting a *Credit Limit*. This section explains how a **credit limit** is set. All new customers approaching a company for the first time and wishing to obtain goods or services on credit should be subject to a credit check prior to business commencing. Companies are there to do business, in times of recession they may be desperate for new business and therefore when approached by a potential new customer there is a danger that they only see this as being new sales and profit. They should realize that this new customer could also mean bad debts.

A system, therefore, should be in place that checks out all new customers to decide whether:

1   the company does not want to do business with them;
2   the company would like to do business with them but will only provide goods and services on credit up to a certain limit.

Below we shall explain how these limits can be set, but it must be stressed that the method is imperfect, it can only act as a guide and does not guarantee that bad debts will not occur. Nevertheless, in an uncertain world with imperfect information it is only by systematically examining the evidence available in a structured and logical way and combining this with good management practice that you can minimize the risks of bad debts.

Bank references

Your first move should be to obtain a **bank reference**. Potential credit customers should be asked to supply the name and address of their current bankers. The bank can be contacted and informed that their client has applied to you for credit and you would like confirmation that the client is in a position to proceed on a normal basis.

Your potential customer is, of course, the bank's client and, therefore, the bank will be very careful in its response, not wishing to breach confidentiality or place its client in a very difficult situation. At the same time they do not wish to mislead potential suppliers. Consequently replies from banks tend to be very guarded and in most cases very uninformative. The bank can, however, answer straight factual questions like

'How long has X Ltd banked with you?' and the answer could be informative in that it can lead to directing other questions at the client and also cross referencing with the client's answer. For example, ask both the client and the bank the same question. If the bank says two years and the client five years your own suspicions should be aroused. Also if the bank currently used has only been involved for two years yet the company has been in existence for ten, who were its previous bankers and why did they leave?

Supplier references

You can also obtain **supplier references**. The potential customer must have current suppliers and it would be interesting to hear from them about their credit level, ability to pay, timing of payment and how long they have traded. It is very worthwhile asking for a telephone number of suppliers and following up their response to your form with a telephone conversation. Many people are reluctant to commit themselves in writing to saying something about a company which may be used against them in law. Verbally, however, much information can be gained as people appreciate that they are all fighting a common cause of minimizing bad debts.

Copies of accounts

You may wish to ask to see a copy of their recent filed accounts (filed with Companies House) and conduct a search in Companies House yourself.

Although there is a limit on what information you can gain from a set of accounts that is 9 or 18 months old, it all adds to the picture you have of this customer, and knowledge that accounts have not been filed for two years could be revealing in itself (Chapter 17 will cover analysis of company accounts).

Credit agencies

Obtaining and analysing the information described above can be extremely time consuming and costly, particularly for small companies. An alternative to completing this analysis yourself is to use the service of a credit agency.

Credit agencies specialize in collecting and analysing all sorts of information about almost every company. This information is held in a database which can easily be accessed. You can pay for one-off reports. Because of the specialist nature of this work many companies have stopped carrying out this analysis themselves and use credit agencies entirely.

Points system

In certain circumstances a points system may be used when a list of criteria is decided upon and then each criteria is given a prescribed weighting. The total score determines the credit rating.

In the example in Table 9.1 a score of 50 points would enable the client to obtain a maximum £2000 of credit. Scores of 30 points and below would be granted no credit at all. In setting such criteria care must be taken to ensure that the questions do not discriminate on the grounds of race, sex or religion.

Table 9.1 Example of credit rating using points system

Criteria	Weighting	Score
House owner	20	20
Car owner	20	0
Bank account	5	5
Dependent relatives	−5	−5
Previously declared bankrupt	−20	0
Is a professional person	10	10
Is in regular employment	20	20
		50

Score	Credit Rating
70	£5000
60	£4000
50	£2000
40	£1000
<30	£000

Regular reassessment

Although great care may be taken in setting initial credit limits, these limits need to be reviewed regularly if they are to serve their purpose. As a customer becomes familiar to you and your confidence grows in their ability to pay you may wish to raise their credit limit. Alternatively knowledge gained about a customer (you hear that other suppliers are taking legal action against them) would result in a review that would lower the credit limit.

Early warning that the credit limit is being exceeded is improved by using a computerized system. Figure 9.2 shows an invoice being posted to customer SL0001, Cardiff Timber Supplies. By inserting code SL0001 you are informing the program which sales ledger account is to be debited but, as you do so, the program

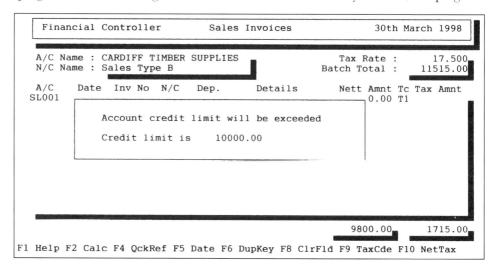

Figure 9.2
Credit limit
warning

takes the current balance on SL0001 and checks that when you add the value of the new order to the current balance it does not exceed the credit limit. If it does, a warning appears, as shown in Figure 9.2. This does not prevent you processing the translation, but it draws your attention to the fact that the credit limit has been exceeded and that the order should either be rejected or the credit limit adjusted upwards.

Terms and conditions of sale

When you have established a credit limit for a customer and have decided to supply him or her with your product you must, prior to the first delivery, obtain the agreement of the customer to your conditions and **terms of sale**. This will be a document that states very clearly what you expect from the customer e.g. normal credit terms 30 days; availability of any cash discount or early payment discount; interest penalties for not paying on time, etc. Without such a document legal action against a customer at a later date may be compromised.

Statements

To leave the customer in no doubt as to his indebtedness to you, regular **statements** should be sent to the customer (at least once per month). These statements will contain details of all outstanding invoices. This provides the customer with the opportunity of checking your statement against his own records and contacting you if a discrepancy exists. If the details of the statement are not challenged then no excuse exists to delay payment of these invoices which are due. Production of such statements from a manual system is a very arduous task indeed. With a computerized system the process is almost effortless, requiring the operator to ensure only that statement stationery has been loaded into the printer.

Aged debt analysis

The **aged debt analysis** is an extremely important tool for controlling debt, and as with statement production, computerized accounting systems produce the analysis with no effort. The analysis will take the total of debtors shown in the sales ledger and show how that debt is aged between different periods. Typically the periods are Current, 30 Days, 60 Days, 90 Days and Older.

Furthermore this information is readily available for each customer. In Figure 9.3 the company should be very concerned at such a profile, particularly the £1410 which is over 60 days old.

During the regular review of individual accounts aged debt analysis is invaluable in highlighting, very early, debts that start to exceed the standard terms and conditions. If there were no special reasons why this debt had not been paid (e.g. dispute over damaged goods) the value of goods in the current period (£1011.75) should never have been supplied. It is a well known business fact that as debt becomes older the chances of it becoming a bad debt increase. Credit controllers should aim never to let any debt enter the 60 day period. Figure 9.4 shows how the aged debt analysis of SL0001 enhanced the credit controllers ability to identify very clearly the status of the

```
┌──────────────────────────────────────────────────────────────────────┐
│  ┌──────────────────────────────────────────────────────────────┐     │
│  │ Financial Controller    Account Balances (Aged)    30th March 1998 │ │
│  └──────────────────────────────────────────────────────────────┘     │
│                                                                         │
│                                              Report Date : 300398       │
│                                                                         │
│     A/C         Future    Current    30Days    60Days    90Days   Older │
│     SL001        0.00     1011.75    646.25   1410.00      0.00    0.00  │
│     SL002        0.00     2820.00    141.00    205.63      0.00    0.00  │
│     SL003        0.00        0.00      0.00      0.00     11.75    0.00  │
│     SL004        0.00      401.85   2585.00      0.00      0.00    0.00  │
│     SL005        0.00        0.00   2338.25    158.63      0.00    0.00  │
│     SL006        0.00      293.75   3102.00      0.00      0.00    0.00  │
│     SL007        0.00      352.50   1468.75      0.00      0.00    0.00  │
│     SL008        0.00     1410.00      0.00      0.00      0.00    0.00  │
│                                                                         │
│                                                                         │
│     Debtor's Control Balance    18357.11    Total Aged Balance  18357.11│
│                   Press  ESC  to cancel   Balance Summary               │
│  F1 Help F2 Calc                                                        │
└──────────────────────────────────────────────────────────────────────┘
```

Figure 9.3
Aged debtors
balances

account when faced with a screenful of information from the account. The balance on the account is £3068 (which is well within the credit limit) but it is only when you examine the age debt analysis of that balance do the 'alarm bells' start to ring and it becomes clear that action needs to be taken.

Activity

1   Explain how aged debt analysis and the credit limit are complementary tools in the control of debtors. Although aged debt analysis normally covers the periods current, 30 days, 60 days and 90 days, can you think of circumstances where these periods are not suitable and would need revising?

2   Your company sells computers and printers and you have been asked to draw up a draft terms and conditions of sale for consideration by your Managing Director. Draft a set of Terms and Conditions of Sale.

```
┌──────────────────────────────────────────────────────────────────────┐
│  ┌──────────────────────────────────────────────────────────────┐     │
│  │ Financial Controller    Transaction History    30th March 1998 │    │
│  └──────────────────────────────────────────────────────────────┘     │
│                                                                         │
│  A/C Ref. :     SL001                  Balance      :    3068.00        │
│  A/C Name :     CARDIFF TIMBER SUPPLIES  Amount paid :      75.00       │
│  Credit Limit : 10000.00               Turnover     :       0.00        │
│                                                                         │
│  No. Tp  Date   Ref       Details       Value      Debit       Credit   │
│    7 SC 221297 C3456  Damaged Keyboard  1000.00  *              1000.00  │
│   12 SI 081297 2345   Correction          75.00  *    75.00             │
│   25 SI 160198 34521  Ink jet printer   1410.00  *  1410.00             │
│   26 SI 120298 34267  Disks              141.00  *   141.00             │
│   27 SI 180298 34376  Scanner           1116.25  p                      │
│                       Amount Outstanding 505.15       1116.25           │
│   28 SI 170398 34445  Second hand printer 400.75 *    400.75            │
│   29 SC 260298 C23420 Goods damaged      611.00                611.00   │
│   30 SI 120398 34652  Replaced goods     611.00  *    611.00            │
│                                                                         │
│              Future    Current   30Days    60Days   90Days    Older     │
│  Aged :       0.00     1011.75   646.25   1410.00     0.00     0.00      │
│                                                                         │
│  F1 Help F2 Calc F4 QckRef F9 PrevA/C F10 NextA/C                       │
└──────────────────────────────────────────────────────────────────────┘
```

Figure 9.4
Transaction history
for a customer

Debt collection procedure

Experience at debt collection has shown very clearly that early action is essential to minimize bad debt. The warnings provided by a credit limit being exceeded or by an aged debt analysis are of no use unless you intend to act upon the information. A procedure must exist within the organization which regularly reviews the management information available and then acts on that information.

Figure 9.1 illustrated the whole process, and in this section we shall concentrate on the lower half of the figure from the issuing of a statement and a review of the aged debt analysis. If the review has revealed that a debt is now overdue and has exceeded 30 days the following sequence of events should begin:

1   Telephone the customer to determine if there is a particular reason why payments have not been made. Although a credit controller must be firm they must also be sensitive to the customer's needs and requirements. The customer in question may be long-standing and providing high sales, so care is needed not to offend the customer unnecessarily. It might well be that invoices have not been received; the customer is disputing an invoice value because goods were found to be damaged on delivery; the customer is awaiting a credit note; a cheque may already be in the post, etc. The first task, therefore, is to ensure that you and the customer are looking at the same picture, that your statement is accepted as being the true position. Unless particular circumstances exist, there should therefore be no reason why payment to you should not be made.

2   If payment is not received within 24/48 hours then further telephone calls may be made or letters sent drawing the customer's attention to the facts, the terms and conditions of sale and the procedure which will be followed if payment is not received. Companies normally have two or three letters that they send to their customers. The first one is used to ascertain the facts and the language of the others become progressively more severe.

3   What is also clear from experience is that if you have procedures you must use them and never make threats unless you intend to act. If you are inconsistent in your approach then you will find that customers will take advantage of you. Unless you have a lawyer working within the company you should have selected a firm of solicitors to represent you. It is important that some of the partners of the solicitor's firm specialize in this type of work and will act quickly on behalf of your company when required to. In most cases, notification by a solicitor that proceedings are commencing against a customer results in payment being made. Some companies play this game of 'bankmanship' to extract extra days of credit without realizing that their actions are being noted by credit agencies who will, as a consequence, reduce their credit rating.

Receipts

The overwhelming objective of managing the sales ledger is to insure that cash inflow is maximized, i.e. debts are collected, the debtors figure is kept as low as possible and bad debts are minimized. The actual management of the receipts when they arrive will be discussed in Chapter 10.

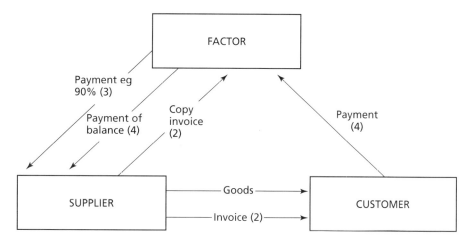

Figure 9.5
Relationship with
factor

Factoring

Over the last 15 years there has been a considerable growth in **factoring**. It is a concept which started in the USA and is now widely used in the UK. Figure 9.5 illustrates the reason why factoring commenced and how it operates.

The exchange of goods between customers and suppliers has always resulted in a conflict. Suppliers want to be paid immediately once the goods are delivered and the customer wishes to wait for a short period before making payment. This conflict has traditionally been resolved by the supplier providing credit to the customer resulting in the supplier having debtors, managing a sales ledger and accepting the risk of potential bad debts.

Factoring is a method of working by which the factor (a finance company) will take the burden of debtors from the supplier and accept responsibility for collecting the debt. With the introduction of the factor, the method of working is as follows:

1 Prior to supplying the customer, the supplier will seek clearance and a credit rating from the factor. The factor will screen the customer and reject or recommend a credit limit.
2 The supplier supplies goods to the customer, issues an invoice to the customer and sends a copy of the invoice to the factor.
3 The factor will send an agreed percentage, say 90 per cent, of the invoice value to the supplier within a few days of receipt of the copy invoice. The factor is now responsible for collecting the debt.
4 When the factor has been paid, the remaining 10 per cent minus interest and factoring expenses will be passed on to the supplier.

The factor, has, in effect taken over the complete management of the sales ledger and providing the supplier does not supply a non-customer and exceed the recommended credit limit the supplier will be protected from any bad debts, i.e. all bad debts are shouldered by the factor because it was on their screening and recommendation that business was conducted. Individual companies must decide whether this approach suits them. It is quite expensive but can, depending upon the circumstances, be cheaper than managing your own sales ledger.

Following the bad debt of one of their customers Bale and Co. had realized it needed to put in a sensible credit control system. Up to now Azina had used all that the computer system could offer in the way of credit control but there were no set procedures and no systematic approach.

They had reassessed every customer's credit limit and had spent some time organizing a new system. They decided, amongst other things, to use a local solicitor to prosecute late payers. They had reviewed their standard conditions of sale and were convinced that if a customer had not paid after receiving two warning letters then legal proceedings should commence. Although this seemed harsh it was essential if they were to minimize bad debts and ensure that cash flow was maintained.

With this in mind Azina phoned one of the customers.

'Hello Mrs Lewis this is Azina from Bale and Co. I'm calling to inform you that, unfortunately, we cannot process your current order because your credit limit has been exceeded. We were expecting a cheque from you yesterday but, as yet, nothing has been received'. Mrs Lewis was concerned. 'You did promise to send a cheque last week. I appreciate you need this order for a customer, but I must insist on payment within the next 24 hours. I have sent you two reminder letters but they have been ignored. If you read our standard conditions of sale you will see that the next step will be legal proceedings. We do not want to do this: we value your custom, but you must appreciate that like you, to survive, we need your payment'. The payment arrived delivered by hand that same day.

Azina now felt confident that the sales ledger was under control. However neither she nor John had really though about the purchase ledger. A few days after the phone call to Mrs Lewis, they were watching TV in the late evening.

'This should be interesting. It's one of those investigative programs and this week it is showing how some unscrupulous companies take advantage of poor systems and procedures with their customers – invoicing them for more goods than they've delivered, and even invoicing them and getting paid when nothing has been delivered.'

One hour later as the credits rolled, John and Aniza looked at each other, the alarm bells ringing loudly in their heads. 'What we just saw is frightening, I didn't realize just how dishonest some companies can be.'

Although the program had concentrated on deliberate fraudulent behaviour, John and Aniza realized that very costly mistakes could be made in a situation where large quantities of goods were being ordered, delivered, stored and sold.

The following morning John had an early appointment at the bank. On the way out he bumped into an old colleague, Michael Wong, and as they chatted he happened to mention the TV programme. Michael had seen it too, but for him the message had come too late.

'It's not just fraud you need to watch for,' he told John, 'I have a real problem with a supplier at the moment.' He had just received the bad news that one of his best clients was seriously threatening to take business elsewhere. Apparently, they had been promised a delivery of new keyboards but the delivery had not taken place. The dispatch manager working for Michael had known about the delivery and had taken the necessary steps to collect and dispatch the keyboards but, the keyboards were not in stock because Intratech, the suppliers, refused to deliver.

Intratech had been a supplier for many years and, by and large, relationships between the companies had been good. Michael had not been able to understand why they hadn't delivered. He phoned the customer services manager at Intratech, to find out their side of the story. Intratech had not made the delivery because some of the invoices outstanding with Michael's company were 60 days old.

Michael had fallen into the trap of paying more attention to managing the sales ledger than the purchase ledger, and the whole purchase cycle in particular. He had forgotten the simple fact that your purchase ledger is someone else's sales ledger. By thinking that he could pay suppliers as and when he pleased, he had upset a very reliable supplier and, as a consequence of non-delivery, was on the verge of losing a very valuable customer.

John went back to the office determined to review the purchase ledger in the same way that the sales ledger had just been reviewed.

The purchase cycle

The **purchase cycle** refers to all the steps that take place from deciding to order new supplies, selection of suppliers, placing an order, receiving delivery and finally, payment for the supplies.

Figure 3.2 in Chapter 3, introduced you to the purchase ordering system and the main documents and steps in that process. We shall now develop those ideas further and ask you to study Figure 9.6. Five steps are shown, and although many organizations will do things slightly differently to suit their particular circumstances, these five steps can form a starting point blue print for any organization and represents the minimum requirements. As in the design of all systems, whenever possible keep it simple. However, one must avoid the temptation of being too simple and consequently having poor internal control. Different personnel must be involved at each of the steps to ensure checking and control. Aspects of control will be discussed in detail in Chapter 18.

Step 1

There must be strict control in all organizations on who can request a **purchase order**, and therefore initiate, the purchase cycle. No organization can have a situation where anyone and everyone can request a supplier to make a delivery. Figure 9.6 shows purchase requests (**requisitions**) coming from three sources. First there is the store manager, who will be controlling stock levels. The Store Manager will have a record for each item in store and each day will examine each record to ensure sufficient stock is available to meet expected demand. When an item of stock falls to what is known as the **reorder point**, a purchase requisition is raised and sent to the purchasing department/manager. Figure 9.6 describes how stock levels vary over time and the key events and terminology used. It is assumed that usage takes place at an even rate during the period. Maximum level means the maximum amount of stock (given current demand) that the organization wishes to hold for that item.

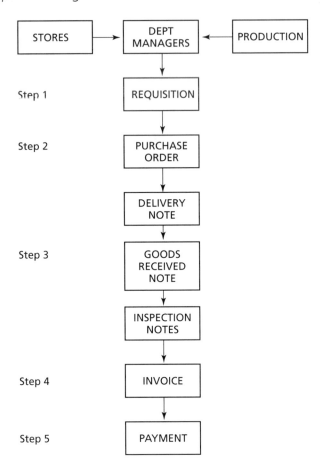

Figure 9.6
*Managing the
purchase ledger*

Buffer stock (also sometimes referred to as safety stock) is there to ensure that an organization does not run out of stock (suffer a 'stockout'). Due to the fact that delivery time and demand cannot be precisely predicted, a buffer stock is required. To suffer a stockout is serious because in a production environment you could have thousands of workers with no work to do, and you can lose customers. New orders are placed (reorder point) when sufficient stock still exists because deliveries will take time (in some cases days, and in others weeks and months) and during this waiting period, current stock levels will be run down. Finally, when a new delivery is made, levels will be restored to the maximum level. Most requisitions will come from the stores manager, although Figure 9.6 indicates two possible other sources.

The purchase manager will not initiate a new order unless he receives a requisition, and that requisition must have a recognized and authorized signatory.

Step 2

On receiving the requisitions, the Purchase manager will place an order with a supplier. In some cases this will involve a supplier search and possibly a tender process

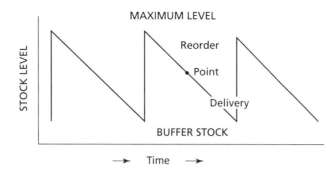

but, for many day-to-day items, a regular reliable supplier will have been chosen and a purchase order is raised.

This is a key document and the purchase order number will need to be quoted on delivery documents and invoices. Most documents will be produced in multiple copies (coloured sets) to inform various members of the organization within the purchase cycle.

For example:

Copy 1 to supplier
Copy 2 files of purchase manager
Copy 3 to originating department
Copy 4 to delivery point
Copy 5 to accounting department.

Physical multiple copies are now becoming a thing of the past as such information is transferred electronically. This information will be used to control the whole process and ensures that the company only accepts deliveries of what has been ordered and only pays for what has been delivered.

Step 3

Step 3 is concerned with receiving deliveries, only accepting what has been ordered and confirming the quality and quantity of what has been ordered. A number of documents will be used and multiple copies will be circulated to inform and update those within the purchase cycle.

When goods are delivered they will arrive with a **delivery note** that has been produced by the supplier. Deliveries should go to a central point in an organization (goods inwards) and those accepting the delivery must check that the goods have in fact been ordered. Goods inward will have a copy of the purchase order describing the goods ordered and will check that the delivery note contains the purchase order number and that the delivery matches the quantity and description/quality.

If goods inward is satisfied that the delivery has been authorized, they will raise a goods received note (**GRN**) to inform members of the purchasing cycle that the order has been received (fully or partially).

In very technical organizations, it may be necessary to test goods when they arrive because a purely visual inspection will not suffice, e.g. components used in the aircraft industry. Goods inward will need to weigh, measure and test components for performance before delivery is completely accepted. To inform members of the purchasing cycle of the results of their tests, an inspection note is circulated.

Step 4

The invoice will arrive and it is now important that its details are checked against the purchase order, delivery note, GRN and, if used, inspection note. The organization must ensure that it only pays:

1 what it has ordered;
2 what has been delivered;
3 what is of acceptable quality.

Step 5

The supplier will send monthly statements and expect to be paid within the agreed terms and conditions. Like the Bale's, many organizations pay less attention to managing the purchase ledger than the sales ledger. Their rightful emphasis on cash flow unfortunately, ignores the fact that if you do not keep your suppliers happy, you may not have anything to sell.

Your computerized system can help you manage payment to your suppliers by providing you with an aged supplier analysis, a cheque printing facility for those invoices you have flagged that you wish to pay, and also by producing a **remittance advice** to accompany the cheque. The remittance advice was discussed in Chapters 3 and 6.

Managing payments

Deciding how much to pay your suppliers each month is, unfortunately, not just a matter of complying with the above procedures and looking at an aged supplier analysis. The decision to pay must also consider how much money will be received that month from customers and the amount of overdraft available. The decision cannot be made by reference to the sales or purchase ledgers in isolation.

A meeting will be held by the financial director who will receive information of expected receipts from the sales ledger and the payments that are due. If it is considered that insufficient cash is available, then it must be decided just how much in total is available and second, who will receive payment. Each organization will have their own method of prioritizing their payments.

Summary

Because the majority of business is conducted under credit, the supplier always has the problem of financing the debtors and accepting the risk of bad debts occurring. Management of the sales ledger, therefore, is an important function in limiting the volume of debtors, minimizing bad debts and maximizing the cash inflow of the company.

Managing the sales ledger is, clearly, more than ensuring that all entries are correctly made in the accounts of each customer. This aspect is, of course, important because it is on the basis of these figures that we act to manage the sales ledger. You must, therefore, learn to use the figures and utilize the power of the computer in generating management information. Management of the sales ledger had been enhanced greatly by using computerized accounting systems. You have seen that by setting up a customer account with a credit limit, transactions are posted just once yet:

1 statements can be produced;
2 aged debt analysis produced;
3 letters sent;
4 sales analysed;
5 special reports produced.

The production of such information is a great benefit, but to work effectively and use such information systems, procedures need to be set up and applied. You have examined every step in such a process from setting credit limits to instructing your solicitor to take legal proceedings.

Remember that management of the purchase ledger is as important as managing the sales ledger. The order process, relationships with suppliers and cash flow complement the management of customers.

Together with stock, the sales and purchase ledger control are vital to good cash management which we discuss in the next chapter.

Key words

aged debt analysis p. 154 • bank references p. 151 • buffer stock p. 160 • credit agencies p. 152 • credit limit p. 151 • delivery note p. 161 • factoring p. 157 • GRN p. 161 • purchase cycle p. 159 • purchase order p. 159 • remittance advice p. 162 • reorder point p. 159 • requisitions p. 159 • statements p. 154 • supplier references p. 152 • terms of sale p. 154

Practice questions

1 Design a form which you intend issuing to all new customers who request credit to enable you to set an initial credit limit.
2 Write a letter to a new customer's bank requesting information to help you establish a credit limit for that customer.
3 Why are banks reluctant to be completely free with the information they have at their disposal when faced with a request from a supplier of one of their clients?
4 Having backed up your case study on a separate disk complete the following exercises as a new and independent exercise
   A Set up the following three customers. Make up your own addresses, telephone numbers and fax numbers.

Acc No.	Acc Name	Credit Limit (£)
SL200	H Coombes	5 000
SL300	E Sheppard	3 000
SL400	S McCarthy	7 000

B Post the following invoices for each customer. The date of posting will be determined by your current system date. If the invoice is current use today's date. Minus 30 and minus 60 means choose a date 30 and 60 days prior to the current date.

Acc No.	Date	Net (£)	VAT (£)
SL200	Current	600.00	105.00
SL300	Current	1 000.00	175.00
SL400	Minus 60	2 500.00	437.50
SL200	Current	1 300.00	227.50
SL400	Minus 30	2 500.00	437.50
SL300	Current	750.00	131.25
SL200	Minus 30	1 200.00	210.00
SL400	Minus 60	500.00	87.50

C Print off the aged debt analysis and familiarize yourself with its layout and content.

D Using the function *Transaction History* examine each account and write a report explaining what action, if any should be taken with regard to each customer.

5 What factors would you consider in deciding who could sign a purchase requisition?

6 Why is it essential to try and use more than one supplier for your key purchases?

7 What criteria would you use in selecting a new supplier?

8 Explain why:
   (i) buffer stock is required
   (ii) new orders are placed when stock levels of the item in question can still be high.

9 Explain the difference between a GRN and an inspection note.

10 List the main objectives to be achieved in successfully managing a purchase ledger.

11 Set up the following three suppliers. Make up your own addresses, telephone numbers, fax numbers, etc.:

Acc No.	Acc Name	Credit limit (£)
PL200	L. Bonetto	2 000
PL300	S. John	3 000
PL400	J. Jones	4 000

12 Post the following invoices for each supplier. The date of posting will be determined by your current system date. If the invoice is current, use today's date. Minus 30 and minus 60 means choose a date 30 and 60 days prior to the current date.

Acc No.	Date	Net	(£)
PL200	Current	100	17.50
PL300	Current	200	35.00
PL400	Current	500	87.50
PL400	Minus 30	2 000	350.00
PL300	Minus 30	100	17.50
PL200	Minus 30	300	52.50
PL300	Minus 60	400	70.00
PL300	Minus 30	20	3.50
PL200	Current	200	35.00
PL400	Minus 30	1 400	245.00
PL200	Minus 30	30	5.25
PL200	Current	400	70.00

13 Print the aged supplier analysis and familiarize yourself with its layout and contents.
14 Using the function *Transaction History* together with the aged supplier report, examine each account and write a report explaining what action, if any, should be taken with regard to each supplier.
15 What factors would you consider in drawing up a checklist of how to decide which supplier will be paid during a month when insufficient cash is available to pay all the supplier accounts that are due.

10 Managing cash flows

Learning outcomes

After reading this chapter you should be able to:
- understand the importance of cash flows to a business
- prepare a bank reconciliation statement
- identify the main internal control and security measures needed to control cash
- record discounts received and allowed
- prepare a simple cash flow forecast.

Introduction

In this chapter, cash is used to mean both cash in hand as notes and coins and on deposit in a bank account. On their own, notes and coins are known as **petty cash**; if only the bank account is involved then it will be called bank. In the last chapter we looked at the need to control the credit offered by a business to its customers and to operate a professional debt collection policy. One of the objectives of this policy was to make sure that the business received the cash from its customers. Cash is important to a business. A company needs to be profitable in the long-term to give its investors a return on their investment and to generate funds for renewal and growth. However it is possible for a business to be profitable but at the same time so starved of cash that it is unable to meet its liabilities as they fall due. Profit is not the same thing as cash. A business can survive if it makes a loss for short periods of time. If a business fails to pay what is due, the creditors can sue for the amounts they are owed. In the extreme case, a receiver will be appointed to seize the assets of the business and in a sole trader's case personal assets as well. The assets will be sold and the money received used to pay off the amounts owed. This has nothing to do with business profitability.

In this chapter we look at the differences between cash and profit, and the basic routines needed to control and monitor cash.

One December morning, Azina opened the post to discover a bank statement for the business account. She was puzzled because it showed a balance of £2743.66 at 30 November. She was sure that the balance according to her records had been different.

Looking up the figures later that day she discovered the figure in the trial balance amounted to £7544.38. The difference shocked her. She had been assuming that if the records showed that there was money in the bank then she could write a cheque. Suddenly she realized that this was a dangerous strategy. If the bank figure was so much lower than they thought then a cheque could bounce (i.e. the bank could refuse to pay out a cheque if insufficient funds were in the account).

She showed John the statement when he got back from a sales trip later that day. He was equally surprised.

'How can it be so little if we are making profits?' he asked and suggested that the bank must be wrong. He and Azina sat down with all their business records to check. They discovered that there was quite a delay in the timing between their records and those in the bank but that one large cheque had gone through much more quickly than most. Azina decided to ring the bank the next day to try to find out why the one cheque had been so quickly processed.

The bank statement is reproduced in Figure 10.1.

Cash and profit – the difference

Cash is a concept most people can understand. Dealing with cash in their personal affairs, it is easy to understand the business needs to have cash and what it means when you say cash has increased or decreased by a certain amount. The amount of cash on hand is a matter of fact. You should be able to go and count it. This does not make it a good way to assess the performance of an organization. A cash balance might be high because you have not made some much needed repairs to fixed assets or have delayed paying creditors who will not be very happy to wait for the money due to them. In other words the balance at any particular moment in time can be manipulated to show a healthy figure but to the detriment of the future of the business. It is also subject to major fluctuations as, for example, when a business decides to invest in fixed assets or raise a loan. This means that neither the actual cash balance at any time nor the change in the balance over a period of time is a useful indicator of business performance. Nevertheless a business needs a healthy cash flow if it is to survive and this makes managing cash an important element in running a business. The availability of cash determines when new equipment can be purchased or expenses incurred.

Profit is a much more complex idea. Economic theory defines profit as 'the amount you can consume in a period and still be as well off at the end of that time as you were at the beginning'. This definition assumes that you can define 'well off'. A simple example might help to make the definition clearer. Assume that you invest £100 in a deposit account offering interest at 10 per cent per annum. The account will be credited with £10 interest at the end of the period. You could spend £10 and still leave your £100 intact to earn another £10 next year. You could be said to be as 'well off' at the end of the year as you were at the beginning in that you are in a position to earn another £10 next year. We would say your profit was £10.

This assumes that interest rates remain the same and that the purchasing power of

Blackshires Bank PO Box 100 Cardiff	Account: Current J and A Bale Statement date: 30.12.XX Sheet No: 1		CONFIDENTIAL Account No: 11272121		
DATE	DETAIL	WITHDRAWAL	DEPOSIT	BALANCE	
1 Nov	Transfer funds		50 000.00	50 000.00	
2 Nov	001560	30 000.00			
	001561	100.00		19 900.00	
7 Nov	001562	150.00		19 750.00	
8 Nov	001565	1 200.00			
	001566	80.00		18 470.00	
11 Nov	001563	423.05		18 046.95	
14 Nov	001567	85.03		17 961.92	
15 Nov	Counter Credit		514.30	18 476.22	
16 Nov	001564	1 558.32		16 917.90	
21 Nov	Counter Credit		418.73	17 336.63	
25 Nov	Blackshire bank DD	700.00		16 636.63	
28 Nov	001568	9 472.00		7 164.63	
	Counter Credit		142.36	7 306.99	
30 Nov	001569	4 631.20		2 675.79	
30 Nov	Counter Credit		67.87	2 743.66	
2 Dec	Counter Crdit		1 398.45	4 142.11	
5 Dec	Counter Credit		4 682.87		
	001572	200.00		8 624.98	
7 Dec	001570	1 280.60		7 344.38	
	Balance to sheet no 2				

Figure 10.1
Bank statement
for Bale and Co.

money does not change. If, for example, interest rates will fall to say 8 per cent in the second year then you could not expect to earn the same in the future and you would not be as well off as you had been. Your future interest would be £8 instead of £10. You would need to save some of the interest from the earlier year to help make good the income in the following years and so your profit could not be said to be £10 in the first year because it is not sustainable. Similarly if inflation reduces the amount that you can buy with the £10 received you would need more in the future to maintain your standard of living.

If the interest was paid out to you as cash, then in our example the profit would equal the increase in cash. However, assume that instead of calculating the profit for a full year, you need to calculate the profit after six months. Income would be £5, but there would be no cash. The money would be owed to the depositor who could not claim it until the end of the year when the bank had agreed to pay out.

Similarly in a business, profit may have been earned but this is not necessarily in cash. A profit has to be calculated by working out the income generated in a time period, even if it has not yet been received, and after making allowance for the resources used up to generate that income even if they have not been paid. As we saw when we looked at valuing stock at the period end, calculating profit is sometimes a matter of judgement rather than fact. There are other similar problems such as making allowance for the cost of fixed assets used up, which we will look at in the next few chapters.

Despite the fact that it is difficult to calculate and it is subjective, profit is useful because it is an attempt to measure the ongoing income that the business has generated and has the potential to generate again in the future. Cash is the means of acquiring the resources to enable the business to generate that profit.

Both cash and profit are useful in assessing the position of a business. They are different aspects of the same organization.

Reconciling cash to profit

It is possible to identify the items which account for the differences in cash and profit. They include changes in debtors, creditors and stock as well as purchase of fixed assets, loans and owners capital injections and withdrawals. They are the result of timing differences between a transaction being recorded in the profit calculation and the actual cash flow associated with the transaction taking place.

Activity

1   Look at the profit and loss account and the bank account for the case study for November.
    Required
    (a) Identify the items which have been taken out of bank but not out of profit.
    (b) Make a separate list of the items in the profit calculation but not in the bank or cash accounts.

It would be possible to present the bank and petty cash accounts as a formal **cash flow statement** indicating where cash for the month came from and how it was spent. This might be useful for Bale and Co. to enable John and Azina to understand where the cash they raised has gone. The ASB has a format for such a statement in FRS1. The cash flow statement for Bale and Co. for November using that format is illustrated in Figure 10.2 You should make sure that you can trace all the figures used in that statement before moving on.

The change in cash represents the increase in the bank and petty cash balances from zero to the balances at the end of November:

Bank	£7 544.38
Petty cash	43.24
	£7 587.62

Cash Flow Statement for Bale and Co. for the month of November

	£	£
Cash from operating activities		
Cash from customer		7 224.58
Cash to suppliers		(9 472.00)
Cash for expenses – Telephone		(150.00)
– Insurnace		(423.05)
– Advertising		(1 280.00)
– Sundry		(141.79)
		(4 242.26)
Servicing of finance – interest paid		(585.00)
Capital expenditure		
Premises	100 000.00	
Equipment	1 558.32	
Carpets	1 280.60	
Office fittings	4 631.20	
		(107 470.12)
Drawings/return to owners		–
Cash outflow before financing		(112 297.38)
Financing		
Owners capital	50 000.00	
Loan	69 885.00	
		119 885.00
Change in cash		7 587.62

Figure 10.2
Cash flow
statement for Bale
and Co.

The statement has some logic to the order. It starts by looking at the cash being generated or used up by everyday operating activities. These are continuing from period to period. Normally for an established business the cash flow from operating should be a positive figure. The statement then takes out the interest paid to those investors who have put money into the business. In a cash flow for a company it would follow this by deducting the amount to be paid in tax before moving to the amounts the owners decided to invest in fixed assets and/or take out for their own use. These last figures can be increased or decreased depending on the decisions of the owners and managers. Finally, any cash outflow as the result of the items already mentioned will need to be financed or used to repay finance raised in earlier periods.

The FRS1 also requires a note to be published which reconciles the profit from operating with the cash from operating activities. In our case study the **reconciliation** would look as follows:

Profit from profit and loss account after interest	£3 051.97
Add back interest	585.00
Profit from operating	3 636.97
Less: Increase in debtors	(8 110.39)
Increase in stock	(8 246.00)
Add: Increase in creditors	8 477.16
Cash outflow from operating	£(4 242.26)

Note that because the debtors and stock have increased from zero to the balances at the end of the month cash has been used to invest in these assets. They are a cash outflow. On the other hand suppliers have given Bale and Co. credit just as if they had organized a short-term loan. This represents a source of cash and increases the cash flow from operating figure.

Cash flows

In this instance, John and Azina did not have a problem with the balance in the account. Two deposits at the month end were cleared. It will not always be so easy. Given the delays in the banking system and the difficulty of ensuring that debtors pay on time, it is necessary to keep a buffer in the account unless an arrangement has been made with the bank for an **overdraft facility**, whereby the bank will honour cheques up to an agreed overdraft limit. Where this has been done the bank will only charge interest if and when the arrangement is used.

To arrange an overdraft the bank will want to see predicted cash flow statements for a period into the future. A predicted cash flow is obviously a bit like crystal ball gazing but without it you cannot even decide if you will need to talk to the bank manager, let alone discuss the amount you may need to cover. The estimate involves making assumptions about the amount you hope to sell, the length of time the customers will take to pay, the expenses you will incur and the credit you will obtain. The cash flow estimate should be set up to show expected cash flows for each month or, if very crucial, each week. It should calculate:

1 expected cash inflows from cash sales, amounts from customers, sales of fixed assets, cash raised from new loans or owners investments, refunds or any other source;
2 expected cash outflows for purchases, expenses, wages, new fixed assets, owners drawings, interest charges or any other commitment;
3 the change in cash for the month;
4 the balance of cash brought forward from the previous month;

Table 10.1 Illustration of a layout for a cash flow forecast

	Month 1	Month 2	Month 3	Month 4
Cash inflows				
Cash from customers				
Cash invested by owners				
Sales of fixed assets				
Total cash inflows				
Cash outflows				
Payments to suppliers				
Purchase of fixed assets				
Payment of expenses				
Drawings				
Total cash outflows				
Change in cash for month				
Balance from previous month				
Balance carried forward				

5   the balance of cash carried forward to the next month.

A possible layout for this is shown in Table 10.1.

Bale and Co. will have difficulty at first in putting together the estimates that are needed to construct the cash flow estimate. They have no previous experience of the problems they might come across. Nevertheless they need to make the attempt. It can always be modified as more information becomes available and as they learn about the market they are operating in. The business has a number of fixed expenses but the key factor for them is the sales figure. This determines not only the cash inflow but also the outflows for purchases. The sales figure is the key or limiting factor for many organizations.

Activity

2   The first attempt at estimating the cash flows for January to March produced the following:
  (i)   Credit sales were expected to drop to £10 000 in January but pick up again to £25 000 in February and £30 000 in March. In addition, the cash sales would be about £750 per month.
  (ii)   Sales prices were on average worked out at cost price plus a third. In other words if an item cost £75 it would be sold for £100. Suppliers had offered only one month credit to the Bales as they were a new business without a track record.
  (iii)   Advertising, starting in January, would cost £5000 per month payable in the month after the adverts appeared.
  (iv)   Vehicle running costs would be £500 per month paid in cash.
  (v)   New equipment is planned for February at a cost of £5000 payable in the following month.
  (vi)   Other expenses (all payable in cash) were estimated at £400 per month.
  (vii)   A telephone bill (£480) and an electricity bill (£350) are expected in January payable in early February.
  (viii)   The opening cash balance at 31 December is estimated to be £7000 in hand.
  (ix)   Assume that debtors will be given 60 days to pay.
  Required
  (a)   Prepare a cash flow forecast for January to March for Bale and Co. (assume that the debtors at 31 December amounted to £26 000 of which £22 000 related to sales in December; and the creditors at 31 December amounted to £13 500).
  (b)   What effect would changing the credit period given to debtors to 30 days have on the cash flow?
  (c)   What effect would obtaining 60 days credit from the suppliers have on the cash flow?

If the statement is set up on a spreadsheet package the monthly balances can be worked out easily. It can also be used to ask 'what if?' questions to try to assess which factors alter the balance. For example you can see how important it is that you receive

Table 10.2 Cash flow budget for January to March for Bale and Co.

	January	February	March
Cash inflows			
Credit sales	4 000	22 000	10 000
Cash sales	750	750	750
Total inflows	4 750	22 750	10 750
Cash outflows			
Purchases	13 500	8 063	19 312
Advertising		5 000	5 000
Vehicles	500	500	500
Expenses	400	400	400
New equipment			5 000
Telephone		480	
Electricity		350	
Total cash outflows	14 400	14 793	30 212
Change in cash for month	(9 650)	7 957	(19 462)
Opening balance	7 000	(2 650)	5 307
Closing balance	(2 650)	5 307	(14 155)

the money from customers within one month rather than two. You can play with the assumptions and figures to minimize any expected overdraft.

A spreadsheet can be updated as actual figures come to hand, giving a constantly updated figure for the cash balances.

An answer to part (a) of activity 2 is given in Table 10.2.

An overdraft facility is not a cheap form of finance and if this is going to be more than an insurance policy then it makes sense to explore other possible sources of finance. Some of these involve negotiating with your customers and suppliers. If a shorter customer credit period can be arranged perhaps by offering cash discounts to customers who pay early then the balance in the bank account will be under less pressure. Similarly if the suppliers can be persuaded to offer longer credit terms or to supply stock at shorter notice then the need for cash to finance the stock holding will reduce, freeing cash to keep the bank balance in a healthy state. Leasing or hiring equipment instead of purchasing could also help spread the cash outflows.

So far we have assumed that the problem is too little cash, and certainly this carries the risk of default and bankruptcy. In the longer term, too much cash lying idle in the bank account is also a problem for the business. The resources of the business need to be invested in assets which can earn money. The owners and investors will want a return on their investment and more than they would receive from depositing the cash in a current account.

Special features of petty cash and bank deposits

Bank balances and **petty cash** present special security problems to a manager. It is an asset which can be stolen easily. The notes and coins belonging to your business cannot be distinguished from those in anyone's pocket. As soon as you have lost custody of the asset it is hard to prove it belongs to you rather than a third party. Cheques are more difficult to pilfer but can still be stolen. It is not unknown for unscrupulous employees to open bank accounts with similar names to that of the employing business.

Payments are also a problem. A cheque made out to the wrong person or for goods or services which have not been received by the company are another form of theft. Controls need to be put in place to ensure that these risks are minimized. We looked at controls in general in Chapter 3. You might like to reread the section entitled 'Control' in that chapter before continuing.

In larger businesses with a number of employees separating out the responsibility for handling cash from that of recording the transactions is the first step. This is obviously more difficult for smaller concerns but in these cases the owners should take a greater part in the handling and security of cash.

As far as cash receipts are concerned it is important that they are recorded immediately, banked as soon as possible and banked intact. Using cash received to pay your own bills is a source for error. All takings should be banked together and the total should agree to the cash takings for the day recorded in the system. Any cash needed for the businesses own use should be withdrawn separately even if this means a small charge for the transaction at the bank.

Receipts should be issued for all cash sales and a control list of the amounts prepared. This can be used as the basis of the recording system. Credit customers may pay by post and the post should be opened by someone with authority who makes a list of cheques received. These should be recorded in the accounting system as soon as possible.

Payments should be made by cheque and supported by authorized vouchers. It is sometimes necessary to operate a small petty cash fund and if this is the case it should be run efficiently. The cash should be kept in its own box in the custody of an authorized employee. The amount needed should be carefully estimated. It is a nonsense to keep topping up the float daily but equally you will not want the security risk of cash lying around unnecessarily. Experience will help to establish a reasonable figure. The amount is known as the **cash float** and is withdrawn from the bank as one lump sum. Assuming the float is £100.00 it will be recorded as follows:

Journal (1) £ £

| Petty cash | DR | 100.00 | |
| Bank | CR | | 100.00 |

Being the petty cash float.

Any amounts paid out must be supported by a voucher such as parking tickets or till receipts. When the cash begins to run low the amounts paid out on vouchers so far are totalled and this amount is reimbursed by a further cheque from the bank. This time however the debit entry in the records is to the expense accounts represented by the vouchers. Note that the petty cash balance stays at the original float figure unless a decision is taken to increase the amount of the float. At any moment in time, the paid vouchers and remaining cash should total to the petty cash float. The main problem with this is recording the VAT. The items in petty cash can include zero rated, exempt and standard rated goods.

In our example, assume that the vouchers for the first week included:

Petrol	£30.00
Parking	2.40
Stamps	5.20
Milk, coffee, tea	8.50
Window cleaner	5.00
Total:	£51.10

These would be recorded as follows:

Journal (2)		£	£
Petrol	DR	25.53	
Sundry expenses – VAT exempt		7.40	
Sundry expenses – Zero rated		8.50	
Postage		5.20	
VAT		4.47	
Bank	CR		51.10

Being the reimbursement of the petty cash expenses

The journal entries are illustrated in T accounts below:

Petty Cash

Week 1	Bank (1)	100.00	

Bank

			Week 1	Petty cash (1)	100.00
			Week 2	Expenses (2)	51.10

Petrol

Week 2	Bank (2)	25.53	

Sundry expenses

Week 2	Bank (2)	7.40	
Week 2	Bank (2)	8.50	

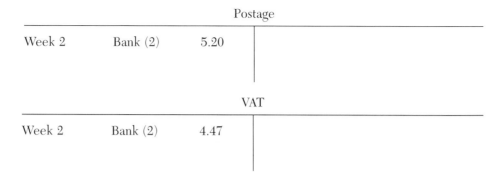

Postage		
Week 2	Bank (2)	5.20

VAT		
Week 2	Bank (2)	4.47

Remember in the Sage system you need to code the items T1, T0, or T9 for VAT and the system can then allocate the expense to the correct category for the VAT return. The payment entries can be made on the bank payments screens in the nominal ledger. Sage has a control feature built in to control cash being drawn out of the bank account. To transfer an amount from the bank to the cash you will need to make a journal entry. As journals should all be scrutinized and authorized by someone in authority, the system is designed to ensure that the management know how much cash is being withdrawn and for what purposes.

Activity

3   Looking at the case study, what level of float does Bale and Co. appear to operate with? How often is the float reimbursed? Do you think the amount of the float is reasonable?

The relationship with the bank

In many ways a business bank account operates in a similar fashion to a personal account. A bank should be chosen with care. Banks differ in the terms which they offer and in the charges which they make. As some transactions take longer to process if not initiated at your branch, it is important to select a bank with a branch which is accessible to you. Take time to read the small print and consider which bank will suit your business. It is worth talking to other business people in the area if possible but do not make the mistake of selecting a bank just because a friend recommends it or because you or your family have always banked with them.

When the account is opened you will have to say who can sign a cheque on the account. The bank will need specimen signatures. Some businesses require two signatures for security reasons but for Bale and Co. that would be restrictive since it would mean that Azina could not operate the account when John was away on business. The terms and conditions should be read very carefully and filed for further reference. All phone calls to the bank should be logged and confirmed in writing for use as evidence should a dispute arise in the future. Owners are generally so busy that these details can get overlooked but the bank account can cost you a great deal of money if things go wrong. Bank charges and interest can be high and the bank is able to take the cash from the account before you realize that it has gone. Banks can make mistakes. Bank managers and staff are moved to different branches and may not be available to confirm your understanding of events. It is important to have the papers to support your case. Credit ratings can depend on a banker's reference and you would not wish to develop a bad relationship with the bank.

A business account will probably be subject to higher bank charges than a personal account, each transaction bearing a small cost. The transactions generally take a time to process just as they would on a personal account. For example, it could take up to five working days to clear a deposit banked in your account. The major banks' timings vary and you should find this out by asking when you can draw a cheque against the cleared balance. Similarly they vary with charges and conditions. The problem encountered by Bale and Co. at the end of November was not due to an error. Office Supplies Ltd, who received a large cheque from Bale and Co. on 29 November, paid for special clearance and the cheque went through straight away. This is a service offered by the banks but does cost money. It might be used where the depositor has a need for the money quickly to clear their own liability or where there is some doubt about the money being available in the account of the drawer of the cheque. The effect for Bale and Co. was to reduce severely the amount available in the account well before they had expected.

Other shocks which can take bank account holders by surprise are bounced cheques for which a charge is made. The business may not know this for some time after the cheque has been presented and rejected. In the mean time they are expecting to draw cheque payments against it.

For these reasons it is dangerous to rely on your business records of the balance in hand at any time. Instead it is sensible to obtain details of the balance from the automatic till available at the bank.

Bank reconciliation

One step in operating a good cash management policy is to check and reconcile the bank statements with the accounting records regularly. This should be done in a systematic way.

You need details of the bank account from the accounting ledger records and the bank statement.

1   Check every cheque paid and every deposit made against the statement ticking them as you go.
2   List all the items on the statement but not in the business records. These will include such things as bank charges and interest, bounced cheques, bank giro deposits and transfers. These latter items if they are agreed as belonging to the business should be entered in the accounting system. Any items not agreed should be taken up with the bank as soon as possible. This stage should give you the 'true' bank balance.
3   List any items that appear in the ledger but not on the statement. These items will form part of the reconciliation.
4   Take the balance from the bank statement and add the outstanding deposits, take

off the **outstanding cheques**, adjust any other items from the list in stage (3) and you should arrive at the true balance calculated in (2).

4   Follow the four steps to complete the bank reconciliation for Bale and Co. at 30 November.

Your answer should come to a reconciliation as follows:

Balance per statement	£2 743.66
Add outstanding deposits	
£1 398.45	
4 682.87	
	6 081.32
	8 824.98
Less outstanding cheque	
001570	1 280.60
True cash at bank balance	£7 544.38

The reconciliation needs to be carried out regularly. For most businesses it is important to arrange to receive statements fairly frequently, at least once a month. As soon as the statement arrives the reconciliation process should be carried out. Any errors or problems can then be sorted out immediately.

Discounts

Discounts can be received from suppliers on purchases or granted to customers on sales. There are two broad reasons for discounts. One is for bulk buying and is often called **trade discount**. The other is for prompt payment and is known as a **finance discount**.

Trade discounts are normally accounted for by recording the invoice and related VAT at the reduced price. The supplier's account will show an amount outstanding of the discounted figure. Finance discounts need to be shown separately because they are the result of good cash flow and credit management. For a business operating with an overdraft, receiving the cash from customers early reduces interest charges but also means accepting a smaller inflow of cash; on the purchase ledger, paying the discounted figure reduces the immediate cash outflow but could increase the interest charges on the overdraft. The manager needs to compare the rate of interest represented by the discount against the interest charged on the overdraft.

For example, consider a situation where interest on the overdraft was being charged at an annual rate of 24 per cent, but the discount on offer from the supplier was 2.5 per cent of the invoiced amount if paid within 30 days. The invoice is for £1000 and without the discount would be due for payment within 60 days. In other words an extra 30 days credit is possible but only if the discount is forgone. If the invoice is paid within 30 days, the amount paid will be £975 (i.e. £1000 less the discount of £25) but this will mean extra overdraft interest of £19.5 (£975 at 24 per cent per annum for 30 days). The business would be £5.50 better off if they pay the supplier early and take advantage of the discount. Note that if the decision had been to ignore the discount, then the later the payment can be made the better and full advantage should be taken of the credit period on offer.

For a business without an overdraft, the manager needs to set the prospect of reduced income against the prospect of receiving the cash early and being able to reinvest it to earn interest.

These finance discounts are part of the financing costs of the business and need to be shown as such. As these discounts affect the amount payable to the supplier or received from the customer they will affect the sales and purchase ledger accounts and so this is where the recording will take place. Customers' or suppliers accounts will show the original gross amount due on the invoice before the discount. The discount is only available if the payment is received or paid on time. When the cash is received or paid it is recorded in the customer or supplier account This will leave the discount amount shown as still owing. It is necessary to write this off separately debiting a **discounts allowed** or crediting a **discounts received** account in the nominal ledger. At the period end the discounts allowed will be debited to the profit and loss account as an expense and the discounts received credited as income.

The entries in the records will be made through the sales and purchase ledger routines. Using the example of the invoice for £1000 from a supplier:

		£	£
(1) Purchases	DR	1 000	
Creditors control account	CR		1 000
(CR Suppliers account in purchase ledger)			
Being the invoice for goods supplied			

		£	£
(2) Creditors control account	DR	975	
Bank	CR		9 75
Being payment of supplier's account less the discount			

		£	£
(3) Creditors control account	DR	25	
Discounts received	CR		25
Being the discount received from supplier			

Sage offers routines in the purchase ledger payments section and the receipts section of the sales ledger to mark these amounts as discounts and automatically record them in the nominal ledger discounts received or allowed accounts. Appendix 6A introduces the discount routine in Sage but we look at posting such a transaction in more detail here.

5 Back up your disks before working through the following illustration. It is not part of the case study and you will not want to alter the case study Sage records to date.

(i)   First create a new supplier or use a supplier account set up from previous work.

(ii)   Post the invoice for £1000 to the supplier account using the tax code T1.

(iii) Pay an amount of £975 using the payment routine.

(iv)   Examine the *Transaction History* to check that the invoice has been part paid.

(v)   Re-enter the payments section and fill in the details but leave the cheque number and amount blank.

(vi)   Select *Manual* as the payment allocation method and highlight the outstanding amount on the invoice.

(vii) At the bottom of the screen you will be asked to select the type of payment. One option offered is *Discount*. Accept this option.

(viii) You will be asked to enter the amount of the discount. If it is the whole remaining balance you can just press *ESC* and post the full amount. Enter the tax code T1 again.

(ix)   Now you can post the entry. The amount will be shown in the discount column and the account balance will be reduced accordingly.

(x)   Check the nominal ledger discounts received account to find the discount figure which will be taken to the profit and loss account.

Summary

In this chapter we looked at the importance of cash to a business and its relationship with profit. Both cash and profit are important to a business and must be monitored. Cash needs to be controlled carefully. Basic cash management procedures were introduced including the need to:

1   plan the amount of cash receipts and payments in advance on a month by month basis;
2   operate a strict system of physical control of cash and cheques;
3   record all payments and receipts promptly;
4   impose a policy of constant monitoring of cash flows to ensure that there is cash to meet obligation as they fall due but that cash does not lie idle in accounts producing little return.

The chapter also looked at the recording of discounts allowed and received, distinguishing finance and trade discounts.

So far we have been looking at the day to day running of the business and the need to record and use the accounting system to provide management information. Periodically it is necessary to summarize transactions to date and to assess performance. To do this we need to look at the results for accounting periods. This presents a number of problems. In the next chapter we introdce these problems and the concepts and methods which accountants have developed to overcome them.

Key words

Practice questions

1   Explain in your own words the difference between cash and profit. Why should a business monitor both these figures?

2   Green and Co. is a small business and cannot afford to employ more staff than at present. Current staff comprise the two brothers who own the business, two sales assistants, a driver who delivers goods and looks after the stock and one accounting assistant who is responsible for all accounting functions. Cash is not banked regularly and is sometimes used to top up petty cash. Unfortunately the accounting assistant is under considerable financial strain at home and seeing the cash receipts from sales for the day decides to borrow them rather than bank them. A week later, opening the post, the assistant finds a cheque from a credit customer for a similar amount. The assistant alters the records in that customer's account to indicate a credit note has been issued. The cheque however is banked and recorded as cash sales to hide the amount stolen.

   Required

   What controls could be operated to discover and prevent such theft?

3   Miro Ltd has received its bank statement for the last month and has started the reconciliation process by checking the statement items with its own records. The following items were found:

   (i)   The balance on the statement at 30 September was £847.04 and the balance in the accounting information system was £5673.24.

   (ii)   Cash takings of £702.20 on 30 September were deposited just as the bank was closing but do not appear on the statement.

   (iii)   The statement includes a giro receipt from a credit customer for £253.00 which had not been recorded in Miros' accounting system.

   (iv)   Cheques deposited at the bank in September amounting to £4090.00 have not been included on the statement.

   (v)   A cheque for £2321.00 from a credit customer banked on 15 September has been returned by the bank. The bank charged a fee of £25.00. The cheque and the fee have been deducted from the statement balance by the bank but are not recorded in the company's records.

   (vi)   Bank charges of £142.00 have been deducted on the statement from the bank.

   (vii)   A standing order for £220.00 has been deducted by the bank. This had been cancelled in writing by Miro Ltd and the bank is in error in continuing to deduct the amount.

   (viii)   Cheques paid by Miro to its creditors amounting in total to £2421.00 have not yet been presented to the bank for payment. These have been recorded in the accounting system.

Required

(a) Calculate the true balance for the accounting records.

(b) Prepare the bank reconciliation statement.

(c) Which items will need to be recorded by Miro in its accounting system?

4   Roger is considering setting up in business, importing art and craft work from South America. He has made the following estimates of the activities for the first year.

(i) He will transfer £10 000 to the business bank account to set the business up on 1 April.

(ii) He will need to rent a small shop at a cost of £800 per month payable in advance.

(iii) Shop equipment will cost £5000 and a further £2000 will be needed for a computer. The equipment is expected to last eight years but the computer he estimates will last about three years. The equipment will be paid for in May but the computer will be a cash purchase in April.

(iv) He estimates sales will be £5000 for the launch in April, dropping to £3000 in May but increasing to £4000 in June and £6000 for July onwards.

(v) He will invest in stock initially at a cost of £10 000 which he will pay for in April. However he estimates that normally he will have two months to pay for the goods but all sales will be for cash. The selling price will be at cost plus 50 per cent. He will reorder stock as soon as it is sold.

(vi) He will need to pay running expenses averaging £300.00 per month.

(vii) He intends to draw out £800 per month as his salary for the first year.

Required

(a) Prepare a monthly cash forecast for Roger for the first year of trading.

(b) Draw up a draft profit and loss account for the first year.

(c) Reconcile the change in the cash figure to the profit for the year.

(d) What level of overdraft would you negotiate with the bank?

5   Sunny runs a wholesale fruit and vegetable business. Different suppliers are offered different terms depending upon the quantity, timing, quality and reliability of supply. Customers negotiate the terms of each purchase with one of Sunny's sales people. This will depend upon regularity of custom, quantity and range of goods required. In addition if customers pay within 30 days they receive a discount of 5 per cent but for payment within 10 days an 8 per cent finance discount.

On 1 December:

Customer 1 Purchased goods with a normal value of £690, less a trade discount of 5 per cent.

Customer 2 Purchased goods worth £2200 normal price, less a trade discount of 10 per cent.

Customer 3 Purchased goods worth £450 normal price, no trade discount given.

Customer 1 paid in full on 10 January.

Customer 2 paid on 29 December.

Customer 3 paid on 6 December.

Required

(a)   Back up previous work on the case study to keep it separate from this exercise.

(b)   Make up three new customers in the Sage sales ledger and enter the above transactions including the trade and finance discounts (take VAT at zero rate).

11 End of period adjustments

Learning objectives

After reading this chapter you should be able to:

- understand the artificial idea of an accounting period
- recognize the implications of accounting periods for the production of accounting reports
- know the difference between preparing reports on a cash basis and preparing them on an accruals basis
- make the end of period adjustments to revenue expenses needed to prepare reports on an accruals basis.

Introduction

So far we have looked at the recording and controlling of data with only a brief mention of the way in which reports are drawn from those records. The database will build gradually day by day, month by month, year by year over the organization's life time. However the owners and managers cannot wait until the end of the organization's life for information on how it is progressing. Reports are drawn up periodically and regularly to assess and monitor progress. As we have seen the records are entered by date. This enables reports to be produced for specific time periods. Problems arise however when transactions do not fit neatly into one accounting time period. In this chapter we look at the implications of drawing up reports for artificially chosen time periods and the adjustments which will need to be made to cope with this.

John was delighted by the apparent profit from the first month's trading but he was concerned that some expenses did not appear in the accounts. When the time comes to prepare accounts for December, John realizes that the telephone and electricity bills for the quarter will be due at the end of January. By reading the meter, he estimates that the electricity used in December amounts to £210.00 and the telephone bill he estimates at £315.00 – both figures before VAT.

He asks Bill: 'we are using the electricity and telephone all the time. Is it right that we charge them all in the month they are paid? And the insurance policies for the car and professional indemnity insurance are for a full year – should they all be taken out of the December profit?'

Privately John and Azina have wondered how much Bill is going to charge them for all the advice he has given them. They decide not to ask him about it yet!

Meanwhile, at a New Year's party John hears from another contact that Customer 1 has been forced into liquidation. His 'friend' buys him a strong drink as he explains that he had known that there were problems with that business all along. John wonders how he is going to break the news to Azina. He also wonders how many other customers might not pay. He had worked hard to put the credit control procedures that Bill had recommended into practice and it was depressing that this customer had slipped through the net. He realized that they would need to make allowance for the debtors who might not pay when they looked at the results for December.

Accounting time periods

Most businesses draw up reports at least once a year. Even if this were not sensible from a management point of view it would be needed to calculate tax liabilities, support loan applications or for some business forms, such as registered companies, it is a legal requirement. To run a business properly it is often advisable to draw up reports more regularly. A lot can happen in a year and management should not wait twelve months to make adjustments such as tightening credit control or reducing stock holdings. Monthly reporting is a reasonable and commonly adopted practice. Problems arise because business does not stop just because the owners would like to look at some information. Transactions can be part way through completion at the date chosen for the report. A product could have been ordered by a customer, or the order could have been processed but not yet sent, or sent but not invoiced, or invoiced but not yet paid for. Which time period should the sale be recorded in? Similar problems arise with expenses. Obviously it is important that a rule is adopted and consistently applied.

Accountants talk about the **realization principle** which treats income as realized or earned when:

1 it is reasonably certain to be received and
2 the amount which will be received is known with reasonable accuracy.

For most UK businesses this occurs when the goods have been despatched and the invoice issued. There is still the uncertainty for credit sales of whether the customer will actually pay or whether it will be lost through bad debts but this risk should be small and, as we shall see, can be provided against. The date the invoice is issued is the one which we have used for the recording system that we have set up for the case study.

Having decided when to record income, the timing of expenses follows automatically. Expenses will be allocated to the same time period as the income which that expense helped to create. This is known as the **matching or accruals principle** and is fundamental to the production of the financial statements. Accounts are assumed to be prepared under this concept unless it is specifically stated that they are not.

Matching expenses to revenue

As we have seen expenses are charged against the revenue which they help to produce. However expenses are not incurred within neat time periods or as revenue is earned.

They may:

1 be paid in advance;
2 be paid in arrears;
3 be paid as a lump sum and last for many years.

The accountant needs to exercise judgement to allocate the expense against the right income and therefore to the right period. We look at the first two situations in this chapter and the lump sum situation in the next chapter.

Prepayments

Expenses are sometimes paid in advance. A typical example would be insurance. Insurance is usually paid annually to cover the following twelve months. Unless the payment is made on the first day of the accounting year, part of the payment will relate to the next accounting period, i.e. it is a **prepayment**.

For example, consider property insurance costing £900 paid on 1 April of Year 1 for the following twelve months. Assuming an accounting year end of 31 December the cost will need to be split.

At 31 December Year 1 there will be:

1 a prepayment of £225
2 an expense for the year ended 31 December Year 1 of £675

This needs to be recorded in the AIS. The first step is to record the initial payment of the invoice for the insurance in the same way as any other invoice.

		£	£
Journal A			
1 April Yr1 Insurance	DR	900	
Bank	CR		900
Being the payment of the invoice			

The second step is more difficult and needs to be thought through in the light of the way in which your system operates.

The easiest way for a small manual system is merely to transfer to the profit and loss account the amount that is required as an expense. This leaves a balance on the expense account which would be picked up in the trial balance as a prepayment.

		£	£
31 December Yr1 Profit and loss account	DR	675	
Insurance	CR		675
Being the transfer of the insurance expense			

However, for a computerized system, this is unlikely to work with the reporting function. These systems automatically pick up the balances in the expense and income accounts to transfer the balances to the profit and loss account at the end of each period. This clears the accounts to record the following period's transactions. It would not be possible to leave the prepayment as an opening balance for the next period. The way to overcome this is to transfer the balance to a prepayment account in the current asset section of the balance sheet records and then reverse the record at the very beginning of the subsequent period. We will look first at the end result that we are trying to achieve using journal entries. Like most computer systems Sage has the ability to automatically adjust for accruals and prepayments once they are set up. It is important however that you understand what the automatic function should do.

First we need to transfer the prepayment and to do that the following journal needs to be put through:

		£	£
Journal B			
31 December Yr 1 Prepayments accounts	DR	225	
Insurance	CR		225
Being the portion of the insurance premium prepaid for Yr 2			

The system will then automatically transfer the remaining balance to the profit and loss account at the end of the time period.

		£	£
Journal C			
31 December Yr 1 Profit and loss	DR	675	
Insurance	CR		675
Being the transfer of the business expense			

The journal B then needs to be reversed immediately after the period end.

		£	£
Journal D			
1 January Yr 2 Insurance	DR	225	
Prepayments	CR		225
Being the reversal of the period end adjustment			

Looking at the result of this using T accounts might make this clearer.

Bank

	1 April Yr 1 Insurance (A)	900

Insurance

1 April Yr 1 Bank (A)	900	31 Dec Yr1 Prepayments (B)	225
		31 Dec Yr1 Profit and loss (C)	675
	900		900
1 Jan Yr 2 Prepayments (D)	225		

Prepayments

31 Dec Yr 1 Insurance (B)	225	31 Dec Yr 1 Balance c/d	225
1 Jan Yr 2 Balance B/d	225	1 Jan Yr 2 Insurance (D)	225

Profit and Loss account (Extract)

31 Dec Yr 1 Insurance (C)	675	

Accruals

Some expenses are paid in arrears, e.g. electricity or telephone. As with prepayments the date of the bill does not necessarily coincide with the accounting year end. To ensure that the correct expense is charged, it is usual to estimate the amount used to the accounting date. For example assume electricity is paid quarterly on 1 February, 1 May, 1 August and 1 November and the accounting year runs from 1 January to 31 December.

The electricity account in the nominal ledger stands at £990 at 31 December being the total of the bills paid in the year to date. At 31 December the company has used two months worth of electricity for which it has not been invoiced. First, it needs to estimate the amount used e.g. by reading the meter or by taking two-thirds of the previous quarter's bill.

In a similar way to the prepayments, the way in which the **accruals** are recorded depends on the AIS. We can use the Sage system, but first we will look at how to make the adjustments using journals. Then we will consider the automatic function.

Assuming the estimate is £345, a journal needs to be put through to record the estimated extra expense in the electricity account:

		£	£
Journal E			
31 December Yr 1 Electricity	DR	345	
Accruals	CR		345
Being the posting of the accrued electricity			

Then the system will automatically transfer the topped-up balance on the electricity account to the profit and loss account.

		£	£
Journal F			
31 December Yr 1 Profit and Loss Account	DR	1 335	
Electricity	CR		1 335
Being the transfer of the expense for the year			

With this system it will be necessary to reverse the journal at the beginning of the following time period.

		£	£
Journal G			
1 Jan Yr 2 Accruals	DR	345	
Electricity	CR		345
Being reversal of estimated accrual for year 1			

When the electricity bill finally arrives, it will be debited to the electricity account in the normal way. We will assume that the bill amounts to £432. Since the account already holds the credit figure of £345 from the previous year, the balance on the account will automatically be reduced by the amount charged in the previous time period leaving only the current year's expense in hand. Again, looking at the electricity record in T form will help make this clear.

Electricity

31 Dec Yr 1 Bank	990	31 Dec Yr 1 Profit and loss (F)	1 335
31 Dec Yr 1 Accruals (E)	345		
	1 335		1 335
1 Jan Yr 2 Bank	432	1 Jan Yr 2 Accruals (G)	345

Bank

		Year 1 Electricity	£990
		Jan Yr 2 Electricity	432

Accruals

1 Jan Yr 2 Electricity (G) £345	31 Dec Yr1 Electricity (E) £345

The effect of accruals and prepayments

As a business continues year by year, the accruals and prepayments need to be adjusted and readjusted each year. Once they have been set up, the effect on profit is not great unless the expense is changing significantly from year to year. This is because the prepayment or accrual adjustment will be made at the beginning and end of each period. Effectively unless the expense changes the opening adjustment will cancel the closing adjustment. This is as it should be. If, for example, a year's rent is £2000 then each year in which the property is rented for a full year should be charged £2000. It is only the first and last year of the agreement when the property may not be occupied for a full year that the charge should be different. Effectively that is what the use of the accruals and prepayments adjustments has achieved.

Accruals and prepayments for the average ongoing expense will not normally affect profit significantly. For this reason while the adjustments should be made, it is not worth spending time on achieving complete accuracy. An estimate will do. So for example taking one third of a bill which finally comes in for a three month period rather than trying to work out exactly how much related to the first month and how much to subsequent months will be quite sufficient. Another way is to take the previous year's bill adding a percentage for estimated price increases. However, be aware that new or one-off expenses need to be looked out for. It is these which have the potential to affect profit more substantially.

Once established the AIS can be programmed to set up and reverse the accruals and prepayment figures at the beginning and end of each accounting period.

Activity

1   You should now be able to make the adjustments to the case study for the accruals and prepayments which John identified. You should do this before moving to the next section. (You should not go back and alter November's figures to take account of the accruals and prepayments noted by John. Where you wrote off expenses in total for the previous month leave them as if they had been correctly processed). You will need to check through the December transactions for the insurance policies paid in December. Don't forget to back up your disks after the entries are complete.

Unpaid and suspect debts

In Chapter 8 we looked at the importance of managing the credit given to customers. However well the credit control department works, there will be times when a debt remains unpaid. A decision eventually has to be made whether it is worth the time and expense of continuing the attempts to collect or whether to write off the debt and get on with more productive work.

Unpaid debts

When a debt is written off, it is taken out of the sales ledger and put in a '**bad debts written off**' account which should be opened in the expense section of the nominal ledger. This means that the debtors control account will be reduced by the amount of the bad debt. The posting has to be done through the sales ledger in order for the individual debtors account to be corrected. VAT also needs to be considered. When a debt is bad, the business has not actually collected the output VAT which it has recorded. Provided the debt is bad, the VAT can be reclaimed by treating it as input tax. In summary then you need to make the following entries.

Account		Amount
Sales ledger		
Individual debtor's account	CR	Gross amount
Nominal ledger		
Bad debts written off	DR	Net amount
VAT	DR	Tax
Debtors control account	CR	Gross Amount

For example writing off a bad debt of £1000.00 net of VAT owed by customer X.

Sales ledger

<table>
<tr><th colspan="4">Customer X</th></tr>
<tr><td>Balance b/f</td><td>1 175.00</td><td>31 Dec Bad debt written off</td><td>£1 000.00</td></tr>
<tr><td></td><td>_____</td><td>31 Dec VAT</td><td>175.00</td></tr>
<tr><td></td><td>£1 175.00</td><td></td><td>£1 175.00</td></tr>
</table>

Nominal ledger

<table>
<tr><th colspan="2">Bad debts written off</th><th></th></tr>
<tr><td>31 Dec Debtors control</td><td>1 000.00</td><td></td></tr>
</table>

<table>
<tr><th colspan="2">VAT</th><th></th></tr>
<tr><td>31 Dec Debtors control</td><td>175.00</td><td></td></tr>
</table>

<table>
<tr><th colspan="3">Debtors control account</th></tr>
<tr><td></td><td>31 Dec Bad debts</td><td>1 175.00</td></tr>
</table>

The adjustments needed can be achieved in Sage through the sales ledger/batched data entry/credit note routine by posting a credit item for the full amount of the debt through the credit postings. Nominate the bad debts account for the nominal code when asked rather than sales returns. You can check the nominal ledger to make sure you have achieved the effect you expected. Alternatively there is a bad debt routine which does the job for you but it is good practice to try both methods and look at the results to make sure you realize the effect that you have on the underlying records. If you just use the routine you may not understand what you are doing and it will be difficult to undo any errors made.

Doubtful debts

A more difficult situation arises at the year end. Experience shows that a proportion of the debtors owing at the year end will eventually not pay, creating what are known as **doubtful debts**. The reasons might be financial problems or just a disputed bill. Either way the 'matching' principle we have been discussing means that we need to take account of the fact that some of the income earned in the period will not actually be received. This is done by creating a **provision for doubtful debts**.

It is different to the situation of a bad debt which we knew would not be received and which could actually be identified. The bad debt was taken out of the records altogether. The doubtful debt is provided for in the nominal ledger with no adjustment to the sales ledger or the debtors control account. The first step is to decide on the amount of provision that is needed. There is no set formula for this. It is matter of professional judgement based on the evidence to hand. A good place to start is the age analysis of debtors which you should print out from the sales ledger. It is undoubtedly true that the older a debt is the less likely it is to be collected. Experience will dictate the cut off period, but anything outstanding a month or more after the credit period which was agreed should be suspect and similarly any item left from earlier periods on an otherwise well managed customer account. A consideration of the proportion of last year's debts which proved to be bad after the year end will give some idea of the percentage of the current debtors balance which might need to be provided for. Check this information against the knowledge of current trading conditions available from the credit control department before making a final decision. A typical decision would be to provide for all debts older than a particular age and for a percentage, say 2 per cent, of all other debts.

Activity

2   Looking at the case study for Bale and Co., they have a particular problem in setting their provision because they have no experience from previous years to fall back on and as they have only just started, an aged debtors analysis does not exist. All debtors arose in the previous month.
    Required
    How would you decide on a method of making provision for Bale and Co.? Make a decision and an estimate of the amount of provision that results from your decision.

In practice you may use the experience of others in the trade and, as the debtors ledger is very small, look at each debtor deciding, from personal knowledge, which could be doubtful.

The next step is to set the provision up. As the sales ledger and control account are not altered, the record can be made by journal in the nominal ledger. If this is the first period for which a provision has been set up then the journal is straightforward. You will need two new accounts. One account will be in the expenses and called 'change in provision for doubtful debts'. The other will be in the balance sheet section next to the debtors and will be named 'provision for doubtful debts' account.

Change in provision for doubtful debts	DR	Full provision required
Provision for doubtful debts	CR	Full provision required

In the end of period statements, the balance on the change in provision account is transferred to the profit and loss account as an expense reducing the account balance to zero. The provision for doubtful debts account is shown deducted from the debtors in the balance sheet and will form part of the opening trial balance for the next period.

In subsequent periods, it is only the change in the required provision that needs to be adjusted in the journal. For example, assume that it was decided in year 1 that a provision of £30 000 was needed.

Period 1

Provision for doubtful debts

	31 Dec Yr 1 Change in provision 30 000

Change in provision for doubtful debts

31 Dec Yr 1 Doubtful debts £30 000	31 Dec Yr 1 Profit and loss £30 000

In period 2 a review of the sales ledger suggests that a provision of £35 000 is now needed. This time the journal will be:

Change in provision for doubtful debts	DR	£5 000
Provision for doubtful debts	CR	£5 000

The expense on the profit and loss account will be just this difference needed to 'top up' the provision to the amount required. The balance in the balance sheet will be £35 000. These new journal entries need to be put through in period 2 as illustrated below:

Period 2

Provision for doubtful debts

	31 Dec Yr 1 Change in provision 30 000
31 Dec Balance c/f 35 000	31 Dec Yr 2 Change in provision 5 000
35 000	35 500
	31 Dec Yr 2 Balance b/f 35 000

Change in provision for doubtful debts

| 31 Dec Yr 1 Doubtful debts | 30 000 | 31 Dec Yr 1 Profit and loss | 30 000 |
| 31 Dec Yr 2 Doubtful debts | 5 000 | 31 Dec Yr 2 Profit and loss | 5 000 |

If the provision required was less than the current balance the change will be a credit item (a negative expense) and the provision in the balance sheet would be reduced by a debit entry to the new smaller balance.

Companies differ in their treatment of the provision once set up. Some companies use it to write off the bad debts in the subsequent period so that bad debts are not recorded unless the bad debts exceed the provision. Others leave the provision intact preferring to write off the bad debts as they come to light. The total charge to the profit and loss should be the same which ever method is chosen. Now you are ready to make the adjustments for Bale and Co.

Activity

3   Using the information in the case study and your backup disks of the system so far, make the provision for doubtful debts and write off the bad debt for customer 1 in the Sage system.
   Required
   (a) Set up the accounts you need in the nominal ledger.
   (b) Write off the bad debt through the sales ledger.
   (c) Put through the journal you need to record the provision you decided was needed for doubtful debts.
   (d) Print off the trial balance and check that the effect is as you expect.

Summary

This chapter has looked at the way accountants divide up a business' life into time periods and some of the problems that this presents for producing information on performance. The realization and matching principles were used to decide when income would be recognized and expenses charged. To action this in the AIS requires accruals and prepayments to be set up through the journal. Finally we looked at the need to provide for income which experience says might not be received in the form of provisions for doubtful debts.

The use of artificial time periods presents other problems. One of these is how to spread the cost of an asset purchased for use over a number of time periods. The next chapter will look at this.

Key words

accruals p. 189 • bad debts p. 191 • doubtful debts p. 193 • matching principle p. 186 • prepayments p. 187 • provision for doubtful debts p. 193 • realization principle p. 186

Practice questions

1   Jamilla's accounting year ends on 31 March. On 1 June in year 1 she took out an insurance policy, paying an annual premium of £120. On 1 October she started a further policy and paid the annual premium of £600.
    (i)   How would this be treated in the accounts for year 1?
    (ii) How would insurance be dealt with in the accounts for year 2 ?

2   Jamilla pays rent quarterly on 30 April, 31 July, 31 October and 31 January in arrears. The quarterly payment is for £600. For any accounting year, how much is:
    (i)   the payment
    (ii) the expense
    (iii) the balance sheet figure

3   After several years Jamilla sublets a room in the premises for a quarterly rent of £160. The rent is payable in arrears on the same date as given in 2. The tenancy commences on 1 August Year 6. How much revenue is earned for Year 6/7 and what balance would appear in the balance sheet?

4   Jamilla made the following payments. Indicate how much is an expense of the year 19X1 (the first year) and how much for the next year.
    (i)   Computer equipment purchased April 19X1 and expected to last five years – £4800.
    (ii) Insurance for equipment taken out on 1st October 19X1 for the following 12 months – £360.
    (iii) Rent of premises paid annually in advance on 1st December 19X1 – £1440.
    (iv) Stationery purchased on 28 February 19X2, one third of which is still in stock at the year end – £168.
    (v)   A special advertising campaign to launch a new product. The campaign was held in January and February 19X2 but the effect on sales is estimated to continue until September 19X2. The product was launched on 1st March 19X2. Cost £18 000.

5   Complete the following table:

	Opening balance (£)	Cash paid (£)	Expense (£)	Closing balance (£)
Goods for resale	3 000DR	75 000		£6 000DR
Furniture to last 10 yrs – no scrap value	–	42 000		
Wages	12 000CR	39 000		1 000CR
Insurance	700DR		2 000	900DR
Rent payable	6 000CR	2 000	2 000	
Vehicle running costs	–	7 400		900CR

6   The following trial balance was extracted from the books of Sandros, a sole trader, at the close of business on 31 January 1996:

	DR (£)	CR (£)
Debtors and creditors	9 660	4 960
Wages and salaries	6 980	
Rates and insurance	1 260	
Drawings	3 240	
Capital account		5 420
Purchases and sales	17 480	37 380
Delivery van	2 400	
Depreciation on van 1/2/95		600
Bad debts written off	1 040	
Cash in hand	80	
Stock at 1 February 1995	4 140	
Rent	3 300	
Fixtures and fittings	1 400	
Depreciation on fixtures 1/2/95		140
Discounts	760	480
Van running expenses	1 220	
Provision for bad and doubtful debts		360
General office expenses	580	
Bank overdraft		4 200
	53 540	53 540

The following information should also be taken into account:
(i) rates prepaid at 31 January 1996 £140;
(ii) stock at 31 January 1996 of £3900;
(iii) rent prepaid at 31 January 1996 – £300;
(iv) wages and salaries accrued at 31 January 1996 of £320;
(v) provision for depreciation should be made as follows:

fixtures and fittings 10% of cost,

van 25% of cost;

(vi) The provision for doubtful debts is to be increased to £460.
Required
Prepare the trading and profit and loss accounts for the year ended 31 January 1996 and the balance sheet at that date.

7 At the end of year 1, Down and Out Ltd had a debtors balance of £53 256. They identified bad debts amounting to £4354 included in that balance. In addition to recording these, they decided to set up a provision for doubtful debts amounting to 3 per cent of the remaining debtors.
In year 2, a debt of £1078 proves to be bad and is written off. At the year end, it is decided to set a provision of 4 per cent of the year end debtor balance of £68 921.
Required
Using a manual system and T accounts, open a bad debts account, a doubtful debts account and a change in doubtful debts account and write up the entries needed to record the above decisions first for assumption (a) below and then for assumption (b):

(a) that the bad debt in year 2 is written off against the doubtful debts provision rather than as a separate expense in the profit and loss account;

(b) that the bad debt is written off separately leaving the provision from year 1 intact

12 Depreciation

Learning objectives

After reading this chapter you should:
- appreciate the meaning of the accounting concept of depreciation
- be aware of the need to exercise professional judgement to arrive at the estimate of the depreciation provision
- be familiar with the operation of the main methods or bases used by accountants to calculate depreciation
- be able to make the necessary adjustments in the accounting records to record the depreciation provisions required by an organization
- be aware of particular difficulties surrounding some classes of fixed asset, e.g. the arguments surrounding the depreciation of property and other appreciating assets.

Introduction

The last chapter looked at the need to prepare accounting reports for arbitrary time periods and some of the problems this presented for accountants. One of these problems relates to fixed assets. These assets will be used in the business for more than one accounting period but most of them will not last for ever. Accountants therefore need to devise a means of spreading the cost of these assets over the accounting periods to which they relate. There are some problems in doing this. When an asset is bought there is no means of knowing how long the asset will be useful in the business or how long it will last. How can the contribution it is estimated to make be measured? What happens if the estimate turns out to be wrong? Does it make a difference if the asset is appreciating in value rather than reducing? This chapter will look at the nature of depreciation and the methods which accountants have devised to overcome the problems.

Bale and Co. have purchased a number of fixed assets and at the end of the first month's trading they just accepted the fact that since they still owned the assets they were properly disclosed in the balance sheet at the original cost. Now that Amina has had more time to look at the figures, she realised that this needs some more thought.

'We've bought all this furniture and equipment but it will not last forever. I know we should be charging depreciation to account for the use we have made of them but I don't know how to go about working out how much is involved or how to record it. Then there's the shop. Do we need to make a charge for using that?'

John didn't know what depreciation meant but agreed that it seemed reasonable they should make some charge for the assets they were using when they calculated the profit. He was not so sure about the building however.

'I hope that the property will be worth a bit more in a few years time,' he said, 'It should give us a nice lump sum when we retire!'

Azina had another look at the accounts. As far as she could tell the fixed assets included:

Shop	£100 000.00
Carpets	1 280.60
Desks, chairs and office furniture	4 631.20
Second-hand shop equipment	1 558.32
Computer purchased in December	2 483.00
Vehicle	6 000.00

She knew how much they had cost the business but what were they worth now? And did it matter what they were worth? Azina had heard the term depreciation used in class but in the example used she had been told how long the asset was going to last and what it would be sold for at the end of its life. It was a bit different when you had to decide all this for yourself. She decided to read the notes she had made in class and then go and see her tutor for some advice.

What is 'depreciation'?

When a fixed asset is purchased it is recorded as a debit entry in the asset account and a credit either to the bank or to creditors if credit terms have been agreed. The asset is to be a source of future benefit to the organization and will appear in the balance sheet. However the ability of the asset to contribute to the business is unlikely to last for ever. There are assets which are considered to have an infinite life, such as land. Most other assets, such as cars, machinery, vans, buildings, etc., all have a finite life. They will not last forever and therefore they will eventually have no future value to the business. It is sometimes said that the asset is 'used up' through its contribution to the organization, but it can become valueless even if it remains unused or at least not used to capacity due perhaps to technological change, deterioration, damage or changing markets and fashions. **Depreciation** is the term accountants use to describe this loss of value.

The accountant uses professional judgement based on the facts available and using generally accepted accounting principles to come to a best 'guess' of the likely outcome. As with all guesses they are unlikely to prove to be accurate with the benefit of hindsight. Making no estimate would mean that the reports and database do not reflect reality and this could be more misleading than including an estimated figure. Depreciating assets is one of those cases where an estimate is necessary.

Accountants try to spread the cost of an asset over the accounting periods to which it makes a contribution. The estimated contribution to any period will be charged against the profit as a depreciation expense. The same amount will be treated as a provision for depreciation in the balance sheet and shown as a deduction from the cost of the asset. The difference between the cost and the depreciation represents the unallocated cost of the asset which the organisation hopes will contribute to the profit of future periods.

So far the market value of the asset has not been mentioned. This is deliberate. The idea of depreciation is to allocate the cost incurred by the business in acquiring the asset. Unless the asset is about to be scrapped, the market value is of no relevance. The figures for fixed assets given in the balance sheet do not reflect a market value. They are the unallocated costs incurred by the business. If an organization buys a new car, the car will lose in market value as soon as it is driven out of the showroom by virtue of the fact that it has had one owner. This reduction in market value is not relevant for the purposes of accounting depreciation because the intention is to keep and use the car for business purposes. The cost of the car will be depreciated over its life and that depreciation will be calculated in such a way as to reflect, as far as possible, the contribution that it will make. The market value will only become important when the decision is taken to sell the car.

Importance

Although it is an estimated figure, depreciation is important. For many businesses the value of fixed assets is such that not only do they dominate the balance sheet but the charge for their use in the profit and loss account can make a big difference to the profit figure. Table 12 .1 gives some examples of the fixed asset values and depreciation charges taken from the reports of UK public companies in different industry sectors and shown as a percentage of balance sheet total assets and of profit before interest and tax. It is therefore important that the calculation is done with care and that the best available information is used as a basis for this calculation.

Value to be depreciated

The cost of an asset includes not just the invoiced cost but also any delivery and installation costs incurred to get the asset to a position and state in which it can

Table 12.1 Table showing the importance of depreciation

Company Accounts for 1997	Depreciation as % of profit before interest and tax	Fixed assets as % of gross assets
Sainsbury plc	30	83
Hyder plc	27	81

contribute to the organization. This amount can be added to if the asset is substantially updated at a later date. For example if a machine has a more powerful engine installed or a computer has new drives added or extra RAM these extra costs will also be treated as part of the cost and will be depreciated in the same way as the original asset.

The depreciation to be charged in any period must be estimated. The asset is an asset because it will make a future contribution. The extent of this contribution in terms of time and/or value needs to be assessed in order that it can be allocated to the relevant accounting periods. This can be a case of crystal ball gazing.

Take the example of a new PC. A lot of time and trouble will have gone into deciding on the most suitable model to ensure compatibility, capacity, ability to cope with the required software and drive the needed peripherals, all within the available budget. Let us say that the PC which is chosen costs £2520.00. The accountant now needs to estimate how long the PC will remain useful to the organization. This involves not just wear and tear but also technical needs and innovations which might make the PC obsolete even though it looks as good as new. The estimate of useful life might be anything from one year to four or five. Will the PC have any value left at the end of this estimated life? There is a second-hand market for PCs but a lot will depend on how long the PC is kept. The accountant will need to come to a decision which reflects the intentions of the business regarding its IT strategy, the market prices available for used PCs and any manufacturers specifications. Past experience will also come into play. Sometimes other organizations' experience can help. In the examples which follow a life of three years with a scrap value of £100 at the end of that time have been assumed for the PC. It is very unlikely that this estimate will prove to be accurate. Forecasts of the future rarely are.

Activity

1   Try some crystal ball gazing for yourself. For each of the assets which the Bales have purchased try to decide on a suitable length of life. What sources of information might be available which would help Azina come to a reasonable decision?

Methods

Having worked out how much is to be charged against profit during the asset's lifetime, the next decision is how to spread the total through the accounting periods to which the asset contributes. In a perfect world a method which reflected the pattern of contribution made by the particular asset would be used. Accountants have developed a number of rule of thumb methods which can be used to allocate the cost. Each makes different assumptions about the pattern of contribution which the asset makes to the business. The accountant selects the method of **allocation** which best suits the pattern of contribution made by the asset.

Three of the most common methods are straight line, reducing balance and unit of production. These are looked at in detail below.

Straight line

The **straight line** method assumes that the asset makes an equal contribution to each accounting period. Once the life of the asset is chosen and the scrap value estimated the rest of the calculation is straight forward. Taking the example of the PC, the cost of £2520 less the amount it is hoped to recover as scrap value £100, will leave £2420 to be spread over the three accounting periods which it is hoped the asset will contribute to. Using the straight line method the amount is simply divided by the time to give:

£2420/3 i.e. £807 to the nearest pound

Note that rounding to the nearest pound is more than accurate enough. Depreciation is an estimate. Do not become involved in too great a degree of calculation accuracy with figures which are only best estimates.

The amount of £807 will be charged as an expense in each of the three accounting periods. The pattern of the expense charge and the net value of the asset in the balance sheet is shown in Figure 12.1.

The straight line method is particularly useful for assets which make a contribution which relates to time elapsed, e.g. leasehold properties which permit the lessee to occupy the property for a set period. The lessee will obtain the same benefit of accommodation each week, month or year. The pattern of charge produced by the straight line method reflects the contribution the asset makes to the organization.

Reducing balance

Under the **reducing balance** method the asset is assumed to contribute less to the business as it ages. Thus the charge for depreciation is highest in the early years and diminishes as the asset reduces in usefulness. To achieve this the method requires a set percentage to be written off the remaining balance sheet value in each accounting period. The percentage needs to be worked out at the amount which will reduce the

Figure 12.1
Pattern of depreciation charge and net book value for the PC using the straight line method of depreciation

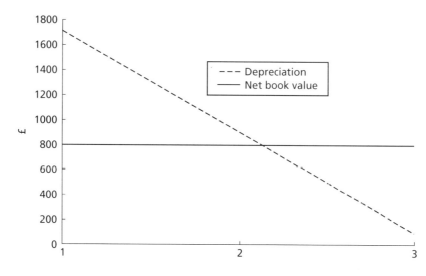

cost to the estimated scrap value over the estimated useful life. There is a formula for calculating this:

$$r = 1 - n\sqrt{\frac{s}{x}}$$

where r is the percentage expressed as a decimal that will be used to calculate the charge;

> n is the estimated life;
> s is the estimated scrap value;
> x is the value to be depreciated.

Using the figures from the example:

$$r = 1 - 3\sqrt{\frac{100}{2520}}$$

This gives a rate of approximately 0.65 or 65 per cent. Using this the amounts to be charged will be:

Depreciation charged:	Balance in balance sheet:
Year 1 £2 520 × 0.65 = £1 638	£2 520 − 1 638 = 882
Year 2 £882 × 0.65 = 573	882 − 573 = 309
Year 3 £309 × 0.65 = 200	309 − 200 = 109

The charge decreases dramatically from the first year, as does the value of the asset shown at the end of year one. Figure 12.2 shows the pattern of the depreciation charge and the asset value over the estimated life.

The reducing balance method is useful for assets where the benefits are received in the early years and performance or contribution falls off over time. This might be the

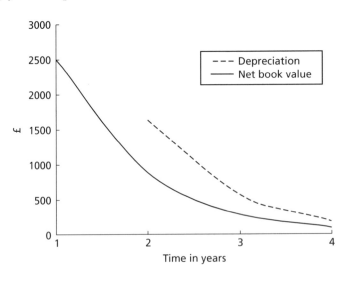

Figure 12.2
Pattern of depreciation charge and net book value for the PC using the reducing balance method of depreciation

case for computer equipment which soon becomes out of date or assets used in the production of fashion items.

Unit of production

Under the unit of production method an estimate is made of the total capacity of the asset using some physical measure of output e.g. the number of hours which a machine can be used for or the estimated total of reserves in a mine or oil well. The cost of the asset is then depreciated according to the measured output in each accounting period. Assume that an estimate is made that the PC will have an output of 3500 hours in total throughout its life. The hours of use in year 1 turn out to amount to 1400. Then 1400/3500 × 2420 will be allocated to depreciation in year 1, i.e. £968. If in year 2 the hours amounted to 1200 but in year 3 due to new technology being made available the hours fall to 400 then depreciation will have been charged as follows:

	£
Year 1	968
Year 2	830
Year 3	277
	£2 075

This means a shortfall of £345 from the estimate. This will be accounted for as a loss when the asset is disposed of. The pattern of depreciation and the balance of value in the balance sheet will depend solely on the use made of the asset and can take any profile. The pattern for the PC we are using here is shown in Figure 12.3.

The unit of production method used to be favoured for mineral reserves since such assets will only be of value when extracted. The owner can choose to wait indefinitely to do this without any deterioration of the asset. The first two methods would be inappropriate for such assets. The use of the method for other classes of fixed asset depends upon the ease of obtaining the necessary data on a period's output. The

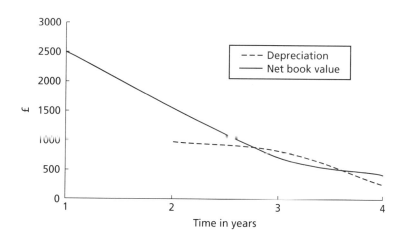

Figure 12.3
Pattern of depreciation charge and net book value for the PC using the unit of production method

method has been used for aeroplanes, for example, where the number of hours flying time is logged.

Which method?

The method should be chosen to reflect as far as possible the pattern of contribution which the asset makes to the organization. However it must be remembered that the figures are based on estimates and judgements about future circumstances. The depreciation provision is a provision because it is an estimate. As such the cost and difficulty of using theoretically superior but time consuming and costly methods of calculation needs to be weighed against the in-built inaccuracy of the data being used. Most businesses select one of the above methods as a best fit for the particular class of asset.

Activity

2   Which method or methods would you advise Azina and John to use for their fixed assets?

Recording the depreciation

Once the estimates are made, the problem is to record them in the system. The first step is to decide when the asset will start to be depreciated. It is unlikely that all fixed assets will be purchased and brought into use on the first day of the accounting period. The purchases will be spread throughout the period. Most organizations make an arbitrary decision on how this will be handled. The choices vary but include the following:

1   no depreciation in the first period;
2   a full period's depreciation in the period in which the asset was acquired regardless of how early or late that was;
3   depreciate assets from the beginning of the month in which they were acquired;
4   depreciate assets from the end of the month in which they were acquired.

The point is to adopt a policy and apply it consistently. Even where accounting reports are produced on a more regular basis, it is normal to decide on depreciation for the next accounting year and not to review or make adjustments other than for acquisitions or disposals until the following year end.

For smaller businesses with limited numbers of fixed assets, the records can be kept adequately in the nominal ledger. In this case, new accounts need to be created to record:

1   the amount of the expense each period, located and coded with the other expense accounts;
2   the accumulated provision to be shown as a deduction from the asset account in the balance sheet.

Each class of asset will need to have its own accumulated charge or **accumulated**

depreciation account and this should be coded next to the asset itself so that the two accounts can be shown in the balance sheet together.

It is possible to use a global expense account to record all the depreciation charges or the period for all classes of asset. If this method is adopted it is not as easy to distinguish which class of asset creates the greatest expense for the business. It is sometimes useful to give different figures for different departments or branches to reflect the greater use of assets by some areas of the business. However it is important to realize that this depreciation is not as easy to interpret as other expenses. The amount will vary depending upon the method used and the age of the asset. A department might look as if it is intensive in its use of assets when in fact the figures merely reflect a new asset which has been depreciated using the reducing balance method.

The entry should be authorized by a senior accountant and put through the journal. Using the example of the PC with the straight line method:

		£	£
Year 1			
Depreciation expense account	DR	807	
Accumulated depreciation	CR		807

The depreciation expense is written off or closed to the profit and loss account

		£	£
Year 2			
Depreciation expense account	DR	807	
Accumulated depreciation	CR		807

Again the expense account is written off to the profit and loss account

		£	£
Year 3			
Depreciation expense account	DR	807	
Accumulated depreciation	CR		807

The 'T' accounts would look as follows:

Accumulated depreciation

	Year 1 Depreciation expense 807
	Year 2 Depreciation expense 807
	Year 3 Depreciation expense 807

Depreciation expense

Year 1 Accumulated depreciation 807	Year 1 Profit and loss account 807
Year 2 Accumulated depreciation 807	Year 2 Profit and loss account 807
Year 3 Accumulated depreciation 807	Year 3 Profit and loss account 807

The asset in the balance sheet is shown as follows:

Year 1	£
At cost	2 520
less accumulated depreciation	807
Net book value	1 713

Year 2	£
At cost	2 520
less accumulated depreciation	1 614
Net book value	906

Year 3	£
At cost	2 520
less accumulated depreciation	2 421
Net book value	99

Activity

3   Using your own estimate of the length of life and the method you have selected, draft the journal entries necessary to record the depreciation for Bale and Co. for December. Remember that this will be just one month, not a full year's charge. Create the necessary new nominal accounts to make the entries and post the entries to the system.

Fixed assets register

For larger businesses, or those with a number of fixed assets, a fixed asset register can be maintained as a supplement to the nominal accounts. In some ways this operates in a similar fashion to a control account for debtors and creditors. It is effectively a detailed record of each fixed asset acquired. The individual records can give identifying details such as machine number, location and custodian and can also be tied in with maintenance, service and insurance needs. Such a register not only assists in the management of the assets, it also acts as a security control. Periodically it makes sense to do a physical check of the register to ensure that the assets do actually exist. This can be combined with a check on condition and expected life reviews.

The register can take many forms including hard copy, e.g. as a card index, but as an integral part of the system it makes sense if it forms part of the computerized system and is compatible with the financial records. However it is recorded, the need for accumulated depreciation accounts for each class of fixed asset and depreciation expense accounts remains the same as for the small business.

Disposing of the asset

Eventually the decision will be made to dispose of or scrap the asset. This should be authorized by a senior manager designated for the role. It is important that the ability to dispose of an asset and to record that disposal are authorized by someone in authority. The scope for theft if this does not happen is wide. The asset needs to be removed from the records together with the accumulated depreciation. If the asset is scrapped or sold the sum received needs to be recorded. It is only at this stage, by comparing the net book value with the amount received, that the business can tell whether the depreciation charged was reasonable or whether it was an over- or under-estimate.

The recording steps are as follows.

1   Another new account is opened in the records to record the asset disposal.
2   The asset account is closed through the journal by transferring the balance to the disposal account.
3   The accumulated depreciation account is closed through the journal and transferred to the disposal account.
4   The proceeds received on disposal are credited to the disposal account normally from the cash or bank account. Where the asset was taken in part exchange for another the allowance will need to be transferred by journal from the new asset account.

Assuming that the PC is sold for cash of £50 at the end of year 3 the records would look as follows:

Cash in hand (extracts)

Year 3 Disposal account	50	

Disposal Account

Year 3 PC at cost	2 520	Year 3 Accumulated depreciation	2 421
		Year 3 Cash	50
		Year 3 Profit and loss account	49
	2 520		2 520

The amount of £49 transferred to the profit and loss account is the balancing figure and represents a loss due to under depreciation of the asset over the three years. If an amount of £150 had been received from selling the PC then a 'profit' of £51 would have been credited to the profit and loss account representing over depreciation charged in earlier years.

What if the estimates prove to be wrong?

In reality there is invariably a profit or loss on the sale of an asset. It is not possible to predict with accuracy the timing of disposal and final scrap value of an item. Matters do become clearer as the asset progresses through its life. For this reason organizations are required to review the estimates of the life of the assets each year, to see whether changing circumstances and experience indicate that a changed estimate is necessary. Note that the method of depreciation should not be changed, but the length of life or estimated capacity and scrap values can and will change. Where this happens earlier years remain unchanged on the grounds that they represented the best estimate at the time they were made. The remaining book value is depreciated using the chosen method over the new estimation of life and scrap value. This may result in an increase or a decrease in the annual depreciation charge. This review is necessary for accounts to reflect contemporary conditions but can lend itself to abuse. The amounts involved are material to the accounts and a different judgement makes a substantial difference to the reported results.

What if the value of the asset appreciates?

The requirement is that all fixed assets with a finite life should be depreciated. This includes buildings although not the site on which they are constructed. This requirement is a matter of some controversy. Buildings are often held as investments for the sale of the capital gain that they will make if property prices rise. Where this happens the owners argue that depreciation is not necessary and in fact ignores the realities of the operation of the business. For investment businesses this has been accepted.

However, if the asset is being used, e.g. as an hotel or a retail premises, then depreciation reflects the fact that the building will eventually reach the end of its life. Given the value of these properties, the depreciation charge, even assuming a life of 50 to 100 years, is likely to be substantial. It is argued that where the property is kept in a good state of repair or constantly refurbished, depreciation is not necessary. This misunderstands the nature of depreciation in accounting. Although the market price may be increasing (or decreasing) it is not the intention of depreciation to adjust the carrying net book value in the accounting records to reflect market value. It is a device to allocate the cost over the useful life. The body setting professional standards argues that however well maintained no ordinary building will last forever. Best practice requires that the asset is broken down into its components, i.e. site – which will not be depreciated because it is deemed to have an infinite life; structure – which could have a long life of 50 years or more; and fittings such as heating systems, facades and lifts – each of which will need to be assessed separately for estimated life span.

Summary

This chapter has introduced the term depreciation and looked at ways in which it can be estimated. Three of the most common methods of calculation found in practice have been illustrated and compared. Depreciation is a material item for many organizations and the basis of estimation and the implications this has for the reports which will be drawn from the data prepared in this way cannot be over emphasized. You need to be aware of the effect that your judgement about life and your choice of method will have.

The principles introduced for recording the provision and charge for depreciation are similar for most organizations.

Key words

Practice questions

1 Hensman purchased a new machine at a cost of £145 000 at the beginning of the current trading year. The brochure from the company who supplied the machine suggested that it should be able to perform well for 10 000 hours of work. At that stage the machine would have a scrap value estimated at £5000. Hensman has used the machine for 3000 hours in the current year but estimates that the use will reduce in the next three years by 500 hours per year. Hensman has planned that it will be in use for four years in total (including the year just completed) but the product that it contributes to is subject to technical change and it is possible that the market will collapse in a further two years. If the machine is scrapped at the end of a further two years the value will be £50 000, but if it is scrapped in three years time that figure will fall to £5000.

Required

Calculate the depreciation on the machine to be charged by Hensman in years 1, 2 and 3 making any necessary assumptions using the:

(a) unit of production method

(b) straight line method

(c) reducing balance method.

State the assumptions you make and the reason for making them.

Which method would you consider the most suitable for this asset?

2 Little and Co. purchased equipment from a new supplier for a list price of £408 000. VAT at 17.5 per cent was charged on this amount. A haulage company charged £2000 to transport the equipment to Little and Co.'s premises and the fitters charged £7400 for installation and setting up. The equipment was insured at a premium of £750.

Required

What amount should Little and Co. include in its fixed assets?

3 During a trading year, Arch disposed of the following items:

(i) Machine A which had cost £12 000 but had been depreciated by £10 000 was given to a local scrap dealer for nothing.

(ii) A fork lift truck which had cost £25 000, accumulated depreciation £15 000 was traded in for a new model with a list price of £32 000. The trade-in allowance was £7000, the balance being paid in cash.

(iii) Machine B with an original cost of £8000 which had been depreciated by £7200 was sold for £1500.

Required

Prepare journal entries and draft T accounts to explain how these items should be recorded in the records of Arch.

13 Financial statements of unincorporated businesses and accounting policies

Learning objectives

After reading this chapter you should be able to:
- produce the profit and loss account for an accounting period and the balance sheet in a form suitable for internal use by managers and including the period end adjustments
- understand the implications for the statements of operating as a partnership as opposed to a sole trader
- recognize the underlying concepts and assumptions on which the statements are based
- appreciate the need for a note to be attached to the statements outlining the accounting policies
- draft a suitable accounting policies note.

Introduction

Earlier chapters have looked at how an organization keeps the records to form the database from which information can be drawn for management purposes. To make decisions the management will need to summarize and organize the information into meaningful reports. The profit and loss account and the balance sheet were introduced in Chapter 7. This chapter builds on those ideas, incorporating the adjustments due to the need to allocate transactions to artificial time periods which were discussed in the last three chapters. Together with the adjustments for stock in hand at the end of the time period, they enable a fully accruals based income report to be produced with its supporting balance sheet. We look at the changes needed to produce statements for a partnership as opposed to a sole trader. Once the regular reporting time periods have been chosen and the adjustments organized, the next problem is to set up the standard format for the required reports. In this way the reports will be produced automatically each time they are required enabling the accountant to concentrate on any changes in the period and to interpret the results.

The information for December should now all have been posted to the system and the adjustments for accruals, prepayments, doubtful debts and depreciation should have been made. The end of the month has come and it is time to run off the end of the month statements to see how the business is performing. The amount of work has increased. Although they had planned that Azina would continue in work for at least the first year, this needs to be thought through again. The work involved in the accounting and administrative function, not to mention minding the shop while John is out means that they need to consider bringing in Azina full time as an equal partner. This would mean altering the form of the owner's capital in the statements but make no difference to the underlying business accounts.

Time periods

Time periods for management purposes can be any length. Some organizations manage with just annual reports. This is quite dangerous. Most businesses need to know how matters are progressing more regularly than this. In a year a lot can go wrong and an owner might not notice a small decrease in the number of customers coming through the shop door, or how a slight increase in each of the bills arriving in the post is building up into a fall in profits for the year. For most businesses a monthly set of detailed reports is about right to keep an eye on what is happening while keeping the time needed for preparation and interpretation to reasonable levels. Bale and Co. adopts this period for the management reports.

Designing standard reports

If the information in the reports is to be useful it is important that it is organized in a standard format. This will make it easier to compare the results over time and trace what is happening to a particular expense or asset for example. It is also important that the results are organized in a way that has some logic to the order. This makes it easier to read and to compare the results of the organization with others. Most computerized recording systems will allow the user to set up standard formats. Usually they permit the user to set up several versions so that they can be used for different purposes.

The reports prepared for managers should be quite detailed and most businesses would not want that amount of information to become available to people outside the business. In any case many investors not involved in the day-to-day running of the business would not want that level of detail and would find a summarized version far more useful. In this chapter we look at designing a report for owner managers, whether sole trader or partnership. We will use the formats introduced in Chapter 7 to present the profit and loss account and balance sheet. In Chapter 16 we will look at the formats required by law for the published statements of companies.

Producing the statements from a template

An integrated computerized system should be capable of producing a range of reports to meet different needs.

The Sage system holds financial information in a huge database. This means that you can use the same information again and again to redraft the statements in different formats for different users while keeping the underlying database secure and unchanged. You just need to learn how to call out the information in the format that you have designed. There are three possibilities with Sage.

1 SAGE offers some default statements which you can call on without further effort. Some of these are very useful. As we saw in Chapter 7, Sage automatically generates the information for the VAT return for the Customs and Excise as a standard. However some of the defaults such as the monthly profit and loss and balance sheet may not be best suited to your business and here it is worth making the effort to draft your own. The default will be a constant irritation while you adjust it to the particular style you need.

2 SAGE can store a number of different statement templates so you can set up proformas to meet the needs of many of the users who you send the information to. Once set up you just need to call up the relevant template to print out the statements you need. The downside is that the number of such templates that the system can store is limited and although detail can be altered, the basic structure is not flexible, restricting the formats that can be achieved in this way.

3 If you have the right software you should be able to capture some of the information from the AIS to download it to a spreadsheet and manipulate it as you wish, e.g. by rearranging it or using 'what if' style questions to see the effect of charging different rates of provision for depreciation or bad debts. This offers the greatest potential for drafting management reports.

We will look at how to set up a template for management use under the Sage system. The same procedure can be used to set up a template for other users.

The template

The template procedure in Sage is separate from the underlying database. The database will not allow the trial balance to fall out of balance. Items might be in the wrong place but the trial balance will be in balance. The template has no such control mechanism. It will print out exactly what you ask it to. This means that it is up to you to get it right.

The first step is to print off the chart of accounts from the database. Every account on this list must be pointed to the correct place in the statements if they are to balance.

SAGE has a facility to set up a profit and loss account with a trading account and the body of a profit and loss account. It has no facility for a balance before and after interest or for appropriations. The profit calculated will automatically be transferred to the profit and loss account in the balance sheet. The balance sheet has sections for fixed assets, current assets, current liabilities, long-term liabilities and capital. Both profit and loss account and balance sheet are in vertical format.

For each section there is a similar screen. The heading for the section is printed automatically. You need to enter the actual words you want typed on the statement in each line under the section heading. Alongside the heading you indicate the codes of the accounts from which you want the balance totalled to give the figure in the printed statement. Note that it only possible to include the upper and lower code in a range.

Sage will include a total of the balances in all the accounts for the range of codes indicated. This is why it is important to design the chart carefully in the first place. Any account out of place will be difficult to include in the total where it is needed.

You should work through the chart making sure that every account in the chart is included in the template somewhere. Then make a trial run to check that the statements balance. If they do not remember that it is the template that is wrong not the trial balance. If you cannot find the error, you may need to draft the statements by hand in the form you need and then check the figures you have produced manually with those in the template. This should highlight where problems lie.

It is easy to go back to the template to make the necessary adjustments. You do not have to start from scratch again. This means that it is straightforward to alter the format as necessary over time as conditions change.

Activity

1   Using the case study material to date, set up a template to produce financial statements in good form for Bale and Co. for their internal management purposes Produce the statements for December including a profit and loss account and balance sheet.

Partnerships

The accounts you have produced are those for a sole trader. Given Azina's commitment to the business it is unlikely that John and Azina would continue to operate as a sole trader. It is more likely that they will adopt a partnership form. Azina is already financially committed to the business in that she signed the personal guarantee with the bank to raise the capital needed when the business started. Given her liability, paying her a wage as an employee would not reflect her real status in the enterprise.

The underlying records would need little change to incorporate Azina as a partner. The nature of the business operations have not changed. It is the ownership that changes. This reflects legal reality. When the change from sole trader to partnership takes place, the original business ceases and a new business is formed. Such a move would have tax and legal consequences which would need to be sorted out before undertaking the change. They would need to inform all the trading contacts such as banks, creditors, Customs and Excise and Inland Revenue.

The decision made, the first step should be the drawing up of a formal partnership agreement. Unlike in the situation of a company this is not a legal requirement. However it does lay down the respective duties and liabilities of the partners together with their rights. A lot of partnerships do not do this due to the cost and time involved. In a case like Bale and Co. where the partners are husband and wife, it is often felt to be a waste of time. However it does make good sense. It is difficult to sort out the relationship when things have gone wrong and there is little goodwill left. There can also be problems if the business goes into bankruptcy or if there is an illness or even death of one partner. In the event of there being no partnership agreement, the law takes over and disputes will be sorted out according to the Partnership Act.

From the recording point of view, each partner will need a separate capital and current account. The capital account will record the amount invested in the business originally. Sometimes the partnership agreement specifies how much this is to be. The partner's current account will record the share of any profits and losses allocated to the partner and the amounts withdrawn. The capital and current accounts for every partner will be shown in the financial statements under the 'financed by' section of the balance sheet. It reflects the financial interests of the owners in the business just as it does for the sole trader with the one capital and current account.

Where the partners have not made equal contributions to the operations of the business there is usually an agreement that the split of the profits should reflect this.

1   There needs to be a reward for investing capital. This is usually met by giving those partners who have invested capital a return on the amount of capital calculated as a notional interest charge. The agreement usually specifies a fixed rate for the calculation. Note that this charge is technically a share of the profit and is not shown as an interest charge in the profit and loss account.

2   There is a need to reward partners for work done. This can be in the form of a salary which is equivalent to the amount that would need to be paid if the work had to be done by an employee. Again the salary is notional and so is shown as a share of profit not an expense in the profit and loss account.

3   The remaining profits are shared out in the agreed proportions as a reward for taking the risk. Senior partners who originally set up the business are often given a larger share than junior partners.

A typical example might be as follows:

Activity

2   Jay, Raph and Geena are in partnership. Jay set the business up originally and has £100 000 invested in the business. He is now semi-retired and works part-time. Raph joined Jay 15 years ago and now carries most of the responsibility for the running of the business. However he has only invested £20 000 of capital in the business. Geena is an expert in a new and growing line of business. She joined the firm very recently bringing with her a number of clients. She has not invested capital in the business.

The agreement reached is that partners should be entitled to 8 per cent notional interest on their capital accounts.

Jay receives £40 000 in salary, Raph £100 000 and Geena £100 000.

They share the remaining profits Jay 20 per cent, Raph and Geena 40 per cent each.

The profits before the partners received anything amounted to £365 000 for the current year. Current account balances brought forward from the previous year amounted to £13 324 for Jay, £2686 for Raph and £876 for Geena. Drawings made by the partners during the year amounted to £72 000 for Jay, £150 060 for Raph and 145 876 for Geena.

Required

Prepare each partners' capital and current accounts for presentation in the balance sheet showing clearly the allocation of profit to each partner.

	Jay	Raph	Geena	Total
	£	£	£	£
Interest on capital	8 000	1 600	–	9 600
Salaries	40 000	100 000	100 000	240 000
Share of profits	23 080	46 160	46 160	115 400
	71 080	147 760	146 160	365 000

The financed by section of the balance sheet would look thus:

	Jay	Raph	Geena		Total
	£	£	£	£	£
Capital	100 000	20 000	–	120 000	
Current accounts					
Balance b/fwd	13 324	2 686	876	16 886	
Add share of profit for year	71 080	147 760	146 160	365 000	
	184 404	170 446	147 036	501 886	
Less Drawings	72 000	150 060	145 876	367 936	
Balance c/fwd	112 404	20 386	1 160		133 950
Total					£253 950

The split between the partners and their separate capital and current accounts might need to be kept manually with the total figures in the system operating as control accounts. This allows a certain amount of privacy for the partners' financial affairs while allowing other staff to work on the system.

Activity

3 Discuss how John and Azina might share profits. Prepare a table to illustrate the effect of your decision for the split of the profits for December.

Accounting policies

As we have seen accountants have a lot of room to exercise professional judgement in arriving at the final financial statements. Even if the underlying system is the same, the end result could be very different. In the preceding chapters we have looked at some of the areas where the differences could occur. Different judgements in areas such as depreciation; stock valuations; and provision for debts can make a very big difference to the end statement. Financial statements are produced with the sole purpose of communicating information. Nothing will be communicated unless the basis for the underlying judgements is known.

Some judgements are the result of applying basic accounting conventions which are the result of accepted practice over many years. It is not usual to actually state that these are used. They are just assumed. For other judgements, there are acceptable alternatives and it is important if you are to understand the statements to know which have been chosen and why.

In 1971 the accounting profession through the ASC, issued a statement (**SSAP 2** Accounting policies) to make it standard practice to attach a note to the statements to explain the assumptions made and the basis of the judgement used. Since that time a number of the ideas in SSAP 2 have been incorporated into company law. More recently there has been a growing debate criticizing SSAP 2 and suggesting changes. We will look first at some basic accounting concepts then at the requirements of SSAP 2, which has not been withdrawn, before turning to the criticisms.

Accounting concepts

All statements are based on assumptions and **concepts**. Some of these are so fundamental that some accountants might not even be aware that they are being used. They would explain what they have done in terms of 'That is the way it is always done' without thinking about why. These assumptions are part of generally accepted accounting practice (GAAP). Some of these you have already met and used e.g.:

1 entity concept;
2 cost principle;
3 matching or accruals;
4 realization principle.

There are others, some of which are described below.

Materiality

Materiality is one example of a concept that is often referred to and applied, but rarely defined. It refers to the way in which accountants exercise their judgement to make sure that items which are fundamental to the understanding of the statements are properly treated and drawn attention to. Items considered to be immaterial are given less attention. For example, in theory a pencil sharpener would be a fixed asset if it is bought for use in the office. It is intended to last, say, three years. However it is too small an amount to warrant being treated as a fixed asset and depreciated. The time and effort would be wasted. Materiality is often thought of as relating to the amount involved but while this is important there are other factors to be considered. For example a case of food poisoning in a firm making baby food may have had a very small financial effect immediately, but the fact that it occurred could have major implications for future sales. Managers would need to know about it. Similarly a very small amount stolen from the business may itself be immaterial until you understand it was taken by a director.

Consistency

Consistency is a basic concept without which it would be impossible to compare what is happening in an organization over time. Once a method has been chosen it is to be used in the same way period by period. The concept applies to the same organization over time, not to consistency between organizations.

The going concern

The **going concern** concept assumes that the organization will continue to operate in the future. If the business has no future then the assets have no use. This has major implications for the values attached to assets and liabilities in the balance sheet. Going concern assumes they will be valued at 'use to the business'. If the business has no operational use for them then the value to the business is the scrap value. Similarly, recording accruals or prepayments for future time periods assumes there is a future time period. Financial statements are prepared on the understanding that there is a future.

Prudence

Prudence or conservatism is an approach to accounting that was popular in the UK. It is often described as requiring a business to make provision for future losses as soon as they are anticipated whereas income should only be recognized when realized, i.e. the realization principle. In suggesting the bringing forward of expenses to earlier time periods, this concept can be in conflict with the matching principle. Until recently it has been common practice where the two conflict to err on the side of prudence. That view is now being challenged as unduly cautious and permitting the manipulation of profits and results. Nevertheless it is a well accepted concept in the UK.

SSAP 2

SSAP 2 names four of these basic concepts as being fundamental. These are:

1 going concern;
2 consistency;
3 prudence;
4 matching.

These concepts are to be assumed unless the accounts actually state they have not been complied with.

It is possible to trace how the application of these has affected items in the statements.

For example, consider the depreciation of fixed assets. Going concern applies as soon as you attempt to depreciate an asset. If the organization was not a going concern then the asset would have been put in at scrap value since it would have no further use within the organization and would be sold. The accruals concept requires that you depreciate the asset in such a way as to spread the cost over the time periods in which it contributes to generating income. This dictates the method of depreciation that should be chosen. Consistency requires that the method of depreciation chosen should be applied consistently from year to year and not changed. Prudence requires that the total contribution to be made by the asset is not over estimated but reflects what is reasonable for the asset concerned.

Activity

4   In introducing the accounting concepts the example of fixed assets and depreciation was used. Stock in hand at the period end also has to be valued.
Required
Describe in your own words how the four basic concepts identified in SSAP 2 affect the way in which stock is valued in the financial statements.
Apart from the basic concepts, SSAP 2 introduces the terms accounting bases and accounting polices.

Accounting bases

Accounting **bases** are the possible accounting methods which have been developed for use by accountants and from which **policies** are chosen. So in our depreciation example, the accountant has the choice from reducing balance, straight line or unit of production method. The actual choice made becomes the accounting policy of the organization.

Accounting policies

SSAP 2 requires that the policy chosen is described in the accounting policy note attached to the statements to enable the reader of the accounts to interpret them accurately.

These notes are now standard in published accounts. Figure 13.1 is extracted from the accounting policy note for depreciation in the published reports of J Sainsbury plc to give you an idea of the sort of language that is used.

Criticisms of SSAP 2

The accounting policies note produced under SSAP 2 is a useful addition to statements. However the standard has been criticized. To start with there is no real reason why it should include the four concepts it has chosen rather than any of the others. Inclusion suggests that they are more important than the others, which is not the case. The ASB amongst others has advocated a different approach. GAAP in the UK has grown from accepted practice. As such it does not have a theoretical framework as a base. Decisions about the treatment of particular problems are made in isolation and this can result in inconsistent solutions and a meaningless result in the overall statements. To take an extreme example, if the decision about how to value fixed assets is

Figure 13.1
Extract from the accounting policies note in the published reports for J Sainsbury plc for 1997

'Freehold land is not depreciated. Freehold buildings and leasehold buildings with more than 50 years unexpired are depreciated in equal instalments at the rate of 2% per annum.

Leasehold properties with less than 50 years unexpired are depreciated to write off their book value in equal annual instalments over the unexpired period of the lease.

Fixtures, equipment and vehicles are depreciated in equal annual instalments to write off their cost over their estimated lives which range from 3 to 15 years, commencing when they are brought into use.'

made with the view that the balance sheet is intended to show assets at their continued use to the business rather than at scrap value, then it makes no sense to value current assets at scrap value (net realizable value) and add the resulting figures together. What is needed is a conceptual framework to establish the overall goals to be achieved by statements which can be used to make decisions on how individual items should be treated. The ASB has tried to do this, but the matter is still one for considerable debate within the profession and it is by no means universally agreed that the approach is the correct one.

Activity

5 Draft the accounting policies note for Bale and Co. explaining the methods you used to depreciate the assets and value stock.

Summary

This chapter has taken a further look at the production of financial statements. You should now be confident that you could prepare financial statements for simple sole traders and partnerships from the underlying records. The chapter also summarized the importance of accounting policies and the need to make these explicit in the presentation of reports. The recording systems we have looked at are similar whichever organizational form has been chosen. However there are some changes which need to be made if the organization chooses to operate as a company. We will look at why this is so in the next chapter and then look at these alterations before turning to interpreting the statements you have been producing.

Key words

bases p. 221 • concepts p. 219 • consistency p. 219 • going concern p. 220 • materiality p. 219 • policies p. 221 • prudence p. 220 • SSAP2 pp. 219, 220

Practice questions

1 For each of the situations described below, identify the concepts which are relevant and decide how the item should be treated in the accounts giving your reasons:
   (i) A has incurred large losses on uncollectible loans which called for repayment over the next ten years. A proposes to depreciate the losses over the ten year period to which they relate.
   (ii) B is being sued by another company for illegal practices. The case is ongoing but likely to conclude that B was liable. No adjustment has been made in the accounts for this possible loss.
   (iii) C is an hotel. It receives bookings for its rooms up to a year in advance. Revenue is recognized as soon as bookings are confirmed in writing.
   (iv) D has a policy of revaluing its plant and machinery each year at realizable value. The change is then used as the depreciation figure.

(v) E built an hotel with 500 rooms. All materials and furnishings with an individual cost of less than £100 were written off immediately as an expense. There were some 100 such items per room.

(vi) F has changed its depreciation policy to write assets off over 12 years instead of the six years that it considers more appropriate to bring its depreciation into line with other companies in the industry.

(vii) G estimates that its executives stayed on average for four years with the company before moving on for more experience. It therefore depreciates the cost of the initial training programme (which all executives undertake) over a four year period.

(viii) H paid for a custom made machine which is impossible to remove being imbedded in concrete. The company hopes to use it for ten years but as it is so immovable and specific to the company the cost has been written off immediately.

(ix) I can borrow a maximum 50 per cent of its assets. It has insufficient assets to provide cover for a much needed loan and has therefore included in its accounts some securities owned personally by the main shareholder.

(x) J is a mining business. It has discovered that one of its mines has much larger reserves of ore than was originally thought. The increase in value has been credited to profit in the year in which it was discovered.

(xi) K is a theatre. A major new show has attracted bookings well in advance. These have been credited to income as they are received.

(xii) L has estimated its doubtful debts provision by taking the previous years' experience of bad debts and doubling it to make sure that there is no under provision.

14 Regulation and control of limited companies

Learning objectives

After reading this chapter you should:

■ understand the need for regulation and control of company reporting and accounting procedures
■ appreciate the factors which determine the approach to regulation and how these differ between countries
■ be aware of the main sources of these controls in the UK and the framework in which companies operate
■ understand that directors have responsibilities and liabilities regarding the companies which they serve as directors – in particular their responsibilities for stewardship, recording and reporting
■ understand what is meant by the term audit and the difference between external and internal audit
■ be aware of the availability of exemptions and reduced regulations for small and medium sized businesses
■ understand the importance of business ethics and corporate governance.

Introduction

In this chapter we build on some of the ideas introduced in Chapter 2 and Appendix 3A. We look at the obligations to investors and the business community which come with being a limited company. The UK developed its own distinct regulatory regime as a combination of law and professional good practice driven by market forces. Other countries have faced similar problems but have approached the problem in their own way, with the result that there are different rules in different countries. This is becoming increasingly difficult as businesses become international and global in outlook. To try to put things in perspective, we look briefly at steps being taken to try to harmonize approaches to corporate control. Finally, not all controls are set in a formal framework. Legal controls tend to be slow to adapt, expensive and the solution of last resort. If the capital markets and the business world are to prosper, a level of trust and good faith needs to operate. Business ethics and corporate governance issues are introduced as the last topic.

REVISITING THE BUSINESS FORMAT

John and Azina survived the problem with the bad debt and large overdraft. However some months later while trading was good and the list of customers growing, cash flow was a constant problem and a constraint on growth. John was depressed about the constant difficulties of monitoring the cash situation.

John took some time off to attend a reunion of his class at university. The weekend went well and unexpectedly he bumped into an old friend who had been a mature student. When Mike Cowley graduated he had started his own business offering systems advice. It had done well but recently he had been offered a large sum by a national organization to buy him out. With some regrets he had taken the offer. The business had been his life but he was suffering from arthritis and found the physical demands of travelling too much to cope with. Now 60, he thought it was time to retire. He had been offered the chance to stay on as an advisor but as he said to John, he had been his own boss for so long he didn't feel he could enjoy working for someone else.

Mike was very enthusiastic about John and Azina's venture and gave John some useful ideas. John found the chat with Mike very helpful and he arrived back home feeling much more positive. He explained to Azina.

'Old Mike knew the problems we are up against. He thinks we could get a better deal with purchasing from a supplier in Birmingham. He told me to mention his name. He's often down this way visiting his daughter and I told him to drop in any time. It was good to be able to talk about things to someone who understands.'

A week later Mike did drop in at the shop. He had brought the names of some contacts he had in the area. Over coffee he told them how much he missed the challenge of business but he knew he could not have continued with the travelling. Jokingly, John told him he could share some of their headaches. To his surprise Mike took him seriously.

'If you were ever looking for a business partner who could bring some cash and some advice, I'd be interested', he said, 'but I could not take on the day-to-day work. I'm just not mobile enough'.

After he had gone John and Azina looked at each other. They had not considered the idea of going into business with anyone else but the more they thought about it the better it seemed. There were some problems however. Not the least of these was thinking out what business form would be the best. John was concerned about the need to pay Mike an income.

'Could we pay him a salary or interest? With our erratic cash flow it would be difficult to meet a fixed commitment.'

'He would want to take an active interest in the business', thought Azina, 'and his contacts would be useful, but I would not want to lose control ourselves after all this effort.'

The price of limited liability

Chapter 2 advised that business form was not something that was decided once and for all. If circumstances changed the decision had to be revisited. One of the main issues in deciding on business form is the desire for limited liability. The idea of limited liability and the possible legal forms that a business could take were introduced in Chapter 2. If you don't remember the discussion in that chapter you might find it useful to revise those ideas by rereading sections of that chapter before continuing.

1 The following quick quiz is intended to help you test your knowledge of the information in the earlier chapters for yourself.
   Required
   (a) What do the following initials stand for:
      FRC
      UITF
      SSAP
   (b) What is the difference between an FRS and an SSAP?
   (c) Name three main accounting professional bodies in the UK.
   (d) What factors determine the choice of organizational form?
   (e) What is the difference between an Ltd and a plc company?
   (f) How do you set up a limited company?
   The answers should be easily found in Chapter 2 and Appendix 3A.

Limited companies are the most popular organizational form for business in the UK. According to Companies House statistics, there were some 1.3 million companies in the UK in 1997. For many small business people, operating as a company as opposed to a sole trader gives a feeling of substance and permanence. For this reason small family businesses are often set up as limited companies despite the costs and the need to give personal guarantees. Others see company status as a means of avoiding liabilities should the economy turn against them. Rightly or wrongly, the building trade has a reputation for adopting this latter approach. The following discussion

Table 14.1 Summary of the main advantages and disadvantages of limited liability

Advantages	Disadvantages
To company:	To company:
Ability to raise finance	Costs of compliance with legal and
Indefinite life	market regulations
Transfer of ownership without closing business	Lack of privacy
Ability to bring in further investors	Possible tax consequences
	Need to operate within company
	regulations
To shareholders:	To shareholders:
Liability limited to the original investment	Lack of privacy
committed	Possible loss of control
Marketability of shares without closing business	Possible tax consequences
Ability to realize part of an investment	

considers the issues involved in deciding to operate as a limited company and Table 14.1 summarizes the ideas.

As far as the owner is concerned, if it can be arranged, limited liability offers an obvious way to limit exposure to risk. Provided a personal guarantee has not been signed, the investor/owner can lose the amount of the investment but if the shares were fully paid up, cannot be asked to contribute anything further to meet the debts of the company. The company is an artificial but legal person which has an infinite life independent of its owners. It can own things, enter into contracts, sue and be sued, borrow and lend money. It has an address and, due to the hard work of public relations specialists, its own image and personality.

The twin ideas of limited liability and the joint stock company allowed business to tap the source of small private savings of millions of individuals to build large capital investments.

However limited liability comes at a price. If investors are to be encouraged to deliver their savings into the control of other people in the persons of directors of companies, there must be some safeguards. In the 150 years since limited companies were introduced in the UK, legislation and controls have gradually been built up to control the abuses. It is not just shareholders who need protection. The impact of limited liability is that creditors, customers, lenders, employees and local communities will bear the brunt of the company failing to pay its debts. These people only have the assets the company owns in its own right to meet the debts its owes. They will not be able to demand payment from shareholders or even from directors. It does not matter that the directors may appear to be wealthy and well able to meet the debts. It is not the directors who are responsible for paying the outstanding debts. It is the company itself.

For this reason it is important that creditors actually check the financial stability of a company before offering credit terms or committing themselves in any way. While credit agencies and bank references may help, one major source of material is the annual report and accounts lodged with the Registrar of Companies at Companies House, which are available to everyone – at a small charge. The purchase price of limited liability is the provision of information. The owners of some small businesses find this off-putting. They don't want everyone to know their financial position and if the business is their main asset, publishing financial statements discloses more about their personal circumstances than they might care for the general public and their neighbours to know.

A regulatory framework has grown up to ensure that the business world has confidence in the limited company. As with any form of control, they have a cost in time and resources which are charged to the company, thereby diverting management's time and attention from the real business of running the company. We will look at the level of these costs and the attempts made to minimize them in recent years when we look at each of these controls in more detail. The cost needs to be borne in mind when making decisions about company status.

One aspect that tends to be little recognized is the potential liability of directors for failing to carry out their duties. If, for example, they continue to trade when they should be aware that the company is insolvent (cannot pay its debts when they fall due) they can become personally liable for the debts of the company. As stewards of other peoples money they carry considerable responsibility Some people feel unhappy about accepting that level of responsibility for others.

Finally, as a legal person, the company has its own tax affairs to sort out, being subject to corporation tax as well as dealing with VAT and the tax affairs of the directors and employees of the company. The transfer to company status may itself have tax consequences for the individual investors concerned.

Activity

2   Consider the position of John, Azina and Mike described in the case study earlier in this chapter. Assume that they decide to explore the possibility of transferring the business to a limited company.
    Required
    Looking at the information in Chapter 2 and the ideas introduced above, advise John and Azina of the advantages and disadvantages of transferring to and trading as a limited company. The position of
    (a) the business
    (b) John and Azina
    (c) Mike Cowley
    should each be explored separately. Try to think of all the issues raised by the decision and not just control issues.

Factors determining how companies are regulated

Financial statements prepared within one country can vary widely depending upon the judgements being made by the accountants concerned. For example we looked at depreciation methods and the judgements needed to set provisions for doubtful debts. A simple change in judgement made major differences to the reported profit. Where the accounts are prepared in different countries even greater variations can appear.

Accounting requirements of different countries were developed in isolation to meet the specific needs of each country and reflected the social, legal and business world in each country. You need to understand how this works to appreciate why the regulations can vary so much and to understand how the UK system developed and why it is likely to change in the future. We look at the main factors below.

Legal systems

In the UK the legal system developed under a system known as common law derived from the Nordic invaders centuries ago. It is based on the idea of precedent so that as legal cases are decided in a court those judgments set a precedent which itself becomes part of the body of law and must be followed by subsequent cases. These cases, some centuries old, together with any relevant acts of parliament make up the body of the law on a subject. In contrast, most continental countries developed a system known as roman law which is characterized by a written codified law. The body of law relating to a particular issue is codified in a statute which is updated as required.

The result is that when it comes to accounting regulations, the system in UK and other countries with common law systems such as the USA, Australia and Canada have evolved as a mixture of professional practice and case law. The profession is resistant to a written code which it sees as failing to allow the exercise of professional judgement and being slow to adapt to the changing needs of companies. In contrast, the continental Europeans find it difficult to understand how the control system can operate if it is not clearly set out in one written document.

Finance markets

The finance markets evolved to suit the needs of the local economy. In the UK private investors' savings were the source of business capital. In Europe business expansion was funded by the banks to a far greater degree, the banks working with their customers far more closely than is the tradition in the UK. Similarly Japanese business is heavily dependent upon bank finance. In countries with less of a capitalist economy, the government also played a significant role in financing business. In the directed economies of former communist countries there was no need for published reports at all and the accounting profession did not exist. Records needed to be kept for government statistics and central planning with the result that information systems concentrated on quantities since there were no markets to establish prices for goods, services, property or wages.

Where business tended to develop in family hands or as directed by governments then investors divorced from ownership were in the minority. Most investors were in a position to know what was happening in an organization without the need for specially produced reports. Accounting and the subsequent need for regulation is more developed in countries where finance markets are highly developed. Where reporting was developed mainly for government purposes, such as tax collecting or statistics for economic planning, this coloured the style of reporting to other users and they adopted a rigid proforma style of providing specific figures rather than trying to explain the workings of the business.

Business forms

Similar to the situation with finance markets, where limited companies were the preferred business form, accounting reports became important to provide the information which shareholders needed. Regulation soon became a necessity. The reporting system was market driven. In contrast where businesses remained family based, the priority was to protect the creditors and ensure against tax avoidance. Investors who didn't also have a connection with management were few and far between and their information needs were less important.

Historical connections

Countries which trade together tended to develop similar accounting requirements. So the English speaking world tended to adopt a system derived from the original UK system. The French system was exported to Spain, but was itself derived from a German system. Recently the UK has been strongly influenced by the EU model.

Development of an accounting profession

The accounting profession developed early in the UK, the first professional accounting body being established in Scotland in 1854. This meant that it had established sufficient credibility to have a strong voice in the development of accounting and company regulation. In other countries the profession was established much later, e.g. in France in 1942 and the regulations were well developed by governments before the profession had sufficient credibility to take an active role.

Academic influence

In some countries instead of the profession regulating itself and training its own professional members, the training function was undertaken to some extent by the universities. Where this is the case the accounting system has more of a conceptual or theoretical base than where it relied on professional and accepted practice. The two main examples of a theoretical base are the Netherlands and Finland. The Netherlands in particular developed a very sophisticated reporting model founded in economic theory.

Regulation models

These differences have led to very different regimes in different countries. They can be classified in different ways for convenience of analysis but it should be remembered that in fact, even where the underlying accounting and regulation regime belong to the same model, the actual requirements may be very different. For example, in theory the UK and US regulatory regimes are classed as belonging to the same model sometimes referred to as the Anglo–Saxon model. However if you look at a sample of financial statements from each country you would find very little in common. Apart from the fact that they would both be written in English, the words, the layouts, the accounting policies and the reported profit would all be very different.

Although it originated in the UK, the Anglo–Saxon model has been developed and changed by the USA which spends an enormous amount of money on research. The model is characterized by its emphasis on the needs of investors plus a framework set in law, with detailed interpretation in the form of a series of accounting standards composed by an independent organization established for the purpose and drawing heavily on accepted professional practice.

In contrast, the continental European model was developed to meet the needs of tax collectors, governments and creditors, and as such, was rigidly standardized and set in legislation. The statements were thought to be far more 'conservative' than Anglo–Saxon based accounts and as such should produce lower profits.

It is wrong to think of these models as set in concrete. New models are appearing. The Islamic world is developing its own model for reporting which is based on Islamic Law. Old models adapt as economic and political influences change. The European model is becoming more like the Anglo–Saxon model as the need to tap world capital markets asserts itself. The UK model is becoming more European as the economy becomes tied more closely to Europe. The Anglo–Saxon model is adapted as East Asian needs begin to influence the business world.

Harmonization

The accounting profession has recognized that there is a need for **harmonization**. Bringing the regulations and reporting requirements in line will reduce time and costs and serve the needs of companies and the users of reports more effectively. Currently where companies operate in many different countries, reporting becomes expensive and time consuming. For their part, investors can be totally misled by the reports produced in a different regime. It had been assumed, for example, that the German reporting system (continental model) was far more conservative than that in the USA (Anglo–Saxon model) and would tend to underestimate profits, but this proved to be a mistake. Consider the case of Daimler–Benz when, in 1993, it decided to go for a listing on the New York Stock Exchange (NYSE). It was the first major German company to take this step and one of the reasons for its reluctance was the requirement to disclose far more information than was needed by the German authorities. Nevertheless the need to tap international money markets overcame this concern and Daimler–Benz took the plunge in 1993. They needed to disclose their results in both German GAAP (to satisfy the German regulators) and US GAAP (to satisfy the NYSE) at the same time. To the surprise of the finance markets the profit of DM168million for the half year disclosed in Germany turned into a loss of DM949 million when using US GAAP. The comments by the Daimler–Benz finance director that the US GAAP reflected the underlying trading performance hammered the lesson home. The sensation this caused was one factor in the announcement in 1995 that the German authorities could tolerate the large German companies wishing to raise finance on the international markets preparing financial statements under international rules.

The International Accounting Standards Committee (**IASC**) was set up specifically to draft standards which would be acceptable worldwide. They act through the accounting professional bodies in each country trying to gain co-operation. While they have had some success, one down side to this approach is that to try to keep everyone happy, the standards they produce are very vague.

More recently the international securities regulatory committee (**IOSCO**) has attempted to encourage harmonization by agreeing to accept IASC standards provided they were comprehensive in cover. Currently IASC is trying to meet the IOSCO requirements.

On a European level, the EU has worked to harmonize reporting requirements since the early 1970s. There has been considerable give and take within the countries concerned. The UK imported the idea of standard formats but exported the idea of a **true and fair view** amongst other changes. More recently, the EU has supported the need for global harmonization and the IASC.

Another major agent for harmonization is the accounting profession itself. With the growth of international companies with global interests, a need to provide professional services for these giants has also grown. The largest accounting firms have merged to keep pace and provide a global spread of expertise and resources in international accounting requirements. In countries without an established accounting profession of their own or a profession inadequate in numerical terms to cope with the extra demands of new regulations, the large accounting firms have a major influence on accounting practice. They have had a significant impact on the development of accounting regulation in Italy for example.

Until harmonization is further advanced it is important to check under which GAAP the reports you are interested in are prepared. Companies produce reports under their home country GAAP, sometimes providing English language translations of these but without changing the GAAP, while at the same time also providing reports in US or IASC or some other country's GAAP. The situation can be confusing!

3   In the last decade a number of countries have introduced a free market system into a previously centrally planned economy. Poland chose to adopt the rules of the EU whereas China has announced that it will comply with IASC standards.
    Required
    Briefly consider which factors would influence the decisions on the regulatory models to follow for these countries.
    What would you think would be the main problems in implementing the decisions?

The UK system of regulation

In the UK, accounting and reporting regulations for limited companies are derived from three main sources:

1   statute and case law;
2   professional standards and accepted practice;
3   stock exchange requirements.

Law

The main statute is the Companies Act 1985 as amended by the Companies Act 1989. There are some requirements of a general nature in other statutes, e.g. the Health and Safety Act specifies some information on meeting health and safety needs but these do not have a major impact on the reports or accounting procedures. Some industries have specific statutes applying to them, e.g. the Building Societies Act, which are only of relevance to the industry concerned. We will concentrate on the Companies Acts requirements which lay down the need to keep records, how companies should be managed and basic reporting requirements. The tradition in the UK is that the law should give the framework but that detailed information on interpreting this is left to the independent standard setting bodies. The reason for this is the need to react quickly to new problems and to find solutions where perhaps no consensus currently exists. The standard setting body should be able to move more quickly to alter or redraft requirements as they prove to be ineffective or unhelpful. It is only when consensus has been established for some years that they are likely to be incorporated into law. The Companies Act does allow some changes to be made by statutory instrument by the government minister concerned. For example the definition of a small company in the Act involves the turnover of the company. The actual amount is set by the statutory instrument and can therefore be altered to take account of inflation.

Professional standards and accepted practice

Reporting standards are governed by the Financial Reporting Council as described in Appendix 3A. In earlier chapters, we have come across a number of the statements they have issued, e.g. SSAP 12 relating to depreciation and SSAP 2 on accounting policies. In addition to the work of the FRC and its subsidiary the ASB, the profession uses a whole host of conventions and ideas such as *materiality* and the *cost principle* which are not defined in any of the sources. Nevertheless, as accepted accounting practice, they are assumed to apply unless otherwise stated. Altogether the law, the standards and accounting conventions make up the generally accepted accounting practice (GAAP) under which reports are prepared. In addition to the controls on the communicating of information, rules were needed to interpret the rules for conducting an **audit**. By law every company over a certain size must have an **external audit**. The standards (SAS) for conducting such an audit are issued by the Auditing Practices Board (APB) which was established by the auditing bodies for the purpose.

Stock exchange

The rules of the stock exchange apply purely to companies which are raising finance on one of its exchanges. Nevertheless the size and dominance of these companies lead to the adoption of their practices by other smaller companies. The listing rules of the London Stock exchange are known as the ***Yellow Book***. We will not be looking at the specific requirements of this book in any detail but you should be aware that it exists for companies which have a listing on the exchange and that it imposes more stringent conditions on these companies. The rules are set by the exchange itself and are not set in law. However the power to de-list for non-compliance, with all the bad publicity that would bring, is enough to make companies comply. Recently there has been some considerable concern about the way in which companies are governed and a series of reports have been compiled which impose a code of best practice which we will discuss later under the theme of business ethics.

Overview of controls and regulations in the UK

The rules have become very complex over the years and most accountants will use a checklist to reassure themselves that all the various regulations have been met when preparing and auditing the financial statements for publication. Some of these checklists are in paper form but increasingly there are software versions. We give an overview here to build a framework for you to understand what is happening but do not assume that it covers everything. You should look at the relevant standard, act or case for detailed advice.

The controls we will look at revolve around four themes:

1   management and stewardship of resources;
2   communication of information;

3   audit of the communications, records and management;
4   corporate governance and business ethics.

Management and stewardship

The management controls laid out in the Companies Act 1985, s 221 require that directors keep adequate financial records. The records must be good enough to explain the company's transactions, show the financial position at any time and enable the directors to prepare a balance sheet and profit and loss statement which complies with the Act and shows a 'true and fair view'. The records we have been preparing should be detailed enough to do this. In fact they are the basic records that every business should keep to run a business effectively. The Act is really insisting on sound management practice.

The records have to be kept for three years for a private company and six years for others. However VAT and now self-assessment for tax purposes mean that most businesses would need to keep records for six years even if they are not limited companies.

It is the directors who are responsible for thinking up and installing a sound system of internal control and for checking that it is working. Traditionally this was thought of as **stewardship**. You could think of it as the responsibility for the proper use and security of other people's money.

In addition to the accounting records, the company has to keep a number of statutory books and records which are available for inspection. They include registers of directors, charges against the assets of the company, members (i.e. shareholders), debentures, directors interests in the shares and debentures, interests of more than 5 per cent of the company's shares and minutes of directors meetings. Most of these should be kept at the registered address of the company.

Communication of information

Companies have a duty to provide information both to their shareholders and to the public at Companies House.

Under company law they must register an annual return at Companies House and also file an approved set of financial statements every year. The accounts are approved by the full board before they are signed by two directors. These accounts are sent to every shareholder prior to the annual general meeting at which they are to be discussed. In addition the stock exchange requires listed companies to make interim reports available and preliminary profits statements to the shareholders either through sending everyone a copy or by advertising the results in two national papers.

Most of the detailed requirements of the contents of the financial statements are contained in Schedule 4 to the Companies Act 1985 and in the accounting standards. The overriding principle laid down in the Act is that the accounts should show a true and fair view. This is considered so important that any other requirement in the Act or the accounting standards can be set aside in order that the accounts do give a true and fair view. **True and fair** is not an easy idea to work with. It requires professional judgement on behalf of the directors and auditors but, because it is not an exact measurement, it can be challenged in court. Think of the accounts as a picture of the company and its business. Pictures can be easy to recognize, i.e. they show a true and fair view, or, if taken from a strange angle or very close up can be almost impossible to identify, i.e. true perhaps but not fair. It is the recognisable picture that accounts are aiming to deliver.

The Act and the accounting standards lay down detailed rules for the formats and contents of the accounts. It is important to be aware of these when setting up the chart of accounts in a new system. The accounting system should be set up to produce the details required without having to resort to hand calculations of the amounts needed. However some systems cannot be set up to actually print off the statements in the form that is required and here it is necessary to redraft the information from the detail the system has provided. The average set of published statements will include some information to comply with the Act, some to meet accounting standards, some for the stock market and some as publicity or just because the company wants people to know about what it is doing. We will work through examples of the formats and main notes required in the next chapter.

Smaller companies are allowed to provide less information to the public than larger companies. The reasons for the exemptions are not given in the Act, but it seems that smaller companies are thought to have a greater need for privacy since the owners' personal financial circumstances are more closely tied to the results of the company and correspondingly there is less public interest in the results than in those of a large company.

Whatever the reason, the Act allows companies deemed to be 'small' to file modified accounts at Companies House. These have no profit and loss account or directors report and only a summarizsed balance sheet. Some notes are also omitted. Medium sized companies file a modified profit and loss account but a normal directors' report, full set of notes and a full balance sheet. However the shareholders of all companies whatever their size have a right to a complete set of accounts so the modified version is merely for privacy purposes and does not reduce costs or time.

For small companies there is a further concession in that instead of complying with the full set of statements of accounting practice, a special standard known as FRSSE has been drafted in an attempt to make the standards more appropriate for the small business. Where the FRSSE applies the remaining standards and pronouncements of the Urgent Issues Task Force do not. The definition of small and medium are given in Table 14.2. Basically two criteria must be met to fall into the category. The 'balance sheet total' refers to the total of the fixed and current assets.

Table 14.2 Companies Act definitions of small and medium sized companies

	Small	*Medium*
Annual turnover not exceeding	£2.8 million	£11.2 million
Balance sheet total not exceeding	£1.4 million	£5.6 million
Average number of employees not exceeding	50	250

Audit

The Companies Act 1985, s 236 requires that companies' accounts undergo an **audit** by an auditor who is independent of the business. This is known as an **external audit**. The terms of the appointment are set out in the Act. Audits can be expensive since they require professionally qualified people to make a detailed and time consuming review and assessment of the records and reports of the business. Until recently this applied to all companies in the UK. However it has been recognized that for small businesses the audit can in some cases be an expensive and time consuming luxury. Where the shareholders consist of close family members or two partners working together the audit sometimes becomes a formality with little meaning.

In 1994 a statutory instrument was introduced to amend the Companies Act 1985 so that some very small companies, which meet special conditions, can agree to be exempt from external audit. However the directors have to sign to say that the records have been kept as required by the Act and that the accounting reports are compiled in accordance with the law and present a true and fair view.

In addition to the external audit, the directors have a duty to ensure that the company has all the internal controls and checks in place to safeguard the assets, make sure that the records are reliable and deter fraud. A part of this is the **internal audit** which is the process of checking that the systems are suitable and working effectively. Obviously the external auditor can and should look at the work of the internal auditor as part of the external audit but cannot rely on this entirely because it is directed internally and therefore not independent. The internal audit is the responsibility of the directors and they need to report on this in the published statements as part of the corporate governance issues we look at next.

Corporate governance and business ethics

Business **ethics** become a popular topic in periods when the economy takes a downturn and a number of prominent companies fall into receivership or a major fraud is discovered. When people's pensions and jobs are at risk the activities of the directors supposedly in charge of the business world become subject to media scrutiny. In the recession of the early 1990s this was particularly true. Cases such as Maxwell and the Daily Mirror, Polly Peck and BCCI spawned a series of committees to examine the need to set a code of good practice for directors in their role as corporate governors. The City was concerned that unless it took action the government would step in and impose a statutory regime of control. In addition the finance markets were genuinely concerned that the confidence of investors needed to be restored if the markets were to operate efficiently.

The results were contained first in the report of the **Cadbury** committee which dealt with the general issues of boardroom practice, the appointments, duties and roles of executive directors and non-executive directors, the appointment and responsibilities of external auditors and the responsibilities of the directors in ensuring internal controls were in place and operating effectively.

The main report was backed up by later work by the **Greenbury** committee which concentrated on directors' remuneration. A further committee, known as the Hampel committee is set to review the effectiveness of the earlier reports. The danger is that as the scandals and problems fade into the past, the impetus to improve corporate **governance** and impose high standards will be lost. The issue is often discussed in the national press and you should follow the comments made and use your own judgement about the role and remuneration of directors, chairmen and chief executives.

Cadbury and Greenbury require a considerable amount of extra disclosure and while some disclosure was needed, commentators have criticized the scale of the material required. Sometimes facts can be lost in so much detail. Nevertheless the accounts now spell out the duties and responsibilities of the directors and auditors more clearly and the process has highlighted the duties and expectations of the role of 'director'.

Summary

This chapter described the regulatory and control context within which limited companies have to operate. It began by refreshing your memory of earlier work and then looked at the factors which affect the way in which companies are regulated in different countries. We introduced the sources of controls in the UK and looked at some of the requirements. The chart in Table 14.3 summarizes the contents of the published statements of a typical listed company which should help to bring the ideas of this chapter together. The chart tries to indicate the sources which govern the presentation and disclosure in the item concerned. For this purpose the requirements of the corporate governance committees are included as stock exchange requirements since they are policed by the exchange. The presentation of accounts for publication and the role of the audit will be discussed in more depth in Chapters 16 and 18 when

Table 14.3 The required contents of a typical set of published accounts for a listed company

Contents	Legal	ASB	SE	Voluntary
Chairman's Statement				X
Financial and operating review		X	X	X
Ten year Financial Record			X	
Financial calendar				X
Investor information				X
Report of the directors	X			
Report of the remuneration committee			X	
Statement of directors' responsibilities			X	
Report of the auditors on corporate governance			X	
Report of the auditors to the shareholders	X			
Accounting policies	X	X		
Profit and loss account	X	X		
Balance sheet	X	X		
Cash flow statement		X		
Statement of total recognized gains and losses		X		
Reconciliation of shareholders' funds		X		
Notes to accounts	X	X		
Environmental report				X
Registered offices and financial advisors				X

you will have a chance to try some exercises for yourself. You need to remember as you do this that in the UK the goal is to provide statements which show a 'true and fair view'.

Key words

> audit pp. 234, 237 • Cadbury p. 237 • ethics p. 237 • external audit pp. 234, 237 • governance p. 238 • Greenbury p. 237 • harmonization p. 232 • IASC p. 232 • internal audit p. 237 • IOSCO p. 232 • stewardship p. 235 • true and fair view pp. 232, 235 • Yellow Book p. 234

Practice questions

1 Is international harmonization of company regulation desirable and or achievable?
2 'The EU directives require too many disclosures from small and medium sized companies and not enough from enterprises operating transnationally.' Mr Herbert Biener, German government official quoted in the *Financial Times*, 22 May 1995.
   What are the arguments for and against the introduction of different regulations for different sized businesses?
3 You should collect a number of published financial statements to see examples of layouts and the language used. It is also a good way of becoming familiar with the requirements of reports. In the UK you can write to the company you are interested in. The reports are usually sent free of charge.
   (i)   Try a number of reports in a similar industry to see how they differ in accounting policies.
   (ii) Try reports from different industries to see how they reflect the different businesses.
   (iii) Try some foreign companies and compare the layouts and contents.
   (iv) Look for examples of corporate governance statements.
4 Peter has run a successful small manufacturing business for the whole of his working life. He operates as a sole trader, but has now reached the age of 70 and wishes to retire. However he is of the opinion that none of his family (which consists of his three children and four grandchildren) is capable of taking on his business. In particular he has decided:
   (i)   That he wants each of his children and grandchildren to inherit a share of the business but with the children each having twice as much of an interest as each of the grandchildren.
   (ii) He is concerned that his heirs do not actually run the business. The management should be left in the hands of a long-term employee, Jack Jones, although since Jack is not a member of the family he does not wish him to own the business.
   (iii) He does not want the business to have to close just because one of the family wishes to withdraw from the business now or in the future.
   (iv) In the last few years, Peter has become concerned that the likelihood of being sued as an employer or for product liability is increasing. He is anxious that his family do not face the prospect of losing their private assets to meet such claims should he leave the business to them.

(v) He knows that the business will need further long-term capital if it is to maintain its position in the highly competitive market. He is confident that his family will be able to raise this since they own valuable property to act as security.

Required

Explain how the choice of business form could effect each of the issues raised above separately and then consider the overall position.

15 Company finance

Learning objectives

After reading this chapter you should be able to:
- recognise the main categories of finance available to companies and the risks and rewards associated with them
- understand how to record the issue of share capital
- understand how to record the payment of dividends
- set up a Sage system from an existing trial balance
- practice and consolidate the ideas introduced in earlier chapters by extending the case study.

Introduction

So far we have looked at the AIS from the point of view of a sole trader. In this chapter we look at the adaptations we need to accommodate company status. The basic recording system is exactly the same, but the records need to be adjusted to include some items specific to companies. Share capital and reserves will be needed instead of an owners' capital account, dividends instead of drawings, and corporation tax because the company is responsible for its own taxation affairs. To do this we will need to revisit the chart of accounts we designed in the earlier chapters and create some new accounts. These accounts will need to be organized into a new proforma for producing accounting reports for management. Companies' accounts for publication are rather more complex and we will look at those in the next chapter once we have the trial balance and the internal accounts organized.

It is now several years since the Bales and Mike Cowley set up their company and all is going well. Mike's extra contacts and investment of cash combined with the long hours put in by John and Azina, have led to the business expanding rapidly.

The £1 ordinary shares of the company are held as follows:

John Bale	100 000
Azina Bale	100 000
Mike Cowley	50 000

In addition Mike holds 200 000 £1 cumulative preference shares redeemable in 2010. These shares are entitled to a vote if the preference dividend is unpaid in any year until the dividend is made good. This was to guarantee Mike some income provided the company made profits.

All three of the shareholders are directors and receive fees for this. In the current year these were paid as follows:

Mike	£6 000
Azina	6 000
John – Chairman	10 000

In addition John and Azina receive salaries for their work for the business. John receives £50 000 as chief executive and Azina receives £45 000 as finance director.

The initial trial balance for the year ended 28 February 1998 has been extracted and Azina is now working on the end of year adjustments. The Case study at the end of this chapter includes

- the initial trial balance
- the reconciliation of the sales and purchase ledger balances with their respective control accounts
- the end of year adjustments
- some points of concern which have to come to light during the year end preparations and which will need to be put right.

Finance for limited companies

Bale and Cowley has been set up with two classes of shares in issue. They also have a small, long-term loan still outstanding. It is useful to think of the reasons why they have financed the company in the way they have. A company has two main ways of raising finance. They can issue shares or they can borrow. Borrowing for a company is just like borrowing by an individual. The lender will look for security in the form of a valuable asset that they can use to secure repayment in the event of you not being able to pay back the money borrowed or the interest. In addition they will want to assure themselves that you have a sensible plan for using the money and that you will generate enough cash to pay the interest in time. This is difficult for a new company without a track record. Even if the finance can be obtained, loans are a problem in that the interest has to be paid on time and the cash flows in a new business can be erratic. On the plus side, interest is deductible for tax purposes. Provided the company has a strong cash flow, paying interest is cheaper than dividends which are not tax deductible.

Share capital has different advantages and disadvantages. For small unlisted companies, potential shareholders are often limited to the immediate family and close business partners. Nevertheless shares still offer the advantage that whatever class of share is concerned the shareholder will not be able to demand repayment of capital from the company and cannot demand a dividend either. This means that there is less risk in using shares to finance the business than using loans. The problems for the company lie in finding shareholders and in owners not wanting to lose control of the business. From the potential shareholders' point of view the opposite is true. They will be unhappy about investing in a company where there is no market for the shares, making it difficult to realize the investment should it be needed. Without a majority vote it is difficult to force the payment of a dividend. It would be possible if things went wrong to end up with an investment which could not be sold and which paid very little income. More optimistically, the shareholder-investor hopes that the business will grow spectacularly and pay good dividends while the shares rise in price. This possible return must be high to encourage the shareholder to take the risk.

The types of shares were introduced and described in Chapter 2. The two main categories are preference shares and ordinary shares.

1   Preference shares usually have a fixed rate dividend which the holders are entitled to receive before the other shareholders receive anything. They may also be preferential as to capital in the event of a winding up. This means that if the company is put into liquidation and the assets are sold, the preference share holders will be repaid the nominal capital they invested before the remaining shareholders receive anything. This assumes there are enough assets to pay the other creditors in full beforehand. The preference shares do not usually vote although they are sometimes allowed this right if they have not received their dividend. As shareholders the investors in preference shares have no right to sue the company for dividends or capital in the event of default.

2   The other main category of shares are ordinary shares also known as equity shares. Ordinary shareholders stand to gain the most if the shares are profitable but lose most if the company makes losses. They usually control the votes but beware: there are such things as non-voting ordinary shares although these are not common. In theory it is the ordinary shareholders who own the business and through their votes at general meetings appoint directors, auditors and decide on dividends. In practice, much is left to the directors particularly the chairman and chief executive. As most shares are now held by institutions such as pension funds, unit or investment trusts, it is the block votes of these which tend to exercise most control over the activities of the board of directors.

In practice you will find many variants of share capital each with its own specific rights. Companies and their advisors devise new financial instruments tailoring the terms for a share issue to the needs of the company and the state of the market.

Activity

1   The case study used in this text book follows the fortunes of a small business together with its proprietors. The company has been financed by a mixture of ordinary and preference shares together with a small loan.
    Required
    Consider the advantages and disadvantages of the way in which Bale and Cowley is financed from the view point of:
    (a) the company
    (b) Mike Cowley
    (c) John Bale
    (d) Azina Bale.

Recording share capital in the AIS

For a company 'share capital and reserves' takes the place of 'owners capital' for the sole trader. The **share capital** that the company is authorized to issue is laid down in the Memorandum and Articles of Association which set the company up.

Although the authorized amount can be altered in the future, it is usual to avoid the administrative and legal problems of doing that by giving the new company authority to issue far more shares than it needs. The company can then issue the shares as it grows and the requirement for more capital becomes apparent.

The shares in the balance sheet reflect just the shares actually issued at the time. In the UK the shares are given a nominal or par value at which they are recorded in the balance sheet. So for example the company could be authorized to issue 100 000 shares of £1 each or 200 000 shares of 50 pence each. In either case the nominal value of the shares at £100 000 is the same although the number of shares is different.

If the shares were issued at the par value, then each shareholder would need to pay the nominal value to the company in cash. So if the company issued 50 000 £1 ordinary shares at par the records would show:

		£	£
Cash at bank	DR	50 000	
Ordinary £1 shares	CR		50 000

Share premium account

Once the company is operating it is unlikely that it would issue the shares at par. If the business is doing well then the share price for the shares in issue should be higher than £1 par value. Say they are traded at £1.20. The new shares are going to rank with the existing shares in the market so they need to carry a similar price. In this case if the company issues a further 10 000 shares they will be issued at £1.20. The law requires that the issued capital in the balance sheet be shown at nominal value with any premium shown in a separate reserve account.

		£	£
Cash at bank	DR	12 000	
Ordinary £1 shares	CR		10 000
Share premium account	CR		2 000

The name **share premium account** is given in the Companies Act 1985, which lays down rules regarding what can be done with the balance in it. The important point is that it cannot be used to pay a dividend back to the shareholders. It is not a profit the company has earned by its own efforts. It is capital contributed by the investors and as such they expect it to be invested in the assets of the business. Think of it like a deposit in a bank or building society account. As the depositor, you expect income in the form of interest but you expect this to be paid from earnings and that the sum invested will still be there to earn more interest next year.

The share premium will appear next to the share capital account in the final balance sheet and so it will need to be recorded in an account next to share capital in the AIS.

2   Assuming the preference shares were issued at par, and that all the ordinary shares in Bale and Cowley Ltd were issued at the same time, what price do you think the ordinary shares were issued at?

Capital redemption reserve

It is also possible in some circumstances to redeem shares i.e. buy them back. In this case, there are rules to make sure that the capital base of the company is not reduced. Unless the shares are redeemed out of the proceeds of a new issue of shares whose nominal value is at least equal to the nominal value of the shares being redeemed, the company is required to transfer an amount equivalent to the nominal value of the shares redeemed to a **capital redemption reserve**. The required transfer is made from the profit and loss account or other reserves built up out of profit. There are a number of conditions to be met before a company can redeem shares. For example a company cannot redeem shares if to do so would leave no further non-redeemable shares in issue. In other words it cannot end up redeeming all its shares and being owned by no one. Before undertaking a redemption exercise you should check the legal rules carefully and get advice.

The transfer itself is easy to record by means of a journal entry debiting the profit and loss and crediting the capital redemption reserve. An example should make this clear.

Assume company B wants to redeem 1000 £1 ordinary shares originally issued at £1.20 per share. They have agreed to pay £1.50 per share and they do not intend to make a new issue to meet the cost. The nominal value of £1000 will need to be met from profit together with the whole of the premium since there is no new issue. The journal entries would be:

		£	£
Ordinary £1 shares	DR	1 000	
Profit and loss account	DR	1 500	
Cash at bank	CR		1 500
Capital redemption reserve	CR		1 000

Like the share premium account the capital redemption reserve cannot be used for a dividend. Dividends must be paid from realized profits.

Rights issues

Rather than make a fresh issue to the general public, one way of raising fresh capital without diluting the control of existing shareholders is to make a rights issue. Under this method the shares are issued pro rata to the existing shareholders at a price below the current market price. This encourages investors to take up the offer. Any share-holder who does not wish to take up the shares can sell the rights 'nil paid' on the market to new investors. The company gains the capital. The shareholders get a good deal without diluting their interests and the stock market approves of the method. The discount to market price varies depending upon the amount of shares the company is hoping to issue. The more shares the greater the sweetener required in the form of the discount. A discount of 20 per cent or more might be required if it is a heavy rights issue of, say, 1 new share for 3 old shares. A light issue of, say, 1 new share for 10 old shares would get away with a much lower discount on the price. The floor on the price is the par value.

Bonus issues

Another term you might hear is a bonus issue. In this case the company does not gain any new capital at all. A bonus issue merely uses some of the reserves of the company to allocate free or bonus shares to the current shareholders. From the company's view point the issue does have legal and administrative costs but it does indicate to the shareholders that these past profits are permanently invested in the business and will not form part of a future dividend. It will also split the share price which can help the trading of the shares. No cash changes hands. However for some reason the stock market likes bonus issues and the value of the company on the market increases slightly leading to a small capital gain for the shareholders. The alteration to the trial balance involves making a journal entry transferring a balance from the reserves to the **issued share capital**. For example, if a company with 100 000 £1 shares in issue and reserves of £250 000 decided to make a bonus issue of 1 new share for 2 old shares, the company would need to issue 50 000 new shares at £1. The journal would be:

		£	£
Reserves	DR	50 000	
Ordinary £1 shares in issue	CR		50 000

Reserves

The word 'reserves' is often, mistakenly, thought of as representing piles of money stashed away in a vault in case of need. Unfortunately in accounting the term is used differently. **Reserves** represent the amounts reserved from profit which have not been distributed to the shareholders but retained for use within the business. As with the share capital these reserved or retained profits are already invested in the business and far from being found in treasure chests they are tied up in more mundane things like stock, debtors or a new computer.

The reserves can be given different names in the balance sheet such as general reserve, profit and loss account, retained earnings to name a few. They all appear in the financed by section of the balance sheet after share capital and they form part of the ordinary shareholders funds invested in the business. The reserves, together with the ordinary share capital, are known as the equity in the company.

A reserve is different from a **provision**. A change in provision is a charge against profit and is deducted to calculate the profit for a period. A transfer to a reserve is what happens to the profit once it has been calculated. The recording of a transfer to reserve will be through the journal.

Dividends

The shareholders receive their income in the form of **dividends**. These are not a charge against profit. Like the reserves they are an allocation of the profit once it has been calculated.

The preference dividend is paid at the fixed rate as authorized. The ordinary dividend is declared each year depending upon profits and the needs of the company for reinvestment. Any dividend is a drain on the cash available to the company. For most companies the easiest form of new investment to fund growth is past profit. Nevertheless the needs of the shareholders must be met. Sometimes where the shareholders are also employees of the company they take their income in the form of salaries and leave the profits in the business to finance new investment. This should be reflected in an increase in share price. If the other shareholders are happy to wait for capital growth, possibly because they are investing for the long term or because they pay heavy income tax on dividends, then this strategy will be accepted. Where shareholders rely on their investment for income, however, the company may be forced to pay a dividend regularly and raise the finance it needs elsewhere.

The dividend for the year needs to be agreed at the annual general meeting of the company. It is usual for the directors to make a recommendation and for the share-holders to endorse this. Until the meeting the dividend is known as the **proposed dividend**. A number of companies pay an **interim dividend** during the year as a payment on account. The dividend is usually quoted at so much per share e.g. 10 pence per share. Assuming 10 000 shares are in issue, the total dividend is then the number of shares times the dividend per share £1000 in this example.

The basic recording for the payment of the interim dividend is as follows:

		£	£
Dividend paid	DR	1 000	
Cash at bank	CR		1 000

When the final dividend for the year is proposed the accounts are prepared with a creditor for the liability. In our example, if the final dividend is proposed at 50 pence per share, then a journal to record it would look as follows:

		£	£
Profit and loss account	DR	5 000	
Dividend proposed creditor	CR		5 000

The dividend proposed account would be shown as a transfer from profit and the creditor would appear under current liabilities in the balance sheet.

A more difficult problem lies with the tax situation. Under the imputation system which has been in place since the early 1970s, when a company pays a dividend it also has to pay an advance on the mainstream corporation tax which the company will pay on its profits for the year. The amount is a given fraction of the dividend paid. This advance is known as ACT (Advanced Corporation Tax) and is payable to the Inland Revenue in the quarter when the dividend is paid. Shareholders receiving the dividend in cash also receive a tax credit which entitles them to a credit against their own tax bill. We say that the corporation tax has been imputed to the shareholder. The principle is that the company's profits should not be taxed twice – once in the hands of the company and again in the hands of the shareholder.

Once a dividend is declared the company needs to set up a creditor for the tax payable as a result. Recently there have been suggestions that the government intends to alter this approach. For this reason we will ignore ACT in the examples in this text.

Setting up the new trial balance

To set up a new system for an existing business requires the new system to be tailored to the needs of the ongoing business and the opening data to be entered so that the AIS can be continued.

Setting up the chart

You set up a chart of accounts for a new business in Chapter 5. Setting up a chart for an existing business is similar. You could start with the default chart but in this case you will need to adapt it to your business needs. At first glance this can seem quite easy but it is worth thinking through. The default chart of accounts should be printed off and compared with the trial balance from the existing system. In particular check

1 that the accounts are well ordered and the chart makes sense;
2 that all the items you need for a company are included – you will need several categories of share capital, reserves, dividends proposed and corporation tax;
3 that the accounts in the chart include all the business categories you need for income, expenses, assets and liabilities.

It is unlikely that the default chart will fit the company's needs exactly. You have a choice. You can adapt the chart to your needs or you can start from scratch. In practice it is worth taking the time to create your own chart. It is annoying and distracting continually to be trying to adapt your business to the needs of the chart. More importantly if there are accounts open which you are not intending to use it is easy to mistakenly post items to the unused account particularly if the names of the accounts don't agree with the terms you use in your business.

Entering the opening figures

The opening trial balance will need to be entered. This is usually done with a journal entry but there are two problems which you might need to overcome. First, accounting systems are built with a restriction on the number of characters which can be entered in any field. This means that while the underlying database can hold quite large numbers, the data entry screens for specific inputs can be quite restricted.

3   Open up your computer package and select a data entry screen such as batched
    data entry for invoices or nominal journal. Make up a fictional entry to test the
    number of characters you can enter.
    Required
    Make a record of the number of characters that you can enter in the debit or
    credit columns of the journal data entry routine.

You might find that the number you can enter is much lower than the numbers you
need to enter to set up the trial balance. The underlying system could record the
numbers, the problem lies in the entry screen. The answer is to divide the amount
which you need to enter into numbers small enough for the screen to accept. For
example, you might divide an item into ten amounts and make ten entries in the same
ledger account in order to post the full amount.

   As a one-off exercise to set up the system this might be acceptable. If your business
regularly throws up transactions which need to be posted in this way you should
reconsider the suitability of the software package you have chosen. Dividing items
up is time consuming and a source of errors. You should avoid it if you can.

   The journal necessary to enter the opening balances will be very large. Remember
that you must have balanced the debits and credits before you can post the item. You
should make sure that you have time to complete the operation before you start.

   The second problem you will come across is the difficulty of setting up the sales and
purchase ledgers. If you enter the debtors control account and the creditors control
account with the journal (as you will have to do to make the journal entry balance)
then you will have a system where the control accounts show a balance but the
underlying sales and creditors ledgers will have no accounts in them. The personal
accounts in the sales and creditors ledgers will need to be set up separately just as you
did in Chapter 5. When you have the accounts ready you can post the balances in the
batched data entry invoices screen as dummy invoices. This will automatically debit
the individual accounts and debit the debtors control account in the nominal ledger.
The important point to remember is to post the credit for the dummy invoices to
either

1   the mispostings account in the nominal ledger for later journal to the credit of the
    debtors control account; or
2   if the system will let you, post the credit directly to the debtors control account to
    cancel the unnecessary debit.

Finally once entered you need to print off the trial balance and debtors' and creditors'
lists and check them with the original.

4   Assume that Bale and Cowley are setting their AIS up on a new system. They will
    need to enter the trial balance in the new system and make the adjusting entries
    ready to enter the next years' transactions.

Required

(a) Redraft the chart of accounts to fit the needs of Bale and Cowley Ltd and print it off.

(b) Enter the trial balance before adjustments on the SAGE system.

(c) Make the entries necessary to take account of the adjustments in the case study above.

Summary

This chapter has looked at the changes which are needed to the AIS to accommodate the status of a company. In working through the case study example you should reinforce the work done in earlier chapters as well as understand the differences between sole trader and company status. The finance available to a company is different to that of a sole trader and this chapter discussed the factors that should be considered in making the decision on organizational form. The analysis of the balance of finance will be looked at in Chapter 17, when we look at interpretation techniques. First we need to understand how the accounts of a company are presented for publication. This will be the topic of the next chapter.

Key words

capital redemption reserve p. 245 • dividends p. 247 • interim dividend p. 247 • issued share capital p. 246 • proposed dividend p. 247 • provisions p. 246 • reserves p. 246 • share capital p. 244 • share premium account p. 244

Practice questions

1   Are the items listed below charged in calculating the profit for the year or appropriations of the profit?
   (i)   change in provision for doubtful debts
   (ii)   transfer to capital redemption reserve
   (iii) directors' fees
   (iv)   interim dividend
   (v)   interest on debentures
   (vi)   fixed rate preference dividend
   (vii) proposed dividend.

2   Company X wished to make a rights issue to raise further finance. A shareholder has written to the chairman with the following comment 'I cannot understand why you need to make a rights issue when the balance sheet shows that you already have all those unused reserves under the financed by section. I propose that you use those first.' Draft a reply to the shareholder explaining the meaning of 'reserves' in the balance sheet.

3   The summarized balance sheet of Friend plc is given below:
   Required
   (a) How many ordinary shares are in issue?
   (b) What does the term par value mean?
   (c) If you know that the preference shares were issued at par, and all the ordinary

Fixed assets		£750 000
Current assets		
Stock	£140 000	
Debtors	135 000	
Cash	5 000	
	280 000	
Current liabilities	70 000	
		210 000
		960 000
11% Loan capital		100 000
		860 000
Financed by		
25p Ordinary shares		500 000
8% £1 Preference shares		200 000
Share premium account		50 000
Profit and loss account		110 000
		860 000

       shares were issued at the same time, how much were the ordinary shares priced at when issued?

(d) Why would the company issue loan capital at 11 per cent if it can issue preference shares on which they only have to pay 8 per cent?

(e) What would happen if the company failed to pay the interest on the loan?

(f) What can the preference shareholders do if the company fails to pay the preference dividend?

(g) What would the ordinary shareholder receive per share if the company was wound up and the assets less current liabilities realised only £500 000?

(h) What is the equity in the company? What is the equity per share?

(i) If the current share price is £1.20 why might this be so much higher than the par value?

(j) Why is the share price different to the equity per share?

(k) If the profit for the year amounted to £110 000 before interest and corporation tax, the corporation tax amounted to £20 000 and the company declares a dividend of 2p per share, complete the bottom of the profit and loss account to calculate:

       the profit after interest and before tax
       the profit after tax
       retained profit for the year.

(l) What are the journal entries necessary to record the payment of the dividends?

(m) One of the shareholders has complained that the dividend should be a lot higher. How much could the company pay as a dividend? Can you see any problem with paying the dividend the company has already declared?

4   Distinguish a rights issue from a bonus issue.

5   The following data are extracted from the balance sheet of Woolman Ltd.
    Required
    Redraft the balance sheet to show the effect of making:

Fixed assets		£570 000
Current assets	360 000	
Current liabilities	92 000	
		268 000
		838 000
Financed by		
50p ordinary shares		£500 000
Profit and loss account		338 000
		838 000

(a) a rights issue of 1 for 5 at 60p

(b) a bonus issue of 1 for 10.

CASE STUDY

END OF YEAR 28 FEBRUARY 1998

Bale and Cowley Ltd

Trial balance at 28 February

	Dr (£)	Cr (£)
Sales		7 623 949
Purchases	5 266 910	
Directors' fees	22 000	
Wages and salaries	687 420	
Directors' salaries	95 000	
Heat and light	25 506	
Postage and stationery	16 455	
Telephone	12 943	
Advertising and promotion	52 562	
Rates and insurance	32 859	
Vehicle running expenses	33 759	
Sundry expenses	11 980	
Repairs to buildings	29 840	
Interest paid	13 500	
Repairs and renewals	8 564	
Sale of van – proceeds		5 000
Accounting	12 000	
Interim dividend	5 000	
VAT		14 087
Stock at 1st March	563 927	
Bank current account	24 453	
Debtors control account	863 105	
Land and buildings° – at cost	1 077 500	
– depreciation		32 500
Fixtures and fittings – at cost	97 121	
– depreciation		29 136
Office equipment – at cost	93 477	
– depreciation		35 054
Computer equipment – at cost	75 311	

– depreciation		21 324
Vehicles – at cost	142 895	
– depreciation		34 261
Provision for doubtful debts		29 000
Ordinary £1 shares		250 000
Share premium		25 000
Cumulative redeemable 8% £1 preference shares		200 000
Profit and loss account		340 089
General reserve		120 000
Debentures 9%		150 000
Creditors control account		354 687
	9 264 087	9 264 087

* *Note*: Land and buildings include the value of the site at £265 000, the remaining balance relates to the buildings.

List of debtor balances

	£
Adams supplies	223 126
Brooke and company	47 689
Carter and Son	113 546
Davids Plastics	167 600
Ebbots Ltd	19 451
Frank Brothers	97 624
General Supplies Ltd	83 667
Harry and Jarvis	110 402
Total	863 105
Balance per debtors control account	863 105

List of supplier balances

	£
Alan and Company	123 402
Bank's Office Equipment	47 621
Clement's Computers	34 702
Davies Computers	86 354
Edward's Ltd	62 608
Total	354 687
Balances per purchase ledger control	354 687

End of year adjustments

At the 28 February there is an estimated amount of £587 outstanding for electricity and £353 outstanding for the telephone. The insurance includes prepayments of £500.

Depreciation on fixed assets will need to be calculated according to the following rates on a straight line basis assuming no scrap value:

Buildings	2%
Fixtures and fittings	10%
Office equipment	8%
Computer equipment	25%
Vehicles	25%

During the year a vehicle was sold for £5000 which had originally been purchased for £15 000 although it had been depreciated by £7500. The only entry made for this was to debit the bank with the cash received and credit 'Sale of fixed asset' account.

Looking at the age analysis of debts, Azina and John have agreed that the provision for doubtful debts needs to be increased to £45 000. In addition the debt due from Ebbots Ltd needs to be written off as a bad debt.

A provision for corporation tax will need to be made estimated at £354 000. The dividend will need to be agreed but Azina thinks they should be in a position to pay a final dividend of 5p per share. In addition a transfer to general reserve is required amounting to £100 000. Closing stock has been counted for at £642 611. Finally a provision for Bill's audit fee of £4000 is needed.

Points of concern

- Adams Supplies have a credit limit of £220 000. Should Azina be concerned that their current balance is £223 126? What should she do next?
- A cheque to the value of £5500 received from Frank Brothers has been returned by the bank.
- A credit note for £12 300 has been posted to Carter and Son instead of Frank Brothers. Azina had received a very irate phone call from Simon Frank the managing director of Frank Brothers after he had received the monthly statement.
- Harry and Jarvis had also phoned querying the balance on their statement. They claimed they had sent a cheque to the value of £14 575 in December and wanted to know why it had not been posted against their account. Their bank statement showed that the cheque had not been presented. After exhaustive checks Azina phoned to inform them that it appeared that the cheque had been lost in the post. She advised them to cancel the cheque with their bank and requested from them a replacement cheque.
- During a visit from the VAT inspector three invoices were found to have been missed out when posting to the ledgers.

	Net (£)	VAT (£)
Brooke and Company	3 200.00	560.00
Davids Plastics	1 740.00	304.50
General Supplies	672.00	117.60

This was quite worrying as John and Azina thought that their systems would not allow this to happen. What can they do to ensure that this does not happen in the future?
- A cheque sent to Alan and Company for £5675.00 had been posted to the account of Clements Computers.
- A credit note received from Davies Computers for £10 728 gross had been posted against Edwards Ltd.

■ In January a delivery of printers from Alan and Company were found to be damaged. Of the ten printers delivered four had been returned and Azina had requested a credit note for £3120.00. She now noted that although Alan and Company had agreed that the printers were damaged in transit, no credit note had been received.

■ An electricity bill for £643 had been posted to the telephone account.

■ Postage and stationery worth £184.34 had mistakenly been posted to advertising and promotion.

16 Published company reports

Learning objectives

After reading this chapter you should be able to:
- prepare the published balance sheet and profit and loss account for a company from the trial balance in good form
- draft the main notes required to attach to the published statement
- be familiar with the layout of published financial statements produced by plcs.

Introduction

For management purposes the financial statements for each period will be similar to those of the sole trader. They will contain detailed breakdowns of expenses and income information to enable the managers to assess the performance of different lines of business and different departments. However the company would not want all this information to be made public and investors and creditors would not want all the detail. The information to be published by a company is subject to controls and regulations. In this chapter we will build on the introduction given in Chapter 14 on regulation and control, to look at the formats given in the Companies Act 1985 for published financial statements for companies. The full publication requirements are very detailed and include the accounting standards produced by the ASB and its predecessor. One chapter cannot cover all these requirements and we are going to concentrate on the basic Companies Act regulations. The ASB standards expand and illuminate the requirements of the Act. This makes the Act a good place to start to gain an overview or framework for the publication requirements.

Azina has now corrected or solved the points which concerned her about the draft trial balance and she has made the final adjustments. The trial balance is now in a position to be printed off in a form fit for publication as required by the Companies Act 1985. This is not as easy as just calling up a print off from the screen and Azina usually makes sure she gets advice. She has found that the requirements change year by year and she needs to make sure that no new regulations have been introduced or even some old ones she has not previously needed to worry about suddenly have become relevant. Keeping up to date with all the changes is difficult when she is busy running the business on a day-to-day basis. However this has been a very good trading year, with several major contracts completed. They have all worked very hard and are keen to see the final results. John thinks it is unlikely that such big contracts can be repeated the following year but nevertheless the fact that they handled the contracts successfully has given the whole team a boost of confidence. Azina starts work on the results for publication.

The Companies Act formats – the background

One of the results of the influence of the EU on company reporting practice in the UK is the introduction of formats for the profit and loss account and balance sheet. Continental countries have traditionally used a strict format. This is partly because the primary purpose of the reports was for tax and government statistical purposes or for creditors. The use of a standard format made it easier to compare the results of companies and impose taxes. The French system takes this even further by imposing a national chart of accounts. Every business in France has the same code for the same expense. The accounts are then drawn up by adding the required codes together and filling in the correct total. Ironically this is now seen as an advantage since the standardization of the recording process enables standard default charts to be built for accounting software. As some accounting packages begin to dominate the software market, the standardization process is taking place through market forces rather than law.

The UK, with its emphasis on informing the investor, considered that the format should be flexible to enable each company to present its results in a form which was considered by its directors as being most informative. UK accountants were not at all happy about the imposition of what they saw as a straightjacket in the **Companies Act** of 1981.

In the event, the requirements have been left flexible enough to enable a considerable amount of judgement to be used in the presentation and the formats have not proved the problem they were originally thought to be. Looking at the reports from different companies you might find it difficult to believe there is any set format at all.

The format rules

The **formats** are laid out in Schedule 4 to the **Companies Act** 1985. Companies have a choice from four profit and loss accounts and two balance sheets. In fact, as far as information disclosed is concerned, the choice is not as great as this. The two balance sheets, for example, require the same information but one format organizes it in a horizontal format and the other in a vertical format. Similarly, in reality, the profit and loss accounts offer only two different approaches, each being offered in horizontal or vertical format. In the work below we will use the vertical version because these are used by the vast majority of companies in the UK. You should be aware however that continental and US reports are frequently in horizontal format.

The choice boils down to the selection of a profit and loss account. The difference is that one format summarizes the expenses by the nature of the expense, e.g. all the depreciation expenses are together with all the wages and salaries; the other organizes the expenses by function, e.g. all the expenses associated with cost of sales are put together with all the selling expenses. The choice is for each company to make for itself but having made its choice, the company must be consistent from year to year. Slightly more than half the companies in the UK reportedly use the format which organizes expenses by function. This is the format which we shall use. The horizontal format for the balance sheet and the horizontal format organizing the expenses by function are reproduced in Tables 16.1 and 16.2.

You will notice in the balance sheet format that some items appear more than once. Prepayments for example and called up share capital not paid. These are alternative positions which can be used for the items concerned. Another feature is the lack of subtotals. Although some subtotals such as net current assets are named and therefore must be put in, others such as the total for fixed assets or the total of share capital and reserves are not given. This does not mean they should not be calculated and shown. If the statements are to make sense then some totals must be put in.

The formats as displayed in the Act are not easy to use, or indeed to identify in a published set of accounts until you understand the rules which go with them. As for all the other presentation requirements in the Act, the 'true and fair' override applies to using the formats. If to show a true and fair view it is necessary to ignore the format requirements then you should do so. Marks and Spencers plc has always used this override to state specifically that in its opinion the analysis of expenses required in the Act does not give a true and fair view and it has therefore chosen to analyse its expenses in a way it considers to be more informative. Marks and Spencers has been open about its policy. Other companies have a similar disregard for the analysis of expenses required by the Act but do not draw attention to the fact.

Despite this apparently lax policy in the UK, it is necessary to study the formats because they do provide the basic structure of the statements on which the accounting standard programme has built other features.

The published statements must give the figures for the current year and the previous year. You are not required to reproduce the letters and numbers in the published version of the statements although they are produced in some continental versions of the formats.

The headings indicated with letters or roman numerals form the basic framework of the statements and should be reproduced in the order given. You should include these headings unchanged in the published statements unless there is nothing under that heading in either this year or the last. Note you should not change the wording of the headings. However you are permitted to add to, rearrange or adapt the arabic numeral (1, 2, 3, etc.) headings where required by the special nature of the business. This has been used to justify a number of adaptations such as the analysis of expenses discussed above. It is permitted to amalgamate the arabic headings into one heading on the face

---

Table 16.1 Balance sheet format 1 from the Companies Act 1985 Schedule 4

A   Called up share capital not paid
B   Fixed assets
      I   Intangible assets
           1. Development costs
           2. Concessions, patents, licences, trade marks and similar rights and assets
           3. Goodwill
           4. Payments on account
      II   Tangible assets
           1. Land and buildings
           2. Plant and machinery
           3. Fixtures and fittings, tools and equipment
           4. Payments on account and assets in course of construction
      III   Investments
           1. Shares in group companies
           2. Loans in group companies
           3. Shares in related companies
           4. Loans in related companies
           5. Other investments other than loans
           6. Other loans
           7. Own shares
C   Current assets
      I   Stocks
           1. Raw materials
           2. Work in progress
           3. Finished goods and goods for sale
           4. Payments on account
      II   Debtors
           1. Trade debtors
           2. Amounts owed by group companies
           3. Amounts owed by related companies
           4. Other debtors
           5. Called up share capital not paid
           6. Prepayments and accrued income
      III   Investments
           1. Shares in group companies
           2. Own shares
           3. Other investments
      IV   Cash at bank and in hand
D   Prepayments and accrued income
E   Creditors: amounts falling due within one year
           1. Debenture loans
           2. Bank loans and overdrafts
           3. Payments received on account
           4. Trade creditors
           5. Bills of exchange payable
           6. Amounts owed by group companies
           7. Amounts owed by related companies
           8. Other creditors including taxation and social security
           9. Accruals and deferred income

Table 16.1 Balance sheet format 1 from the Companies Act 1985 Schedule 4 (cont)

F		Net current assets (liabilities)
G		Total assets less current liabilities
H		Creditors amounts falling due after more than one year
		1. Debenture loans
		2. Bank loans and overdrafts
		3. Payments on account
		4. Trade creditors
		5. Bills of exchange
		6. Amounts owed to group companies
		7. Amounts owed to related companies
		8. Other creditors including taxation and social security
		9. Accruals and deferred
I		Provision for liabilities and charges
		1. Pensions and similar obligations
		2. Taxation including deferred taxation
		3. Other provisions
J		Accruals and deferred income
K		Capital and reserves
	I	Called up share capital
	II	Share premium account
	III	Revaluation reserve
	IV	Other reserves
		1. Capital redemption reserve
		2. Reserve for own shares
		3. Reserves provided for by the articles of association
		4. Other reserves
	V	Profit and loss account

Table 16.2 Profit and loss account format 1 from Schedule 4 Companies Act 1985

1	Turnover
2	Cost of sales
3	Gross profit or loss
4	Distribution costs
5	Administrative expenses
6	Other operating income
7	Income from shares in group companies
8	Income from shares in related companies
9	Income from other fixed asset investments
10	Other interest receivable and similar income
11	Amounts witten off investments
12	Interest payable and similar charges
13	Tax on profit and loss on ordinary activites
14	Profit and loss on ordinary activities after tax
15	Extraordinary income
16	Extraordinary charges
17	Extraordinary profit and loss
18	Tax on extraordinary profit and loss
19	Other taxes not shown above
20	Profit or loss for the financial year

of the statements and give the required breakdown by way of note. This has become standard practice in the UK.

Finally where an item with an arabic numeral is considered immaterial it can be amalgamated with another heading. However no guidance is given in the Act regarding what is to be considered to be immaterial.

To illustrate the presentation we will use the information in the last chapter for Bale and Cowley Ltd. If you have not already done so, it would help if you produce a set of management reports from the adjusted trial balance you produced in Chapter 15. It should be possible to print these off from the system.

The profit and loss account

Format 1 for the profit and loss account requires the expenses to be allocated to one of three headings:

1   **cost of sales;**
2   **administrative expenses**;
3   **distribution costs**.

The Act gives little guidance on what to include under each heading. Apart from saying that these three headings should include depreciation and provision for diminution in value, you are left to decide this for yourself. The result is that you should be wary of comparing one company's split of expenses with another. Different finance directors have different ideas.

Activity

1   To which of the three expenses headings given in format 1 would you allocate the following expenses:
    (i)   production director's salary
    (ii)   sales director's fees
    (iii)   depreciation of building
    (iv)   maintenance of canteen available to all staff
    (v)   packing materials.

Your answers may differ depending upon how you thought the business concerned operated. The production director's salary would be considered to be part of the cost of sales by some companies but as administration by others. This might reflect slight differences in role or a genuine difference of opinion on where it belongs. The lesson must be not to take the split of expenses as an important factor in assessing a company against its peers. However, it should be possible to compare the trend within one company year by year because they are required to be consistent.

Although there are few subtotals indicated by headings in the format, in the UK it is standard practice to add these as you did for the sole trader. It is useful to assess the level of profit at different points in the profit and loss account and there is nothing in the Act to stop this being done.

Coming to the headings relating to extraordinary items, while in law they still exist, the advice from the ASB is that there is no transaction that they can think of which would be so unusual as to require being put under these headings. This means that you will not find an example of an extraordinary item in a recent set of published financial statements in the UK. Even the losses incurred by the Daily Mirror pension fund under Maxwell were considered to be part of normal activities. There is a reason for this. The extraordinary items appear in the format after profit after tax. In the UK, investors look at this profit figure as the important indicator of performance. If a company wanted to show its results in a good light and disguise a problem, then calling it extraordinary made sure that it was deducted after the profit figure which analysts were using to assess the company. It was to stop this possible loophole that the ASB put its moratorium on extraordinary items.

Finally you will find that the format stops suddenly at profit for the year. There is no indication of where dividends and appropriations from profit are to be shown. This means that following the formats to the letter makes it very difficult to link the profit and loss and the balance sheet figures for capital and reserves. Without such a link it is possible to make adjustments which shareholders know nothing about.

The Act does require details of the dividends and movements on reserves and shareholders funds to be disclosed although no format is given. The ASB has gone further than this and requires a **Statement of Total Recognized Gains and Losses** (**STRGL** for short) as an additional primary statement in published reports. The requirements for this are set out in FRS3 Reporting Financial Performance which expands the profit and loss account to make it more informative. It is this standard that effectively removed extraordinary items. The STRGL takes the profit for the year before the dividend and adds any unrealized profits on revaluation of assets or foreign exchange translation differences and calculates the total gains for the year which the company has recognized. In a simple case like Bale and Cowley the total recognized

Table 16.3 Bale and Cowley Ltd – Movement on reserves, reconciliation of shareholders funds and Statement of total recognized gains and losses

Movement on reserves

	Share premium (£)	General reserve (£)	Profit and loss (£)	Total (£)
At the beginning of year	25 000	120 000	340 089	485 089
Transfer from profit and loss for the year			891 591	891 591
Transfers from profit	–	100 000	(100 000)	–
At end of year	25 000	220 000	1 131 680	1 376 680

Reconciliation of movements on shareholders funds

Profit for the year	925 091	
Dividends	33 500	
	891 591	
Opening balance of shareholders funds	935 089	
Closing shareholders funds		1 826 680

Statement of total recognized gains and losses

Profit for the year	£925 091

gains and losses is the same as the profit for the year and a statement to that effect is needed. The STRGL is a separate statement to the movement on reserves and the reconciliation of movements on shareholders funds. The three statements for Bale and Cowley Ltd are set out in Table 16.3.

Activity

2   Taking the trial balance or the draft profit and loss account for Bale and Cowley, decide how you will allocate the expenses and try drafting the profit and loss account for publication.

Table 16.4 gives a profit and loss account drawn from the figures given for Bale and Cowley which is in a form for publication. Note that instead of finishing at the profit for the year the dividends are shown as a deduction. This follows common practice amongst companies and illustrates that the company is paying its dividends from this year's profits. It also highlights the proportion of the profit which is being retained for reinvestment within the business.

The Act stipulates a number of notes giving further disclosures which need to be included with the published reports. If you look at some published accounts you will see that it is usual to reference these to the relevant figure in the statement where it relates to a particular item.

The required notes to the profit and loss account include:

I   Turnover needs to be analysed according to class of business and geographical area.
II   Rentals received from leasing land and buildings owned by the company where the figure is a substantial part of the income.
III   The interest payable needs to be analysed between

Table 16.4   Bale and Cowley Ltd Profit and Loss Account for the year ended 28 February 1998

	Notes	£	£
Turnover			7 629 561
Cost of sales			5 185 106
Gross profit			2 444 455
Distribution costs		120 611	
Administrative expenses		1 031 253	
			1 151 864
Profit before interest and tax			1 292 591
Interest payable and similar charges			13 500
Profit before tax			1 279 091
Tax on profit or loss on ordinary activities			354 000
Profit or loss for the financial year			925 091
Dividends:			
Preference		16 000	
Ordinary Interim		5 000	
Final		12 500	
			33 500
Retained profit for the financial year			891 591

- interest payable on bank loans and overdrafts and other loans repayable within five years;
- interest on all other loans.

IV Hire charges for equipment.

V Auditor's remuneration.

VI Depreciation.

VII Directors' remuneration indicating:
- remuneration for services to the company giving separate figures for the fees, other emoluments, pensions, and compensation for loss of office;
- the Chairman's emoluments, the emoluments of the highest paid director and a table giving the number of directors falling into bands rising at £5000 intervals;
- the number of directors who have waived their emoluments for the year.

VIII Regarding employees:
- the weekly average number employed in total and by category (defined by the directors);
- amounts paid to employees giving figures for wages and salaries, social security costs and other pension costs;
- the number of employees whose earnings fall into rising bands of £5000 beginning with £30 001.

IX Taxation – the basis of the tax charge and any significant circumstances affecting the amount.

X Amounts set aside for the redemption of share capital and loans.

XI Separate figures for dividends paid and dividends recommended on each class of share.

Activity

3 Take the information for Bale and Cowley and draft the balance sheet using the format 1 given in the Companies Act 1985. Compare your answer with the one given in Table 16.5.

Notes to the balance sheets include:

I Share capital. Details should be given of authorized share capital; the number and aggregate value of each class of issued share; details of the date for redemption of any redeemable shares; details of any share issue.

II Debentures: Details of any issues and redemptions in the year.

III Reserves and provisions for liabilities and charges should give the opening and closing balances and any movements in the year explained.

IV Creditors: details of any charges over the assets given as security and a breakdown of other creditors to show details of dividends, taxation and social security costs.

V Fixed assets: details of the opening and closing balances of cost and depreciation, movements in the year, including revaluation, and the net book value. Where a valuation was undertaken, the name or qualifications of any valuers and the basis of valuation. Land and buildings should be split between freeholds, long leaseholds

Table 16.5   Balance sheet for Bale and Cowley Ltd

Balance sheet at 31 December 1997

Fixed assets	£	£	£
Tangible assets			
Land and buildings			1 028 750
Fixtures, fittings, tools and equipment			229 353
			1 258 103
Current assets			
Stocks: Finished goods and goods for resale		642 611	
Debtors: Trade debtors		806 427	
Prepayments and accrued income		500	
Cash at bank and in hand		23 116	
		1 472 654	
Creditors amounts falling due within twelve months			
Trade creditors	351 567		
Other creditors including taxation and social security	402 510		
		754 077	
Net current assets			718 577
Total assets less current liabilities			1 976 680
Creditors: amounts falling due after more than one year			
Debenture loans			150 000
			1 826 680
Capital and reserves			
Called up share capital		450 000	
Share premuim account		25 000	
Other reserves		220 000	
Profit and loss account		1 131 680	
			1 826 680

and short leaseholds. Leaseholds with longer than 50 years to run are thought of as long.

VI   Investments: split the investments between listed and unlisted and the stock exchanges where they are listed; the market value of listed shares; details of any holding in another company greater than 10 per cent.

VII   Loans to directors and to other employees to enable them to buy shares in the company.

VIII   Stocks: any material difference between market value and book value.

IX   Details of any charges over the assets of the company or any contingent liability together with pension commitments provided for and those not provided for.

These lists are not exhaustive but give you some idea of the range and detail of the requirements of the Act. In addition to these there are the ASB standards and the rules of the Stock Exchange. The cost and time of producing the information can be very high especially when, like Bale and Cowley, in house expertise is limited. If you remember, in Chapter 14 we discussed the reduced requirements for small and medium sized companies.

4   From the previous chapter check the definitions of small, medium and large companies and the modifications to published reports that results from the classification. Compare this with the statements you have prepared for Bale and Cowley. Assume Bale and Cowley employed 34 people on average during the year.
Required
Is Bale and Cowley classified as small, medium or large in company law? What modifications to the rules for publication is the company entitled to?

Summary

This chapter has concentrated on the legal requirements for the publication of financial statements. The rules are detailed and are best drawn up from a checklist rather than from memory. The best place to see the rules in action is to send off for examples of published statements. Increasingly you will find the results published on the Internet. This can be interesting but from the point of view of learning the requirements are not nearly as useful. Published reports are so long that reading them on screen is not easy. Looking at the real thing will give you an idea of the language that is used and examples of how specific problems have been handled by others. The reports also contain comments on corporate governance and the directors' responsibilities for internal control. This is the topic that is considered in detail in the final chapter. Before that, we look at how to make good use of the information in the reports you have produced and the limitations from the users point of view.

Key words

administrative expenses p. 262 • Companies Acts p. 258 • distribution costs p. 262 • formats p. 258 • statement of total recognized gains and losses p. 263 • STRGL p. 263

1   The following trial balance has been extracted from the accounting system of Pendle Ltd at 31 March 1998:
The finance director has asked your help in presenting the information in a form suitable for publication.
You have been given the following extra information:
   (i)   The company's leasehold property has a 999 year lease. It was revalued at £1 800 000 in March 1998 by J.R. Fox, chartered surveyor. The directors wish to use the valuation in the reports.
   (ii) The company made a bonus issue of 2 ordinary shares, fully paid for each share held, on 1 October 1997. No entries have been made in the records for this issue.

	£	£
Ordinary £1 shares		1 000 000
Retained profit at 1 April 1997		2 078 000
10% Debentures 2012		600 000
Leasehold land and buildings at cost	800 000	
Computer equipment at cost	2 600 000	
Accumulated depreciation		
on computer equipment		1 024 000
Trade debtors	720 000	
Prepayments	20 160	
Stocks of raw materials	1 808 000	
Work in progress	160 040	
Bank balance	536 000	
Provision for doubtful debts		30 000
Creditors		703 000
Sales		6 124 800
Cost of sales	4 083 200	
Office expenses	433 800	
Marketing expenses	300 800	
Bad debts written off	17 400	
General repairs	50 400	
Debenture interest to 30 Sept 1997	30 000	
	£11 559 800	£11 559 800

(iii) The directors propose to pay a dividend of 5p per share for every share in issue on 31 March 1998.

(iv) The company purchased new fittings on 30 March 1998 and these were delivered to the company on 31 March 1998 but not recorded, paid for or used before April. The invoice for £240 000 came with the equipment.

(v) Depreciation has not yet been adjusted. It is to be provided on the reducing balance method at 25 per cent on all computer equipment in use at the year end. Ignore the fittings in (iv) above.

(vi) Corporation tax of £300 000 is to be provided for.

(vii) The company's authorized share capital is 4 million ordinary shares of £1 each.

Required

Prepare the profit and loss account and balance sheet for publication in the formats required by the Companies Act 1985.

2 As far as possible from the information available, draft the notes to the published financial statements for Bale and Cowley Ltd.

17 Interpretation and ratios

Learning objectives

After reading this chapter you should be able to:
- explain the limitations of financial statements and ratios as a source of information
- know the need for and the difficulty in selecting a yardstick for comparison
- calculate a basic set of ratios as an analytical technique
- select a suitable subset of ratios to help to answer specific problems
- analyse and interpret financial statements and ratios as a basis for decision taking.

Introduction

We have stressed throughout the book that the purpose of recording and presenting all this information is for people to use it to manage and control a business and make decisions. Sometimes making sense of the information is not as easy as it looks even if the reports have been well designed. There are so many figures that it can be difficult to understand what is going on and how they all relate to each other.

Ratios are used to help to understand and interpret the financial statements. In this chapter we will look at the ratios in common use and what they can tell us. You need to remember that there is no standard set of ratios which everyone agrees on. If comparing two figures will help you then that is a useful ratio. Managers and analysts can and do invent their own ratios as they see the need. Provided they are correctly interpreted there is nothing wrong in this. However, to start you off there are some ratios which are in common use and which you should be able to calculate and use. This chapter will set out a basic 'tool-kit' of ratios which you should find useful. You should be warned however that just as there is no agreed set of ratios, there is no agreed way of calculating them. This is partly because each situation is different. The ratios need adapting to fit the case you are looking at and the information which you have. If you look at other text books you might well find that the calculations are slightly different. We recommend that you stick to one set to start with. As you become more confident you will understand how and why variations might be used equally successfully.

Finally, interpreting financial statements is one of the most interesting jobs for the accountant. It involves a bit of detective work identifying the main issues and looking for possible explanations. You need to use your accounting skills, professional judgement and imagination.

John and Azina were looking at the accounts for the year ended 28 February which had just been produced. John was pleased. Turnover had increased amazingly over the previous year and although the overall net profit to sales figure was disappointing (he had expected it to be more in the region of 20 per cent) the return on equity was tremendous. Azina agreed that it had been a good year.

'We've increased turnover but mainly through one-off sales. We had only one bad debt this year and that must be an improvement. The balance sheet suggests that we are in a stable position financially. I think we should go out and celebrate.'

The subject of the accounts came up again when John met Mike Cowley for lunch later that week. Mike came up with a suggestion.

'I have a copy of the accounts of a company in the same line of business in the North East – Rowe and Davies. They are based in Durham but cover the whole of the north of England and parts of Scotland. If you are finding it difficult to judge your performance why don't you compare your results with that company? They are about the same size but been around for longer. I think they set up in the late seventies.' John was taken with this idea and Mike promised to send him the accounts.

When the accounts arrived Azina and John set about analyzing the figures as they stood. They decided to compare the working capital management, long-term capital structure and profitability ratios.

Activity

1   The accounts for Rowe and Davies Ltd are set out in Table 17.1. The rest of the chapter will calculate the ratios for Bale and Cowley Ltd using the accounts prepared in the last chapter. These have been summarized and redrafted to match the form of Rowe and Davies to help the analysis. They are reproduced for you in Table 17.2.
Required
As you work through the sections of the chapter indicating how the ratios are calculated for Bale and Cowley Ltd, calculate the same ratios for Rowe and Davies Ltd. By the end of the chapter you should be able to write a report for the directors of Bale and Cowley including the ratios and your interpretation of them.

Choosing a yardstick

The first rule for using ratios is that unless you have something to compare your figures with it is pointless making the calculation. Figures on their own mean nothing. To give you an example, you might be told that sales have increased by £100 000. This might be good if you knew that the sales for the previous year were £1000 or bad if you knew that the sales were £100 million in the previous year and that the plan had been to increase those by 20 per cent. John and Azina are fortunate in that Mike has come up

Table 17.1 The summarized accounts of Rowe and Davies

Rowe and Davies Ltd
Profit and loss account for the year ended 31 December 1997

		£	£
	Sales		6 727 200
Less	Cost of sales		
	Opening stock	392 650	
	Purchases	4 086 006	
		4 478 656	
	Less closing stock	442 336	4 036 320
	Gross profit		2 690 880
Less	Salaries and wages	784 000	
	Directors salaries and fees	420 620	
	Depreciation:		
	Fixtures and fittings	14 333	
	Office equipment	15 500	
	Computer eqiupment	11 900	
	Vehicles	22 867	
	Provision for debts	6 450	
	Sale of assets	(4 200)	
	Other expenses	831 410	
			2 102 880
	Operating profit		588 000
Less	Interest		112 000
	Profit before tax		476 000
	Taxation		62 000
	Profit after tax		414 000
	Profit brought forward		653 629
	Profit carried foward		1 067 629

Balance Sheet at 31 December 1997

Fixed Assets	£	£	£
Land and buildings			663 000
Fixtures and fittings			43 000
Office equipment			62 000
Computer equipment			35 700
Vehicles			137 200
			940 900
Current assets			
Stock		442 336	
Debtors		645 074	
Less provision		(6 450)	
Prepayments		127 600	
		1 208 560	
Current liabilities			
Trade creditors	315 836		
Bank overdraft	181 422		
Other creditors	84 573		
		581 831	
Net current assets			626 729

Table 17.1   The summarized accounts of Rowe and Davies (cont)

	1 567 629
18% Debentures	400 000
	1 167 629
Financed by	
Ordinary shares of £1	100 000
Profit and loss account	1 067 629
	1 167 629

Table 17.2   The summarized accounts of Bale and Cowley Ltd

Profit and loss account for the year ended 28 February 1998

		£	£
	Sales		7 629 561
Less	Cost of sales		
	Opening stock	563 927	
	Purchases	5 263 790	
		5 827 717	
	Less closing stock	642 611	5 185 106
	Gross profit		2 444 455
Less	Salaries and wages	687 420	
	Directors salaries and fees	117 000	
	Depreciation:		
	Building	16 250	
	Fixtures and fittings	9 712	
	Office equipment	7 478	
	Computers	3 012	
	Vehicles	31 974	
	Provision for doubtful debts	16 000	
	Bad debts	19 451	
	Sale of assets	2 500	
	Other expenses	241 067	
			1 151 864
	Profit before interest and tax		1 292 591
Less	Interest		13 500
	Profit before tax		1 279 091
Less	Taxation		354 000
	Profit for the year after tax		925 091
Less	Dividends		
	Preference	16 000	
	Ordinary Interim	5 000	
	Final	12 500	
			33 500
			891 591
Less	Transfer to general reserve		100 000
			791 591
Add	Profit brought forward		340 089
	Profit carried forward		1 131 680

Table 17.2 The summarized accounts of Bale and Cowley Ltd (Continued)

Balance Sheet at 28 February 1997

Fixed assets	£	£	£
Land and buildings			1 028 750
Fixtures and fittings			58 273
Office equipment			50 945
Computer equipment			50 975
Vehicles			69 160
			1 258 103
Current assets			
Stock		642 611	
Debtors		851 427	
Less provision		(45 000)	
Prepayments		500	
Bank		23 116	
		1 472 654	
Current liabilities			
Trade creditors	351 567		
Other creditors	402 510		
		754 077	
Net current assets			718 577
			1 976 680
18% Debentures			150 000
			1 826 680
Financed by			
Share capital			
Ordinary shares of £1		250 000	
Preference shares		200 000	
Share premium		25 000	
General reserve		220 000	
Profit and loss account		1 131 680	
			1 826 680

with a company with which they can compare their own results. It is not normally so easy and each possible yardstick has its drawbacks. We look at the main possibilities below.

Cross sectional analysis

Cross sectional comparison means comparing your results with those of a similar business as John and Azina plan to do. The difficulty lies in finding a company just like yours. No two businesses are identical and this needs to be borne in mind when comparing the performance.

The business will probably be financed differently with a different mix of debt and equity, and a different time scale for repaying the debt. The product or service will be slightly different, possibly more luxurious or more mass market. The market will vary geographically and possibly by type of customer with the different marketing and distribution costs that requires. Different management styles or operating strategies may cause different asset requirements. The business will be unlikely to have started at the same time as your own and therefore the age profile of its assets will be different.

When it comes to statements themselves you will find that different accounting policies will need to be adjusted before you can begin to compare the figures. Even then, you have no idea whether the company you are looking at is an example of good practice or whether it has just had an excellent or a very poor year.

Industry standards

Industry standards are an attempt to provide an average for the results of the businesses operating in the same market. They have the advantage that they have averaged out differences in performance. However, if it is difficult to find one company that is a match for your own, it is far more difficult to find a whole industry. It might well include businesses which are not very like yours at all. If you look at the financial pages of the press you will see this illustrated. Share prices are published grouped by industrial sector. If you look at the companies making up such a sector you will see a diverse range of businesses with different aspirations and not necessarily in direct competition with any of the others. The water sector for example not only includes companies operating in very different geographical areas with different storage and supply problems but includes companies which own electricity distributors and civil engineering companies. Similar comments could be made of other sectors. An average for one of these groupings would be a very rough comparison for the individual companies concerned.

Time series comparisons

Time series comparisons involve looking at the results of the organization over a series of time periods. This should enable trends to be determined and comparisons made with planned outcomes. Time series analyses are not without their problems however. The company itself might have changed business direction, merged or taken over other businesses or ceased trading in some areas. Major new competitors may have entered the market. The accounting polices may have changed. Technological change needs to be thought out and also the economic conditions under which it operates. For example a company may seem to be operating with a very low working capital figure in one year but it might be that interest rates were low at that time and money easy to raise quickly. Operating with the same level of working capital in another year when interest rates were very high and it was difficult to borrow may have been suicidal. You need to be aware of these changing circumstances when reviewing a time series.

First steps in interpreting financial statements

Reading the statements

The first thing you should do is read the statements you are analyzing. This is often missed out as people head straight for their calculators and start producing ratios as fast as they can remember them. Yet you often find that an initial overview can give you a framework to work with which will stop you being sidetracked or accepting ratios which are the result of punching the wrong numbers into the calculator.

All you need to do is take a pencil and work quickly down the statements looking across the years or at the comparisons and note anything that stands out – such as changes in assets or sources of financing, a major increase or decrease in an income or expense heading. Is there an interest charge? Are there any exceptional or unusual items?

Background information

The statements should reflect the world in which the business operates. You need to bring to mind and collect any information about the trading conditions and market for the company's products or services that are available. Press comment on the sector or economic conditions generally can be very useful in understanding what is happening. Review the statements in the light of what knowledge you have. For example, if you know the industry is facing major technological changes then you will be looking for investment in fixed assets.

Same size analysis

Same size statements are often a good way to identify major differences in the way companies operate. The technique involves reducing the figures in the profit and loss account and balance sheet to percentage figures. The profit and loss items are usually shown as a percentage of the sales figure and the balance sheet items as a percentage of shareholders' funds. In this way you can remove the differences due to the scale of the activities undertaken and isolate operating financing and performance differences.

Using this technique the Bale and Cowley statements would look as follows:

Profit and loss account

	%	%
Sales		100.0
Cost of sales		68.0
Gross profit		32.0
Salaries and wages	9.0	
Directors salaries and fees	1.5	
Depreciation	0.9	
Provision for doubtful debts	0.2	
Bad debts	0.3	
Other expenses	3.1	
		15.0
Profit before interest and tax		17.0
Interest		0.2
Profit before tax		16.8
Tax		4.6
Profit after tax		12.2

Balance sheet

	%	%
Fixed assets		68.8
Current assets	80.6	
Less Current liabilities	41.2	
Working capital		39.4
		108.2
Debentures		8.2
Shareholders funds		100.0

If you present the accounts of Rowe and Davies in this style you can compare the way in which the companies:

1 priced their goods by looking at the gross profit;
2 managed their overheads by comparing the expenses;
3 operated with the mix of fixed assets and working capital;
4 financed their businesses by looking at the balance of shareholders funds to borrowings.

These figures should give you an idea of which areas are useful to look at further using the techniques given below.

Percentage changes

Percentage changes are useful where a time series is being looked at. This should highlight which figures are changing out of line with other figures in the statements and flag up matters to be looked at in more detail. Using this technique, the change between each year and the next is shown as a percentage of the earliest year.

If we knew the figures for Bale and Cowley's earlier years we could use percentage changes to develop a trend analysis. To show you how the trend analysis works, we will assume the figure for sales in the year ended 28 February 1997 had been, say, £5 868 893; then the calculation would be:

$$\frac{(7\ 629\ 561 - 5\ 868\ 893) \times 100\%}{5\ 868\ 893} = \frac{1\ 760\ 668 \times 100\%}{5\ 868\ 893} = 30\%.$$

Having calculated the figure you then need to ask yourself how? and why? How could you achieve extra sales of this level? Perhaps they have dropped their prices or had a major advertising campaign or perhaps started to sell in a wider area – exports possibly.

The gross profit should increase by a similar percentage unless the company has altered its pricing policy. If the gross profit had increased by only 20 per cent, say, you could explore the idea that they had tried to generate extra sales by reducing the prices. Look at whether the overhead expenses have increased at less or more than 30 per cent. They could have managed to achieve the extra sales without increasing wage costs and office expenses by the full 30 per cent to achieve the greatest benefits of scale. However you may find that selling expenses are higher as advertising, promotional expenses and delivery costs have risen to cope with the extra sales, wiping out the profit.

One final thought – if the company has extra sales it will have increased debtors, creditors and possibly stocks. These need to be financed. A good analyst would look at the working capital to see if the growth of the firm has been properly financed.

All these questions arise from the one fact that sales have grown substantially. Gradually you are building up a picture in your mind of what the business is doing and where problems might have occurred.

Ratios

Ratios are used in time series, cross sectional or industry comparisons. Again they are a way of comparing the underlying performance having removed the differences due to the scale of operating.

In theory, you should have access to the opening and the closing balance sheets as well as the profit and loss account for the intervening year. This is because a number of the ratios compare figures from the profit and loss account with those in the balance sheets. The question is, since the profit is earned throughout the year and the balance sheets are at either end of that time, which balance sheet has the relevant figures?

1 If you have both balance sheets, the answer can be to take the average of the opening and closing balances. The calculation involves simply adding the opening and closing balances and dividing by two.
2 If you do not have both balance sheets then you can improvise by using just the closing figures.
3 If you know that the major changes to the balance sheet took place at the beginning of the year, for example that a large share and debenture issue was made to purchase a major addition to fixed assets in the first month of the year, then it would make sense to use the year end figures for long-term capital employed because they would reflect the capital employed throughout the year more accurately than the average.

The important thing is that you compare like with like. If you are using year end for one set of accounts you should use year end for the set you are using for comparison.

The following sections look at the calculation of a selection of ratios grouped to look at different aspects of the company. We will look at investors ratios, performance ratios and finance ratios. As Mike Cowley only produced year end figures for Rowe and Davies we will introduce the ratios using the year end balance sheet alone. It is a useful exercise to see how these differ from using the average figures and you might like to calculate these as you work through. There is a summary table at the end which can act as a reference of the ratios introduced in the chapter.

Investor ratios

These ratios look at the returns available to the shareholders.

Earnings per share

Earnings per share looks at the return that the company earned on one ordinary share in the previous year. The ratio is often known as eps for short.

$$\text{Eps} = \frac{\text{Earnings available for ordinary shareholders.}}{\text{No. of ordinary shares}}$$

The earnings available for ordinary shareholders is the figure in the profit and loss account for profit after tax less any dividend payable to the preference shareholders. This figure represents the profit for the year after paying out all other investors' interests. For Bale and Cowley the figure would be

$$\frac{925\ 091 - 16\ 000}{250\ 000} = \quad 363 \text{ pence.}$$

This ratio is usually quoted as pence per share rather than a percentage. In our example it is easy to work out. In a large plc the numbers of shares in issue can change so frequently with options and employee share schemes that it can be difficult to work out the number of shares in issue. To help, there is a SSAP 3 to give guidance on its calculation. The figure is worked out for you in a published set of accounts and is usually printed at the bottom of the profit and loss account.

Price earning ratio (p/e)

The price of a share is often expressed as a multiple of the eps figure. So for example an investor may say 'The Bale and Cowley shares are priced at five times earnings.'

In this example the five would be the price earnings or p/e ratio and tells us that the share price is £18.15.

$$\frac{\text{Share price}}{\text{eps}} = \frac{18.15}{3.63} = 5.$$

You will find this ratio used in the city pages of the national daily newspapers. The ratio reflects the market's view of the future potential of the company. If the market thinks the company has good prospects then the ratio will be high, possibly 20. If the market is not so sure of the company's earning or growth potential then the ratio might be low say 3 or 4. It is the future potential not the past which is important here. Given the fact that Bale and Cowley is not a listed company, there will not be a market for its shares. Investors would find it very difficult to turn their investment into money. For this reason the price of the shares would be much lower than for a similar company which was listed.

Dividend yield

Even though the company's earnings are very high it does not follow that a dividend will be paid. The earnings will be needed for business purposes to invest in new assets or finance growth. The dividend yield measures the amount of income that the shareholder can hope to receive in the form of dividends from the company. The reinvested earnings are not lost to the investor. They should lead to an increase in share price. However in an unlisted company, this will be difficult for the shareholder to realize.

$$\text{Dividend yield} = \frac{\text{dividend per share}}{\text{share price}} = \frac{0.07 \times 100}{18.15} = 3.8\%.$$

This seems low. Compare it with the rate you would expect to receive on a deposit account at a bank for example, which would carry much less risk and would be easier to realize in cash if the investor wanted the money back. However it does not reflect the capital growth prospects. You should also be aware that all the shareholders in this company receive an income as salary or preference dividend in addition to the dividend on ordinary shares. This can often be the case for small companies.

Performance ratios

The key performance ratio is a measure of return on capital employed. The calculation involves taking profit as a percentage of the capital invested in the company known as capital employed. The problems lie in knowing which profit figure to use and how the capital employed should be calculated.

You will find that different analysts have their own favourite method for calculating this figure. The important thing to remember is when you have chosen the profit figure make sure you choose the relevant measure of capital employed. This is one of the ratios which compares a figure from the profit and loss account with a figure from the balance sheet so you need to decide whether to use an average of the opening and closing balances or whether the year end will be suitable. We will use the year end.

Returns from operating

If you pick the profit before interest and tax then the profit figure still includes the amount due to the people who lent the company money. Your measure of capital employed should include the shareholders funds and the loans.

$$\frac{\text{Profit before interest and tax}}{\text{Long-term loans} + \text{shareholders funds}}$$

$$= \frac{1\ 292\ 591}{150\ 000 + 1\ 826\ 680} \times 100 = 65\%.$$

Some analysts like to include all the current liabilities as well because some companies manage to finance a lot of their activities from trade credit and overdrafts. This capital employed is the same as taking total assets (i.e. fixed assets plus current assets) and it is sometimes referred to as return on total assets.

$$\frac{\text{Profit before interest and tax}}{\text{Total assets or Total capital and liabilities}}$$

$$= \frac{1\ 292\ 591}{754\ 077 + 150\ 000 + 1\ 826\ 680} \times 100 = 47\%.$$

This is a figure which measures the returns made by the company from its underlying business activities regardless of how it is financed. It is a useful ratio for comparing with other companies and as a starting point for analyzing the operating performance of a company. It is called Return on Capital Employed and known as ROCE for short. It is the primary ratio.

The percentage here looks high by any standards. You would question whether it could be sustained in future years.

Return on equity

If you look at the profit after interest, tax and the preference dividend then you have the profit available to ordinary shareholders and the capital employed will be the ordinary shares and the reserves. This is usually known as Return on Equity (ROE)

$$\text{Return on equity} = \frac{\text{profit after interest, tax and preference dividend}}{\text{Ordinary share capital and reserves}}$$

$$= \frac{909\ 091}{1\ 626\ 680} = 56\%.$$

The pyramid of ratios

The ratios which examine the factors which affect the ROCE can be organized into a **pyramid of ratios**. The relationships between the ratios in the pyramid are given in Figure 17.1 but we will look in detail at how each of the ratios is calculated. The key ratio in the pyramid is the ROCE that we have already calculated.

The return on capital employed can be increased in two ways:

1   The profit per sale can be increased. The profitability ratios can explore these opportunities.
2   The number of sales generated from the same capital employed can be increased. The activity ratios analyze this aspect of the business.

The two strategies reflect different business strategies. Some businesses collect a

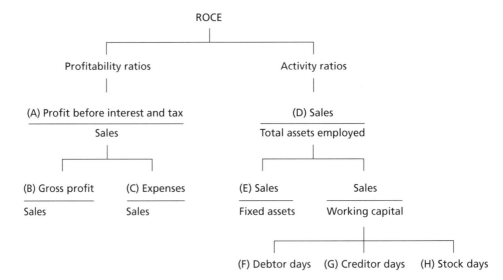

Figure 17.1
The Pyramid of ratios

minimum of profit per sale but the low prices should help to maximize the number of sales generated. Fast food outlets tend to use this strategy. Alternatively, it is possible to work at the luxury end of the market and try to maximize the profit per sale although the number of sales will be restricted. The restriction on sales may actually drive the price higher. Exclusive restaurants adopt this strategy. Most organizations operate somewhere between the two extremes.

The profit per sale ratio multiplied by the sales to capital employed equals the ROCE ratio.

Profitability ratios

With profitability ratios there is no conflict with deciding on opening, closing or average balance sheet figures. Both parts of the ratio came from the profit and loss account. If you have used the same size statements discussed above, then you will have already calculated these ratios.

$$(A) \quad \frac{\text{profit before interest and tax}}{\text{sales}} = \frac{1\ 292\ 591}{7\ 629\ 561}$$

$$= 17\%;$$

$$(B) \quad \frac{\text{gross profit}}{\text{sales}} = \frac{2\ 444\ 455}{7\ 629\ 561}$$

$$= 32\%;$$

$$(C) \quad \frac{\text{expenses}}{\text{sales}} = \frac{2\ 102\ 880}{6\ 727\ 200}$$

$$= 31\%.$$

To examine the expenses you might want to break the figure for expenses down further and look at the relationship of each individual expense to sales. This might happen if the expenses stood out in the comparison with previous years or with the competitor as being over large or increasing too fast.

Activity ratios

Activity ratios compare the activity level measured by sales purchases or cost of sales with the amount of capital tied up in assets. They are sometimes called the **turnover ratios** because they look at the number of times assets are 'turned over' in the period. Turnover is another name for sales.

$$(D) \quad \frac{\text{Sales}}{\text{Fixed assets}} = \frac{7\ 629\ 561}{1\ 258\ 103}$$

$$= 6.06 \text{ times.}$$

You need to be very careful in interpreting too much from this ratio although some analysts like it. The problem is, as we have seen, fixed assets are bought to last and some of them included in a balance sheet may be decades old. The net book value is just the balance of unwritten off original cost. Little value can be found in comparing this figure with the fixed assets of another company which might have bought its fixed assets last week.

The working capital turnover ratios are rather more useful. It is easier to interpret them if they are quoted in terms of days or months. We will use days. Rather than use just sales as the measure of turnover it is more meaningful to use cost of sales for stock and purchases for creditors since these figures do not include an element of profit.

Consider the stock figure. The cost of sales figure is what it says it is i.e. the sales at cost price. Stock is also at cost. Divide the cost of sales by 365 to give the average cost of sales per day. Dividing this cost per day into the stock figure shows how many days stock is in hand at the year end or on average.

(E) Stock days $\qquad = \dfrac{\text{Stocks}}{\text{Cost of sales per day}}$

$$= \frac{642\ 611 \times 365}{5\ 185\ 106}$$

$$= 45.2 \text{ days.}$$

This tells us that at the year end the company had enough stock in hand to cope with 45 days sales before having to order more.

The same calculation can be used for debtors, but this time using sales instead of cost of sales:

(F) Debtor days $\qquad = \dfrac{\text{Debtors}}{\text{Sales per day}}$

$$= \frac{851\ 426 \times 365}{7\ 629\ 561}$$

$$= 40.7 \text{ days.}$$

This tell us that at the year end the company was giving debtors an average of 40.7 days to pay for their goods.

(G) Creditor days $\qquad = \dfrac{\text{Creditors}}{\text{Purchases per day}}$

$$= \frac{351\ 567 \times 365}{5\ 263\ 790}$$
$$= 24 \text{ days.}$$

This tells us that at the year end the company was paying its creditors in 24 days.

Putting these figures together we can work out that if the company holds stock for 45 days before it is sold and then has to wait 40.7 days for payment by the customer, but has to pay for those items in 24 days, then the company must invest enough money to wait the extra time after paying for the goods and before it receives the cash owing. According to our calculations 61 days of credit will have to be funded.

This gives the analyst a good idea of the capital that will need to be invested in working capital.

Finance ratios

These ratios look at the way in which the company has borrowed money and the ability to repay the debt and the interest. We will look first at the long-term finance ratios or gearing and then at short-term liquidity.

Gearing ratios

The ROCE we looked at indicated how well the company is operating. If you look at the ROE calculated above you will see that although the ROCE shows a return of 47 per cent the ROE was much higher than this at 56 per cent. The equity shareholders have received a higher return than the company has made on the capital it employs. The reason it can do this is because the company has managed to borrow at a lower interest rate than it can earn on the money. We are told the debentures are paid 18 per cent interest. This is much lower than the 47 per cent that the company earned on that money this year. The shareholders benefit not just from the fact that the company is earning incredible returns at the moment but also because they have the use of cheap money. This idea is known as gearing. The return to shareholders has been geared up.

Gearing can be measured in a number of ways. Basically it looks at the proportion of debt finance to equity finance in a company. If the debt is high then the company is thought to be of greater risk than one which borrowed very little. This is despite the higher returns that could be achieved by borrowing. As we discussed in Chapter 15 the problem is that borrowers run the risk of not being able to meet the debts when they fall due. Although the preference shareholders do not have the right to sue for payment if their dividend is unpaid, nevertheless they are entitled to a dividend before the ordinary shareholders. As such they are part of the **prior charge capital** and are paid a lower return than the ordinary shareholders expect. They are included in the ratios as part of the borrowings to reflect the 'gearing' of the ordinary shareholders' returns.

Measuring gearing can be done in a number of ways:

$$\frac{\text{Prior charge capital}}{\text{Shareholders equity}} = \frac{150\,000 + 200\,000}{1\,626\,680}$$

$$= 21\%;$$

$$\frac{\text{Prior charge capital}}{\text{Shareholders equity} + \text{prior charge capital}} = \frac{150\,000 + 200\,000}{1\,626\,680 + 150\,000 + 200\,000}$$

$$= 17.7\%;$$

$$\frac{\text{Long- and short-term creditors}}{\text{Shareholders equity long- and short-term creditors}} = \frac{150\ 000 + 200\ 000 + 754\ 077}{1\ 626\ 680 + 150\ 000 + 200\ 000 + 754\ 077}$$

$$= 40\%.$$

Provided you compare like with like by using the same ratio in the comparative company then the choice is yours. If your company has bank overdrafts and heavy creditors then it makes sense to include the short-term creditors in the calculation.

Interest cover is shown by:

$$\frac{\text{Profit before interest and tax}}{\text{Interest for the year}} = \frac{1\ 292\ 591}{13\ 500}$$

$$= 96\ \text{times}.$$

In this case there is obviously no problem meeting interest charges. Even if profits fell drastically, there should be no problem with the company's ability to pay. However for many companies this can be a problem, particularly if profits fluctuate from year to year.

Liquidity ratios

Another aspect of finance that ratios can help to analyse is the working capital management. A common ratio used is the **working capital ratio**, also known as the current ratio.

$$\text{Working capital or current ratio} = \frac{\text{current assets}}{\text{current liabilities}}$$

$$= \frac{1\ 472\ 654}{754\ 077}$$

$$= 1\!:\ 1.95.$$

This ratio is intended to indicate the extent to which the liabilities which are repayable within the next twelve months are covered by the current assets which should be available to meet those liabilities. The problem is that some of the liabilities included in current headings are actually not payable immediately. The company has time to receive money from new sales or make new arrangements to meet the liabilities when they do fall due in anything up to twelve months time. A more immediate indicator is the **acid test ratio** or **liquidity ratio**. This should include as current assets only those assets which will be turned into cash quickly and at a known value. The liabilities included are those which can demand payment immediately. For example, banks can demand repayment of overdrafts at any time but the tax bills have agreed due dates and the tax authorities cannot demand payment before those dates. The ratio is usually stated as:

Liquidity ratio or acid test

$$= \frac{\text{Current assets} - \text{stock}}{\text{Current liabilities payable immediately}}$$

$$= \frac{1\ 472\ 654\ -\ 642\ 611}{754\ 077}$$

$$= 1 : 1.1.$$

Note that by convention these are actually expressed as ratios and not as percentages or 'times'. Both the working capital and the acid test ratio can be manipulated. Delaying payment of creditors for example or not purchasing stock can change the ratio. This is known as window dressing, and can be difficult to detect by the analyst. Until you have worked out a similar figure for Rowe and Davies you can say little about the ratios produced.

These ratios reflect the terms of trade normal to the industry concerned. A super-market selling goods on cash terms for example would have no trade debtors and the stock would be kept to a minimum and bought on credit terms. The result would be that the company would have a negative working capital figure and the working capital and acid test ratios would look very low. In contrast, a service business operating around the world might have very heavy working capital needs. The customers would take time to pay, they would have work in progress under stock for current contracts being worked on, but, as their main inputs of staff wages would be paid as incurred, they would have few creditors.

So the business determines its working capital needs. You need to compare with other companies in the same sector to assess the working capital management. The company needs enough to be able to meet its liabilities as they fall due. If the company has too much tied up in working capital then it is wasting resources; stock sitting on a shelf can deteriorate, be stolen or go out of fashion. The older a debtor balance is, the less likely it is to be paid. Cash balances sitting idle would be better invested in expanding the business. If the company cannot earn more than the deposit rate at the bank then the money should be returned to the shareholders.

If the company seems to have a working capital problem, then you should use the activity ratios for working capital items discussed above. You need to assess the company's ability to collect its debts, manage its stock holdings and negotiate its payments to creditors.

Activity

2   Calculate the ratios for Rowe and Davies and compare their performance with Bale and Cowley.
    Required
    For each ratio:
    (a) Is the ratio lower or higher than that for Bale and Cowley?
    (b) From Bale and Cowley's perspective, is this a good sign, a bad sign or can you not tell?
    (c) What reasons can you think of to explain why the difference has occurred?

(**d**) Is this explanation supported by any other ratios you have calculated?

(**e**) Should Bale and Cowley do anything as a result of these differences?

(**f**) Is there any other information which would help you analyze the performance?

Table 17.3 Summary of ratios

eps	Earnings available for ordinary shareholders / No of ordinary shares in issue
p/e	Share price / eps
Dividend yield	Dividends / Share price
ROCE	Profit before interest and tax / Total assets
ROE	Profit after interest tax and preference dividends / Ordinary shares in issue and reserves
Net profit to sales	Profit before interest and tax / Sales
Gross profit to sales	Gross profit / Sales
Expenses to sales	Expenses / Sales
Sales to capital employed	Sales / (Average) Total assets
Fixed asset turnover	Sales / (Average) Fixed assets
Stock days	(Average) Stocks / Cost of sales per day
Debtor days	(Average) debtors / Sales per day
Creditor days	(Average) creditors / Purchases per day
Gearing ratio	Long- and short-term creditors / Shareholders funds + long- and short-term creditors
Interest cover	Profit before interest and tax / Interest charge for the year
Working capital ratio	Current assets / Current liabilities
Acid test	Current assets − stock / Current liabilities payable immediately

(g) How would you assess the overall performance of Bale and Cowley after looking at the performance of Rowe and Davies?

Summary

This chapter has introduced the techniques used to analyze financial statements. The ratios become easier to use as you become more familiar with them. They are summarized in Table 17.3 for ease of reference. The results of your analysis of the Rowe and Davies figures should indicate that they have a higher gross profit than Bale and Cowley suggesting that they charge higher prices. On the other hand the overhead expenses are higher. They seem to achieve higher activity rates from other fixed assets but this could be due to the fact that the assets are older and therefore carried at a lower net book value than Bale and Cowley's. Rowe and Davies do appear to have better terms of trade in that they give less credit to customers, hold stock for less time and have longer credit from their suppliers. All this makes a significant difference to the working capital required. They are more highly geared than Bale and Cowley but they have no apparent problem with meeting the interest charges. The overall return is lower but still looks respectable. The next step for Bale and Cowley is to find out why the working capital is different. Does it reflect different conditions or the fact that being more established Rowe and Davies has access to better terms from its creditors? Perhaps Bale and Cowley ought to be looking at increasing the gearing to increase the return to the shareholders.

Key words

acid test p. 284 • activity ratios p. 281 • cross sectional p. 273 • interest cover p. 284 • liquidity ratios p. 284 • percentage changes p. 276 • prior charge capital p. 283 • pyramid of ratios p. 280 • same size statements p. 275 • time series p. 274 • turnover ratios p. 281 • working capital ratio p. 284

Practice questions

1 Bill was interested to see the results of the analysis of the competitor's accounts and he called in at the office just as John and Azina were discussing their findings. He listened for a while and then commented that there were other features of the competitors accounts that they needed to be aware of. He listed the following points:

(i) The depreciation rates for the competitor were different to those of Bale and Cowley. According to the notes Rowe and Davies used the straight line method but with the following rates:

Buildings	0%
Fixtures and fittings	12.5%
Office equipment	12.5%
Computer equipment	25%
Vehicles	12.5%

(ii) The fixed assets were all at cost not valuation, but they should remember that most of the property had been purchased when the company was formed. This was in the late 1970s and it was therefore likely that the book value was much lower than it would be at current prices even with the fall in the property market. A figure of £1 million was a more likely comparison.

(iii) The bad debt provision is only 1% of debtors.

(iv) Directors' salaries were very high. The dividends in contrast did not exist. The directors had apparently decided to take their earnings in the form of salary rather than dividends on their shareholdings.

(v) The debtors include an amount of £123 000 relating to an advertisement campaign which had been run six months earlier but which the directors believed would still be benefiting the company and should not be written off against profit in one year.

Required

Consider the effect of the points raised by Bill on the report you prepared in the chapter. Rework any ratios you consider would have changed to support your comments.

2   The latest accounts of Rhys Ltd are outlined below:

Balance Sheet at 30 June 1998

		(£) (000s)	(£) (000s)	(£) (000s)
Fixed assets	Land and buildings	320		
	Plant and machinery	240		
	Vehicles	120		
			680	
Current assets				
	Stock	230		
	Debtors	215		
	Bank and cash	122		
			567	
Current liabilities				
	Creditors		126	
	Proposed dividend		44	
			170	397
				1077
Long-term loans				200
				877

Balance Sheet at 30 June 1998

	(£) (000s)	(£) (000s)	(£) (000s)
Financed by:			
Share capital			
8% £1 preference shares			200
Ordinary shares 25p			400
Reserves			<u>277</u>
			<u>877</u>

Profit and loss account for the year ended 30 June 1998

Sales			998
Less cost of sales			<u>598</u>
Gross profit			400
Less distribution costs		150	
Administration expenses		<u>70</u>	
			<u>220</u>
Net operating profit			180
Less interest			<u>20</u>
			160
Less tax			<u>67</u>
			<u>93</u>
Less dividends			
Interim paid	Preference	4	
	Ordinary	24	
Proposed	Preference	4	
	Ordinary	<u>40</u>	

(i) What is the difference between expenses and appropriations?

(ii) Which of the following would be considered to be appropriations and which expenses?
- Depreciation
- Preference dividends
- Directors fees
- Provision for doubtful debts
- Interest on loans
- Transfer to reserves

(iii) What is the difference between provisions and reserves?

(iv) What rate of dividend has Rhys Ltd declared per ordinary share as an interim dividend and as a final dividend?

(v) What is the value of year end equity in the balance sheet of Rhys Ltd?

(vi) Calculate the following ratios.
- Working capital ratio
- Acid test
- Net operating profit to sales
- Return on year end equity
- Ratio of long-term debt to total long-term finance

(vii) If the ratios for a close and successful competitor for the same period were as indicated below, comment on each of the ratios obtained in (vi) above and summarize any overall advice you would give Rhys Ltd.

Working Capital ratio	2: 1
Acid Test	0.8: 1
Net operating profit to sales	20%
Return on year end equity	16%
Ratio of long-term debt to total long-term finance	40%

18 Internal controls in computerized systems

by Marlene Davies

Learning objectives

After reading this chapter you should:
- understand how important it is to secure the computer not only as an asset but as an information bank
- appreciate the importance of implementing controls to ensure data security and integrity
- be able to identify the possible consequences of control weaknesses within an AIS
- understand the importance of installing appropriate controls as systems are designed and developed
- be able to identify the relationship between the controls associated with computerized systems and those of the traditional internal controls discussed in Chapter 3
- understand why computerized software packages require in-built controls to help prevent the destruction and disruption of the program and its properties.

Introduction

You should now have a good understanding of the workings of an AIS system and the importance of ensuring that the data processed and produced reflect company activities. In this chapter we shall look at the security and control measures that are important for the effective and efficient operation of the accounting system.

When Azina and John first started their business Azina kept a close eye on all the expenditure relating to the business. She could almost tell exactly how much money was outstanding at any one point without looking at the records. As the business grew and more and more customers appeared along with a variety of suppliers, this meant that keeping a close eye on the level of income and expenditure became more difficult. Azina would rely on looking at the AIS for confirmation of the figures. Now that the record keeping has been delegated to a member of staff, Azina and John rely on the accuracy and integrity of the data produced by the computerized accounting system to help them plan their business.

Hindia is a school leaver who has just started working for John and Azina, she has five GCSEs and is keen to make a good impression with Azina. She has a limited range of computer skills mainly on word-processing packages, but is a quick learner and is keen to start on the accounting package.

Hindia's opportunity comes sooner than expected when Terry the accounting system operator suffers a severe attack of RSI (repetitive strain injury) and has to take two months off work. Hindia's first task is to enter the cheque income from outstanding debtors on the system when they arrive each morning. She notes the amount, debtor name and, where it exists, the invoice number. Hindia follows the **Sales Receipts** procedure as outlined in Chapter 6. After a few days Hindia feels very confident in using the system although she does not understand why there is a big fuss about matching reference numbers, invoice numbers and debtor listings. John and Azina, in the meantime, are quite happy with Hindia's work and Azina congratulates herself on appointing Hindia as she seems such a competent girl.

Just before Terry's return to work a very irate letter arrives from one of the company's best customers, Anthony Wong. Anthony is not at all amused by the fact that he has received a final demand for payment when he had already paid the amount within the time period that qualified him for an early settlement discount.

'How did this happen?' asks John,

'I shall check the records myself,' replies Azina.

Indeed when the records were checked it did indicate that Anthony Wong had not paid, however when Azina double checked with the bank, Anthony's cheque had been paid into the business account. This meant that somehow the income had not been properly recorded on to the system.

Azina checked with Hindia as to how she posts the entries and discovers that Hindia was not following the proper procedures for posting the entries. If Hindia did not find a corresponding invoice number or reference number on the receipt she merely looked for a debtor who has an outstanding amount that matched the amount received. She then proceeded to make up the information as she went along.

Hindia said to Azina: 'I thought that if the money was recorded and banked, then as long as the money was secure that there was nothing else to worry about, debtors would all pay up eventually and it would balance'.

Azina suddenly had visions of similar letters arriving from irate customers and instantly blamed Hindia for her lack of common sense. Later that morning Hindia left clutching her coat and in tears, declaring that she would never work for the company again.

The following weekend there was a break-in at the office, very little was taken apart from the coffee and tea kitty that were kept on the shelf behind the door. However when Terry tried to access the accounting system on Monday morning he found that all the previous months' records had been deleted and all new transactions failed due to a virus that had appeared on the computer.

'I thought you and I were the only one who knew the password,' he said to Azina.

'I must have given it to Hindia when she did some inputting for me while you were away.' replied Azina

Fortunately Terry had made backup copies of all entries up until the previous Thursday so it meant that only one day's records had been lost. These required re-entering once the computer had been freed of all viruses. Disappointment struck however when the backup files could not be located, the intruder had overturned a small wooden filing cabinet that contained the disks, the disks had fallen out and were now in disarray amongst the earth and water of the potted plant that had lived on top of the cabinet. It was impossible to identify the backup disk for the previous Thursday.

'There's nothing left to do but start collating the information from the invoices and individual statements of debtors,' said John.

'But it will take weeks,' replied Terry,

'Just as well your RSI is better then,' snapped John.

Later that morning, after the police had gone, John suddenly remembered Hindia talking about her boyfriend who was obsessed with computers and was forever developing new programs and trying to hack into systems. Somehow he could not but feel uneasy about the events of the weekend.

The importance of computer security and controls

In Chapter 5 we looked at the importance of computer security and the importance of ensuring that adequate procedures are in place not only to secure that asset but to secure the data by making backup copies of the information held on the hard disk. We will now look at other aspects of computer security and controls within computerized accounting systems that need further consideration.

Why is security important?

The impact that the theft of a computer can have on an organization is not so much the replacement value of the asset, but the knock-on effect of the loss of information that the computer held. As more and more data processing is computerized and operations become more centralized there is a concentration of data held within the computer which if lost or destroyed can mean complete business failure. Companies will not be able to establish the amount of outstanding debtors, the current level of orders not processed or the reordering level of stock. In addition a great deal of time and money may be spent on recreating data at the expense of income generating activities. Safeguards need to be in place, therefore, to ensure that there is little or no opportunity for data loss, and that there is protection against hardware and software damage whether it be accidental or malicious.

The security of data is of paramount importance as the data held on the computer are probably the company's most valuable resource. Data security is essential because without it then there is a possibility of:

1 financial loss,
2 computer fraud,
3 failure to comply with legislation, Data Protection Act, etc.;
4 competitors gaining an edge in the market due to unauthorized access to sensitive information.

Why are controls important?

Controls exist to prevent errors or fraud occurring during data capture and data processing, and thereby to ensure that data are accurate, complete and valid to the organization.

The likelihood of errors and fraud occurring is much greater when systems have been computerized, mainly due to the volume of data handled and the speed of the computer in dealing with transactions. Under the same reasoning the probability of discovery is much less. Controls are therefore very important when it comes to the operation of computerized accounting systems. There is an increasing level of **business dependency** on the computer as the main source of information but businesses are also therefore more vulnerable to the dangers of business failure should anything happen to this source.

Large organizations invariably have sophisticated computerized accounting systems which in turn have more in-built controls to ensure data accuracy, completeness and integrity. Smaller businesses on the other hand tend to have smaller computers that do not always have sophisticated controls. The characteristics of micro systems means that special consideration needs to be paid to the existence of the appropriate controls.

Micro system data processing has a number of characteristics which demand the existence of adequate and reliable controls, these are identified here as:

1 the opportunity to change data without any trace, whether accidental or deliberate;
2 the possibility of unauthorized access to files and data;
3 the ease at which data can be lost when files are copied;
4 the susceptibility of files becoming lost through fire, flood or theft;
5 the processing capabilities of the computer are enormous, very often there is no human input which means that great reliance is placed on the computer;
6 the volume of data is large but the files themselves are physically small;
7 the direct entry of data via keyboards and the storage of data on disk means that very often there is no regular printing out of output as the information is easily accessed by reading off the visual display unit (VDU), thereby leaving no trace of activity;
8 quite often source documents are not retained or sorted in the same way as the computer record, and this makes any cross referencing difficult;
9 amendments to the data may not be documented, leaving only the most recent transactions retained on the computer;
10 the computer lacks judgement which means that errors which may have been a one-off in a manual system will continue in a computerized system until detected;

11 the systems require no special environment, providing open access facility and the opportunity for sabotage;

12 the computer is often only fully understood by one member of the organization, creating an ideal situation for fraudulent activity;

13 the user friendly operating facility of the micro computer means that lower grade staff can operate it without any prior training – this may appear to be an advantage, but a lack of staff knowledge can mean that errors can go undetected.

These characteristics also contribute to what the auditor refers to as the *loss of* **audit trail** within AISs. This is the facility to trace transactions through a system from source (e.g. customer order) to completion (for example turnover in the final accounts) or vice versa. A number of these characteristics are also true of computerized systems in larger organizations where there is a certain degree of decentralization to the accounting function.

The Sage accounting package has an audit trail report that lists every transaction that has been entered into the accounting system. According to the British Computer Society an audit trail is 'a record of the file updating that takes place during a specific transaction. It enables a trace to be kept on files.' Note how this overcomes some of the problems outlined above when we identified the characteristics of computerized accounting systems, especially those of small computerized systems.

Security

John and Azina were quite happy with their accounting system until something went wrong. Some basic rules could have been employed to safeguard against the incidents that occurred in terms of the errors by Hindia and the break-in at the weekend. Physical security is straightforward: how did the intruder mange to break in? Are the windows secure, does the door have adequate locks and is there an alarm fitted in the building or even a security camera?

In a number of instances the size of the company and the amount of valuables on the premises as well as the cost will be weighed up against the potential loss. In some instances the insurance policy will dictate the rules of the game.

The security policy employed by John and Azina in respect of the data held, however, did fall short of the ideal situation. The intruder managed to access the files probably because he or she knew the password. Changing the password when Hindia left would have been quite easy to implement and could have avoided the situation they faced now. If they had followed a basic set of rules in respect of information security then they may not have experienced such a disastrous Monday.

British Standard BS 7799

In 1993 a joint venture was set up between the DTI (Department of Trade and Industry) and a group of managers from leading British and International companies to provide practical advice on how to manage information securely. This was implemented in 1995 as a British Standard BS 7799. This relects the British government's view of how important information management has become in the UK.

The BS 7799 standard has ten key controls that it considers an organization should follow. These are:

1 the establishment of an information security policy document;
2 the allocation of security responsibilities to named individuals within the organization;
3 the establishment of an information education and training programme;
4 a review to ensure that there is compliance with the security policy;
5 an awareness of and compliance with specific information security legislation, e.g. the Data Protection Act;
6 the documentation of any security incidents;
7 the existence of a procedure that ensures the securing of the organization's records;
8 the establishment of a virus protection policy;
9 the existence of controls to restrict any proprietary software copying;
10 the establishment of a business continuity planning programme.

As you can see this standard broadens the security issue from that of the computer equipment security to **information security**. This standard is likely to become the basis for an International Standard for managing information which recognizes the increased level of cross border information exchange.

Data Protection Act 1984

The implication of the Data Protection Act as far as John and Azina are concerned relate to the fact that they hold personal information on their computer in respect of individuals. The background to the Act is that there was a growing fear that information stored and processed using the computer could be misused. It was felt that an individual could be easily harmed by the existence of computerized data relating to that individual that was inaccurate or misleading. There was also the fear that the information could be transferred to unauthorized third parties at high speed at very little cost. The Act is therefore an attempt to provide a measure of protection to the individual.

The terms of the Act cover data about individuals and not corporate bodies, and data that are processed mechanically, by 'equipment operated automatically in response to the instructions given for that purpose'. This is important because:

1 manual data records are excluded from coverage by the Act;
2 data records that are covered include data processed not just by computer, but also by other equipment that processes personal data automatically.

Controls

Let us now consider the control aspects in respect of computerized systems. Control systems for computerized systems fall into two categories, **general controls** and **application controls**. Controls cost money to develop and operate, and this means that when an organization considers the controls that should exist within its system it must strike a balance between the degree of control desired and the cost of achieving

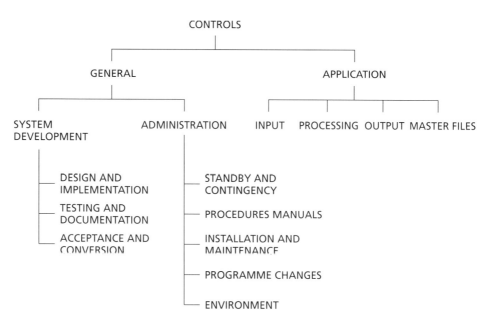

Figure 18.1
Internal controls in
a computerized
accounting system

KEY CONTROL EXAMPLES

PASSWORDS; SECURITY MEASURES; TESTING; TRAINING; CHECKING; AUTHORIZATION; SEGREGATION
OF DUTIES; VIRUS CHECKS.

those controls. When an off-the-shelf accounting system is purchased it is important to identify the level of control that exists within the package. If a system is tailor made or developed in-house it is important to specify the controls that should be contained within that system. This is where the advice of the auditor comes into its own by providing guidance in terms of recommending controls which may be missing and in identifying any risk attached to the existing controls. In the same way, when an item of hardware is purchased, it is important to ensure that provision exists to combat any malfunction or breakdown, while a regular maintenance agreement and repair facility in itself constitutes a control that safeguards against unwanted mishaps.

General controls

General controls are defined as those controls that relate to the accounting environment within which the computerized accounting system is developed, operated and maintained. General controls can be either programmed or manual. The objectives of general controls are to ensure the systems are properly developed and implemented and to ensure the integrity of the program, the data files and the computer operations.

General controls fall into two categories, *administrative* and *system development*. General administrative controls are concerned with the integrity of data, program files and of computer operations. General system development controls are, as the words imply, concerned with the development and implementation of the system.

Application controls

Application controls relate to the transactions and data belonging to each computer based accounting system. The objectives of application controls are to ensure the completeness, accuracy and validity of accounting records. These controls can either be manual or computerized, a manual total of receipts for future comparison is just as valid for ensuring completeness as a computer check on creditor number recognition for validity.

It is worth pointing out here that the distinction between general and application control is not always clear cut: password controls are important general controls to ensure file integrity but they are also application controls that ensure the validity of input in terms of restricting access to only those authorized to input information.

Files

'Files' is a general term for stored data. **Data files** will hold a variety of information that can be classified into the following headings:

1   *Programs* – which are sets of instructions which dictate all sequential functions that are to be undertaken inside the central processor
2   *Transactions data* – this term refers to the data that can be read off the computer which relate to the current period's activities: e.g. cash received, goods and services invoiced, hours worked, stock movements. These are the data that are fed into the computer and which it uses to update the master files by following the programmed instructions within the programs mentioned above.
3   *Standing data* – is the term used to describe data that are of a permanent nature such as price lists, employee codes, overtime rates, creditor names and addresses, debtor reference numbers, stock codes.
4   *Master files* – as the name implies, are files that are of lasting or continuous importance, the term master files also refers to files whose content is subject to frequent changes but are none the less important, e.g. stores ledgers sales and purchase ledgers.

When reference is made later on to the controls applicable to the various categories of files, the above explanation will help to clarify the type of data under discussion.

Examples of controls

In this section we will look at examples of controls that should exist within a computerized environment. As controls exist to ensure the smooth operation of computerized information the examples discussed below will show how their existence can help to prevent any of these situations occurring.

The examples used will quote the same controls for more than one preventative activity, as this highlights the importance of certain controls that can often be taken for granted and not seem significant but when considered in the full context of what it does, the control becomes a cornerstone for ensuring business continuity. Password controls, division of duties, operations manuals, and authorization are some of the controls that will appear on more than one occasion in the following examples.

Examples of general administrative controls

1   *Controls to protect the computer environment* – While the modern computer is less susceptible to environmental hazards, humidity, dust and temperature can still lead to incorrect processing and data loss. The equipment, like all electrical equipment, can overheat, while magnetic or electronic fields anywhere near the machine or the stored data represent danger. Apart from the obvious in terms of the safe location of the computer to avoid theft, these controls include arrangements in respect of vandalism, sabotage, fire or flood, adequate insurance cover, inventory of hardware and software as well as standby facilities and disaster recovery plans. Included within these controls are **virus checks** in respect of viruses introduced accidentally or deliberately. These virus protection controls come as specific software packages and need to be regularly updated in order to combat all new viruses. These controls are therefore an attempt to ensure the continued existence of the computer in a format that ensures continued activity for the business.

2   *Controls to ensure that system software is properly installed and maintained* – The proper installation of systems software is an essential element of the efficient and effective operation of the computerized system. It is necessary therefore to have procedures in place to ensure that the software is installed under a controlled environment. Only authorized personnel should deal with the installation in order to monitor exactly what is installed. This avoids system overload, and provides a record of all installations for the maintenance and upgrade facility. As far as software access is concerned, there has to be an access control facility that is set up in such a way that it provides access only to the relevant personnel for system operation and processing.

3   *Controls to prevent unauthorized amendments to data files* – Unauthorized amendments to data files can lead to disastrous results, making the data that are deemed reliable to become meaningless. These amendments can be either accidental, malicious or fraudulent. The controls that need to be present here include password protection that both prevents unauthorized access and identifies access attempts. These passwords need to be regularly changed and subject to termination at set times to ensure that they do not become common knowledge. Other controls are the authorization of jobs prior to processing to ensure that only relevant processing applicable to the system software is undertaken and the physical protection of data backup files and set procedures in respect of authorized and required amendments, which in turn identify those which are unauthorized.

4   *Controls to prevent or detect unauthorized changes to programs* – These controls exist to prevent accidental and fraudulent corruption of program logic during program maintenance or program execution. This means that segregation of duties, training of personnel, and supervision of staff controls should be in place for program maintenance as well as the other controls of authorization of jobs prior to processing. The recording of program changes, integrity of backup copies, and comparison of production copies to controlled copies. Controls such as restricted access, the investigation of unusual delays and rotation of duties all help in ensuring the prevention and detection of unauthorized changes to programs.

5   *Controls to prevent or detect errors during program activity* – Controls here

include the existence of an operations manual in order that all personnel involved in using the computer are aware of how to operate the package. In addition the manual will give the procedures that need to be followed before, during and after the task is complete. There is a need to set up a job scheduling programme in order to ensure that adequate cover and supervision is provided by appropriately qualified staff. Emergency backup procedures need to be made known to personnel and the staff involved with operating the computer need the correct training and supervision. The training programme of personnel also rests on the quality of personnel appointed initially. There is a requirement for the appointment process to include job descriptions and for those appointed to have the basic skills that can be built upon during training. This appointment process also has to take up references to ensure that staff appointed do not have a past history of computer sabotage or fraud.

6   *Controls to ensure continuity of operations* – As businesses can fail due to computer failure there has to be a good set of procedures in place to ensure continuity of business. Controls here are represented by regular testing of good backup facilities, protection of the power supply and a review policy by designated individuals of the emergency and disaster recovery plans. Failure to implement these when they are required will render their existence worthless. Maintenance agreements and insurance policies must be periodically reviewed to ensure that any amendments or additions to the computer facility have been noted and appropriately accounted for. The protection of equipment against fire, flood and smoke damage must also be reviewed. Consultation with the chief fire officer if necessary will ensure that all the up to date precautions have been installed and are operating properly.

7   *Controls to control access to the operation of terminals* – Physical restriction for controlling access comes in a variety of formats: locked rooms with the distribution of keys to authorized users only, smart cards and code locks. A password logging on system restricts access to the operation of software in terms of programs and files. These files need to be accessible only to those with the right level of password accessibility. In other words some data may not be accessible to all users of the files in which case the data need to be appropriately sectioned into areas for different users. If an attempt is made to access data without the appropriate password then an error system should be set up in such a way as to lock off a terminal from the system. As terminal activity should be logged, the unauthorized or invalid access attempt can be identified. Where continued attempts are made at the same terminal then the situation should be investigated to determine whether the access attempt is merely an employee error or whether there is a serious unauthorized access attempt.

Examples of general systems development controls

1   *Controls over system development* – As inadequate systems can cause large losses it is important to ensure that standards exist to prevent poor design specifications, inadequate testing and implementation of systems. There should exist a plan of activity that identifies the role of specific personnel in the system development. This plan should consider user needs, time scales and issues such as cost-benefit

analysis to ensure that an application is computerized only if it is beneficial to do so. A basis needs to exist for management to be able to review and understand the system. This is where a proactive internal audit section can be involved to provide advice based on past experiences or technical knowledge of the controls expected to exist within a computerized system.

2   *Controls to ensure proper documentation is kept* – A good standard of documentation promotes an efficient and effective operation by users and computer personnel. When amendments are set up, an amendments register should be completed as well as when any recovery measures have to be undertaken after a disaster. It is important therefore to have good quality documents, well-written standards that are followed and an enforcement policy to adhere to these standards. Once a proper and complete system documentation is created it needs to be maintained and reviewed. Specific officers need to have responsibility for ensuring that records are maintained and that the appropriate standards are followed.

3   *Controls to ensure that all program amendments are tested and documented* – Controls are important to avoid new errors in the program and to deter any element of fraud. Program changes require authorization by user departments in writing and at the appropriate level of authority. The changes need to be assessed by a systems analyst and amendments specified in sufficient detail to enable the programmer to make the changes. Once the changes have been made they must be tested and the amendments documented and monitored when it 'goes live'. Program changes can range from a minor alteration of an exception report to a major redesign. The majority of installations have a set of standards for testing and documenting changes. These standards ensure that testing procedures are adhered to, with appropriate approval and recording of the changes by the users and management. This enables a record to be kept of all changes, thereby ensuring that should it be necessary to back track then the information is available. It also provides a record of who authorized the changes to be made. Segregation of duties, training and supervision controls are important here because, without the appropriate training, amendments may be made without consideration for the impact on other facilities within the computer.

Examples of application controls

Application controls deal with the controls over data in terms of input, processing output and master file entries.

1   *Controls to ensure data input is complete, authorized, accurate and valid* – Input data can contain errors: human error is one of the greatest data security weaknesses and minimization of errors is therefore essential. Staff training and supervision are manual controls that can help in reducing the potential errors. Data input documents need to be designed in such a way that the input operator can complete the task properly without missing any important or relevant information. When data input is via the keyboard then the screen should be formatted to help the operator input the correct data. Staff who enter the data need to be encouraged to look for errors. This includes visual checks of the data that appears on the

VDU screen while batch input data totals should be checked against computer produced listings of the input data. Data input needs to be completed in a set time, relevant payments and recording of data into time periods ensures that the financial information produces a meaningful picture. This means that apart from manual agreements of control totals other checks such as sequence checking and programmed matching of input are required. Programmed matching involves the input is matched to a control file that contains details of expected input. There also has to be a procedure to deal with the re-submission of rejected input data.

Data input authorization involves the checking of transactions for the appropriate authorization. Invoices, for example, need the proper authorization code or signature to confirm the payment is due or that goods have been received and that no prior payment has been made. It is important that manual checks are undertaken on authorization prior to input, clerical review of the control totals after processing should also be undertaken to ensure that no unauthorized items have been entered. Authorization limits can be programmed to detect any payments or amounts exceeding the limit set. This control ensures that payments, even if authorized, are identified as being in excess of pre-set limits – these controls are called *confirmation limits*. In such instances transactions will require either further authorization or be rejected from the system.

Controls in respect of data input are required to ensure that data fields are accurate, these include items such as the amounts, account numbers and payment date on invoices. Batch control totals provide a check on accuracy but more importantly programmed checks ensure data verification for accuracy and validity. Programmed controls are check digit verification, reasonableness checks and existence checks. *Check digit verification* checks enable reference numbers to be arithmetically checked for the required relationship to the rest of the number to be checked. *Reasonableness* checks look for the logical relationship between files, and *existence* checks look for valid codes when data are input. Controls also exist to ensure that all input data are subject to *completeness* checks – these ensure that each record that is created contains sufficient information to make the *audit trail* effective.

2   *Controls to ensure all data are processed accurately and completely* – Once data have been input, the computer is expected to process the information accordingly and this is why control totals are written into the programs to ensure that no records have been lost, no records have been duplicated, the input files have been read fully and that all records have been written to the output files. The controls for processing are similar to those applied to the input of transactions, controls batch reconciliation ensures completeness and accuracy although now the reconciliation is made after the update and not after the initial entry. Summary processing is a method by which individual values are totalled and compared to total amounts elsewhere. The sum of the depreciation of individual assets can be compared to the depreciation of the total asset value.

Data may be rejected or fail to be processed after the initial input. Controls need to exist to ensure that when the data are valid they can be re-entered into the system. This often requires a separate activity that identifies the mishaps and thereby avoids any possibility of duplication. Invoices that may have been entered correctly for the correct amount may, during processing, be subject to a hiccup in the system rendering the amount incorrect. There is a possibility that the computer may reject the second input as the invoice details have already been identified and processed. In such circumstances authorized re-input of the transactions has to be recorded.

3   *Controls over the output of computer transactions* – In a batch entry system where data are batched and put into specific sections or departments, there should be a check to ensure that the output matches the original input to confirm that all the processing has been undertaken. Any input records that have failed to complete the loop in terms of input–processing–output need investigation to determine the cause of the error. Once the output has been checked it must be correctly distributed and appropriately recorded.

4   *Controls over the use of correct master files and standing data files* – Master files and standing data file amendments must be complete, accurate and authorized. The controls used during transactions input are the same for these amendments. Validity of the data and the files is essential, the opportunity to amend the incorrect master file or standing data file must not occur. Due to the importance of these amendments there is a need to implement a more stringent control procedure of a one to one checking coupled with record count or batch total each time the file is used. All amendments that include additions and deletions can be confirmed by a simple comparison of the original totals plus additions less deletions, and this ensures the continuing correctness of master files and standing data files. A specific cyclical check on the correctness of these files by users will also ensure that any invalid data amendments are identified early and acted upon accordingly.

Computer fraud

Computers provide their own special opportunity for fraud. Concealment is easier while the absence of monitoring and supervision gives the fraudster the opportunity to undertake the fraudulent act. Centralization of systems enhances the opportunity of perpetration and also concealment. Automation makes the small fraud worthwhile when repeated on countless occasions. It also enables the fraudster to 'set up' indefinitely by amending program instructions or diverting output activity in terms of cheque destinations and payee names. All of this can continue to operate with the perpetrator having left the scene.

It is impossible to combat all the problems associated with computer fraud. However the existence of strong controls can act as a means of combating the problems associated with computer fraud. Hackers and fraudsters succeed because others let them in, either on purpose or unwittingly. Control aspects are therefore important in the fight against computer fraud. The safe custody of passwords and authentication codes, segregation of duties between the setting up and the processing of transactions are some control requirements.

Summary

This chapter has identified the importance of ensuring that proper controls exist within the computerized accounting system of an organization. There are two compartments in which to place controls – general and application.

General controls provide the protection under which the computer is developed, maintained and implemented. Application controls relate to the running of the computer in terms of the inputting, processing and output activities of the system as well as the operation of the master file.

Businesses depend more and more on the computer, making the computer important for business continuity. The computer should to be treated as a major asset for the organization because of the amount of business activity that revolves around it.

Key words

application controls pp. 296, 298 • audit trail p. 295 • business dependency p. 294 • data files p. 298 • general controls pp. 296, 297 • information security p. 296 • virus checks p. 299

Practice questions

1 What are the two main categories of computer system controls?
2 What are the controls that should exist when systems are designed and developed?
3 What are the controls that relate to the environment within which the computer exists?
4 What controls would you expect to see in respect of data input?
5 What are the controls relevant to the processing of data?
6 Which controls would you expect to exist to confirm the accuracy and correctness of data output?
7 What are the controls for ensuring the accuracy and validity of master file and standing data file amendments?
8 Describe the different controls that an organization can implement to safeguard against computer insecurity.
9 What general controls do you think John and Azina should introduce in light of their recent experience with the break-in and loss of data?
10 What application controls would you advise John and Azina to introduce for data input and master file amendments?

Index

Numbers in bold indicate figures or tables.